Radical Thoughts on Ethical Leadership

A volume in
Ethics in Practice
Carole L. Jurkiewicz and Robert A. Giacalone, *Series Editors*

Radical Thoughts on Ethical Leadership

Ethics in Practice

edited by

Carole L. Jurkiewicz

University of Massachusetts Boston

Robert A. Giacalone

John Carroll University

INFORMATION AGE PUBLISHING, INC.
Charlotte, NC • www.infoagepub.com

Library of Congress Cataloging-in-Publication Data

A CIP record for this book is available from the Library of Congress
http://www.loc.gov

ISBN: 978-1-68123-988-0 (Paperback)
       978-1-68123-989-7 (Hardcover)
       978-1-68123-990-3 (ebook)

Printed in the United States of America

Dedication

Spencer and Crosby Jurkiewicz, and Lincoln Barber.
Three extraordinary young men who are models of ethical leadership,
and who give us hope for the future.
—CLJ

Karen, Elizabeth, and Joshua Giacalone, the three topmost reasons
why an ethical world is so important to me.
—RAG

CONTENTS

FOREWORD

The *Ethics in Practice Series* provides a forum for exploring and discussing organizational ethics issues that may otherwise be overlooked in the usual professional venues. The focus of the series is interdisciplinary, which includes not only a focus on ethical issues in the public, private, and non-profit sectors, but on the body of knowledge on ethics that can be found in other disciplines as well. The series, therefore, seeks to help readers better understand organizational ethics from a variety of vantage points, including business, public and nonprofit administration, psychology, sociology, anthropology, criminology, and victimology.

As editors, our goal is to provide scholars, instructors, and professionals interested in ethics and social responsibility with a meaningful collection of books in key areas that expand thinking on issues of research and pedagogy. We see the series as a forum where new ideas can be surfaced and explored, future inquiry can be stimulated, and old ideas can be seen through different lenses.

This edited volume, *Radical Thoughts on Ethical Leadership* offers the reader such ideas. The thoughts articulated in this volume challenge and extend current business ethics research on ethical leadership using different disciplinary lenses. The chapters, all from the perspectives of well-known, scholars working in within different disciplinary foundations, provide innovative ideas that address a basic theme: extending our understanding of ethical leadership beyond the scope generally found in the mainstream scholarly literature.

We believe these original chapters will motivate and inspire new studies of organizational ethics and ethical leadership in different business sectors. But equally important, we hope these chapters will impact how business ethics and social responsibility are taught to business students and will serve to improve the practice of ethics in organizations.

—**Robert A. Giacalone**
Carole L. Jurkiewicz
Editors, *Ethics in Practice*

PREFACE

That there is an overwhelming need for ethical leadership in 2017 is not a radical thought. In fact it seems like a statement of the obvious. The world feels like it is changing rapidly, and for many, that change is an uncertain and quite frightening one. For millions of people, 2017 has started with a deep sense of unease over a national and international future that seems far less certain than previous years or even decades.

Despite its apparent obviousness, then, our initial statement begs a number of other questions. Where is the place of ethical leadership in a post-truth world? From whom? And to what purpose?

This book makes a significant contribution to these and myriad other questions. It brings together leading scholars from around the globe to present a range of perspectives from both theory and practice to advance our understanding of ethical leadership and where it stands today. Its radical thoughts can be found in the breadth and depth of the research presented here and it offers some positive paths for the future. But can thoughts on ethics ever be radical enough? I would respectfully suggest that there are a number of fundamental ideas about our understanding of ethical leadership that are too infrequently discussed.

The first of these is more of a plea to intellectual honesty. We appear to have now entered an age where untruth is official policy, whether this is shielded under the rubric of "alternative facts" or by simple, blatant repetition. But we need to remember that falsehoods have always played a significant role in the public realm. Exaggeration, confabulation, misdirection, etc. can all be traced in the histories of politics, business, the media, and

Radical Thoughts on Ethical Leadership, pages xi–xiii
Copyright © 2017 by Information Age Publishing

just about every institutional pillar of public life. Sadly, lying to the public is not a new development, even if its current manifestation seems more nakedly aggressive than most.

Yet the promotion of dishonesty arguably goes much deeper, and a more radical perspective, then, asks us to acknowledge that huge swathes of the entire Western political philosophical canon is either predicated on falsehoods (of a variety of shapes and sizes), or else promotes dishonesty as a legitimate act of leadership.

Let's start with Plato. Let us not forget that it was the musings of Socrates in *The Republic* that not only suggested that "noble lies" be told to the populace to keep them loyal, but that a leader's education should be manipulated to inculcate a sense of patriotism and duty. There was no room for truth, except of the partial kind through a blend of censorship and restricted content. Sounds remarkably familiar.

Aristotle's *Politics* was in many ways more benign, and his famous declaration—that "He who is unable to live in society, or who has no need because he is sufficient for himself, must be either a beast or a god"—rarely fails to inspire. That is, until we recall that the political life did not pertain to women, or slaves, or those outside the polis. Factor in this inherent and unashamed elitism, and Aristotle does not seem a million miles away from the dehumanizing effect of modern political rhetoric.

St. Augustine's *City of God* perpetuates a different kind of deceit; that of predestination and man's unquestioning obedience to a ruler, no matter who that ruler may be. When Augustine writes, "Earthly kingdoms are given by Him to good and evil men alike," he is telling us to accept our lot and that no matter what tyranny we live under, we should do so without murmur. He places an imposition on man not to try and effect any change, even against authoritarianism.

Machiavelli, of course, exhorted us to act like both fox and lion, but at least his leadership advice was entirely context-bound, a fact either forgotten or ignored by the majority of his detractors. There was never an indication that deception was a universally regarded standard of behavior.

And so onto those writers who still inspire much of our political thinking to this day—the social contract theorists. It would be unfair and unwise to accuse Hobbes or Locke (and others) of promoting lies, but perhaps they did something far more dangerous—mythologizing power. This was done not only through the formulation of the state of nature in its various incarnations, but with the idea of the social contract itself. Nobody has signed a social contract and they never did; it is nothing more than a convenient fiction upon which to offer post hoc rationalizations for the status quo.

A more generous reading would argue that these social contracts were never meant to be taken literally, that they were hypothetical constructs designed to act as a foundation for other theories. That is a reasonable point, but it does not remove the inherently manipulative character of such hypotheses. At least Rousseau, of all the social contractarians, was honest enough to admit this: "The first man who, having enclosed a piece of ground, bethought himself of saying 'This is mine,' and found people simple enough to believe him, was the real founder of civil society."

Even a modern giant such as Rawls can be seen in this tradition. Directly situating his work in terms of social contract, Rawls describes his own version of it, the original position, as "a purely hypothetical situation characterized so as to lead to a *certain conception of justice*" (my emphasis). The construct does not, of course, invalidate his principles of justice, nor suggest that they are inherently bad, but it clearly shows that they are the product of a rigged game, designed to appear neutral but resulting in pre-ordained principles.

I fully acknowledge that I can be accused of cherry picking my arguments here. Hopefully, however, they are illustrative of a number of radical positions. First, that ethical leadership does not necessarily have a very rich tradition, particularly in terms of political discourse. Yes, this is arguably because social values change and thus what may have been an acceptable position once is no longer the case. But that leads to a second concern, that moral fluidity makes it difficult to establish norms and values for future generations. Will the readers of this book wake one morning to find that their values are no longer acceptable to society's decision and taste makers?

The only way to combat these issues is for fearless debate and continual reflection. Morality and ethics are not set in stone and we need to be ever vigilant that our values do not slip. This is particularly important today with a quite explicit attack on evidence and knowledge. We live in an almost paradoxical world; where more information is available to us, and more rapidly, than ever before, and yet truth seems harder than ever to find. Not for nothing has recent debate in the United States, United Kingdom, and mainland Europe questioned the very nature of expertise, and even truth. Alternative facts, anyone?

All of which underlines the importance of this book. Its authors take concepts old and new and recast them in the very latest research. In so doing they provide not only a wealth of knowledge, but more importantly a safe space for open thinking and honest reflection, which is now and forever will be crucial to our own development of practice.

That there is an overwhelming need for ethical leadership in 2017 may not be a very radical thought, but it is a crucially important one. This book goes some way in offering constructive ideas in responding to our need.

—**Michael Macaulay**

CHAPTER 1

YOU CAN LEAD A MAN TO OUGHTA, BUT YOU CAN'T MAKE HIM THINK

The Disparity Between Knowing What is Right and Doing it

Carole L. Jurkiewicz
University of Massachusetts Boston

Robert A. Giacalone
John Carroll University

ABSTRACT

The foundation of effective leadership in any sector is built upon ethical competence, or at least the perception of it. What an individual asserts are his/her values do not necessarily fit with what that person thinks or how they act, but rather who they want the world to see. Generally, people believe they are more ethical than those surrounding them, and they tend to disparage the level of ethicality in the milieu in which they work. While this may serve to inflate one's sense of self, such beliefs can also justify unethical and perhaps evil

Radical Thoughts on Ethical Leadership, pages 1–20

behavior by those espousing quite the opposite. Advances in ethics research have detailed a number of factors that can create a more ethical leader, but the disparity between knowing what is right and doing it is a function of many variables. Beyond formal ethics education, this chapter explores what can be done in the workplace itself to facilitate ethical leadership, and identifies the ethical traps that can, and often do, derail these efforts.

A substantial body of research indicates that leaders who are ethical have improved employee physical, psychological, and job well-being (Giacalone & Promislo, 2010; Valentine, 2014). Given that, whether through omission or commission, leaders are a primary influencer of their employees' ethics (Jurkiewicz, 2012), as well as the overall organizational climate (Schminke, Ambrose, & Neubaum, 2005). The impact of their level of ethicality is discernable at both the individual and organizational levels. By focusing on the long-term impact of ethical leadership, the connection to positive organizational advantages are clear. So what can be done to ensure the highest level of leader ethicality? Using the research base in leadership, ethics, and behavioral science, we propose different approaches: hire the most ethical individuals, develop formal ethics education, use ethics as an organizational strategy, understand factors that inaugurate unethical leadership, and measure unethical behavior.

HIRE THE MOST ETHICAL INDIVIDUALS

It is much easier to hire and develop an individual who enacts the values they espouse rather than to reform one who has a history of unethical behavior—and doing so enhances job-related well-being across the organization. Research suggests that such hires have significant and positive impacts on organizations, both directly and indirectly, by developing the ethical followership, leadership, and climate of the organization.

Hiring and developing the most ethical individuals translates into diverse forms of job well-being resulting from the ethical climate that develops. An organizational team that develops a higher ethical work climate (Mulki, Jaramillo, & Locander, 2008), or whose top leadership supports ethics (Viswesvaran, Deshpande, & Joseph, 1998), is positively related to job satisfaction. When leadership has incorporated ethics into its decision-making processes (known as ethics institutionalization; Singhapakdi & Vitell, 2007), or have developed a dynamic ethics code (Valentine & Barnett, 2002), higher organizational commitment results. A higher ethical climate created by hiring ethical employees and leaders is also known to enhance employee retention (Stewart, Volpone, Avery, & McKay, 2011), decrease conflict with coworkers (Babin, Boles, & Robin, 2000), enhance person-organization fit (Valentine, Godkin, & Lucero, 2002), decrease individual misconduct (Andreoli & Lefkowitz, 2009), increase the ability to attract employees (Sims & Kroeck, 1994), increase job performance (Jaramillo, Mulki, & Solomon, 2006) and improve group creativity (Valentine, Godkin, Fleischman, & Kidwell, 2011).

FORMAL ETHICS EDUCATION

Effective ethics education is critical for leaders and followers alike. Research has demonstrated that ethicality can be outlined, taught, and measured, and that its effects are long-lasting (Menzel, 2017). As Darley (1996) and Hejka-Elkins (1988), among many, have pointed out, individuals rarely do what is right without targeted intervention, meaning education, training, or other behavioral intercession. Employees report wanting to maintain higher ethical standards in the workplace but that leader directives, his or her policies, and the culture the leader creates is the major impediment to behaving ethically (Jurkiewicz, 2000). Ethics education also has a profound influence on whether leaders or employees can withstand the pressures or pitfalls to behave otherwise (Jurkiewicz, 2002), and those without such instruction are largely unaware of the ethical importance of their decisions (Kennedy & Malatesta, 2010).

Effective ethics education connects an individual's developing moral awareness to the applied theory of ethics (Jurkiewicz & Grossman, 2012) as opposed to what is frequently used as the basis for ethics training: compliance requirements with a focus on the legal ramifications of violating them. Laws change with time and compliance training disassociates ethics from behaviors beyond the completion of required forms. And who could argue that those who craft our laws are moral exemplars (Rassmussen, 2010)? Thus, legalistic approaches to ethics education do not address the development of cognitive complexity needed to make effective ethical decisions. This type of learning occurs when such instruction employs specific methodologies (Jurkiewicz, 2002; Jurkiewicz & Nichols, 2002; Kohlberg, 1981, 1986; Norman et al., 1998;). Kohlberg's stage theory of moral development and ethical reasoning (Kohlberg, 1976; 1986) is the foundation for much of what we know to be effective. His model parses ethicality into interactionally-structured, integrated conceptual structures that form individual understanding, and which can be operationalized and assessed (Jurkiewicz, 2012).

The principal components of effective ethics education, as detailed by Jurkiewicz (2012), are: applied moral philosophy and moral arguments; differentiating between ethical issues distinct from other issues such as management or resource distribution; learning to reason logically in seeking solutions to ethical issues; clarity regarding one's own ethical framework and the realization that others likely do not intuitively share that view; and the skill to function ethically in an unethical environment. The educational tools viewed as most effective include the use of diagnostic instruments; experiential exercises; case analysis; lectures; and group discussions (Jurkiewicz & Giacalone, 2002), with the emphasis being on motivating ethical behavior, and the introduction of tools for ethical reasoning and the opportunities to apply that knowledge in a variety of venues through facilitated interaction. Leaders and followers without effective ethics education usually ignore ethical issues completely or deal with them only at a superficial level, or react to them from emotion in quite idiosyncratic ways (Cooper, 2006).

ETHICS AS AN ORGANIZATIONAL STRATEGY

Ethics is a powerful organizational strategy for those who know how to harness and apply it. The three key methods by which to attain the greatest impact in this regard are creating an ethical culture, instituting effective training programs, and building and maintaining trust. Each of these will be considered separately.

Culture

Leaders who create a positive ethical culture are creating a strategic advantage for the organization. By creating a system of shared values, the leader distinguishes his or her organization from others that bonds employees together and strengthens their degree of organizational commitment, enhances the organization's reputation meaning greater employee retention and easier recruiting of qualified and talented individuals, greater levels of employee health and job satisfaction, and greater financial stability (Promislo, Giacalone, & Jurkiewicz, 2012; Valentine, 2014). The leader creates the culture of an organization as a function of their behavior, attitude, treatment of others, and consistency in performance. It's a comprehensive, top-down feature of organizations and is created whether through default or intention, and something that needs to be proactively reinforced through policies, practices, and reward systems (Jurkiewicz & Grossman, 2012).

While most organizational cultures develop through default, a leader can use this important influence on employee ethical behavior with proactive, targeted acts. Acting as a visible role model for the behavior you expect from others is essential; employees' behavior is shaped much more by what leaders do, rather than what they say. Communicating ethical expectations often and in various venues, and in supporting the ethics training program. Visibly rewarding ethical acts, and punishing unethical ones, to the same extent one would achieving production or sales goals. Emphasize that the means used to achieve the goal are as important as achieving the goal itself. Support employees for taking calculated risks that hold the promise of innovation, and discourage unbridled competition. Finally, ensure that viable, anonymous, and responsive protective mechanisms are in place for those who report unethical behavior.

Training

Creating and maintaining an effective ethics training program can be a powerful strategic tool (Sekerka, 2013). Generally, an ethics officer who operates separately from the human resources department and one who reports only to the Board should be appointed to oversee the program. Based on organizational and sector data, s/he would decide upon content, format, frequency, hire the trainers, and evaluate the program for continual improvements. The program needs to be targeted to the audience, be clear and applicable, interactive, supplemented with materials, widespread and frequent, and include ethical issues from across the hierarchy. Areas of risk and concern should be addressed, a discussion and instruments to measure values are essential, and encouraging attendees to discuss actual ethical issues they have faced are key.

To be most effective, training should be mandatory for everyone in the organization, be up-to-date and cover different topics across all annual sessions. Integrating stand-alone training with regularly scheduled meetings to include brief elements for discussion is ideal. Code development is also a function of the ethics officer and should be a comprehensive, rather than a top-down effort. Ensuring all have a voice in expressing what the organization should uphold in terms of values and mission, without regard to hierarchical position, is essential; this can be accomplished through the application of the nominal group technique in small group meetings. Communicating that the code is dynamic, and needs to discussed, tweaked, updated, and tested for real-life relevance is important if the code is to have the intended impact. Regular ethical and social audits are additional tools that can have powerful impacts.

Trust

Trust can be intentionally created between leaders and employees, and is difficult to repair once broken. The benefits of being a trustworthy leader have been demonstrated in the literature: higher morale and productivity, reduced turnover and greater loyalty, healthier employees, stronger financial performance, greater collaboration, and increased trust-worthiness of employees. Less than 26% of employees, in recent surveys (Jurkiewicz & Giacalone, 2016), say they trust their managers. In an absence of trust, employees presume that all behavior has a hidden purpose and they'll spend time seeking it out rather than focusing on work. They will suppress performance; engage in power plays and personal conflicts; gossip; broadcast organizational problems to outsiders including vendors, suppliers, and customers; engage in sabotage and revengeful activities; will experience more stress and illness; be absent more often; and whistle-blow.

Leaders can build trust by enforcing transparency and accountability, engaging in open communication and admitting mistakes, showing respect for others, being honest and consistent, following through on obligations, setting reasonable expectations, and sharing credit where it is due. Further, trust is created by resolving conflicts head-on, providing direct positive and negative feedback, demonstrating trusting behavior, be accessible and walk the talk, be accessible, and express vulnerability as appropriate. Leader behaviors that destroy trust include making promises that go unfulfilled, rewarding and punishing unevenly, expressing emotional extremes, giving ambiguous directives and frequently shifting goals, lying, pitting employees against one another, focusing on outcomes at all costs, and acting at odds with the organization's mission or top leaders' directives.

FACTORS THAT INAUGURATE UNETHICAL LEADERSHIP

While it would be difficult if not impossible to argue that leaders are unaware of what constitutes ethical leadership and the advantages to the leader and the organization in behaving ethically, some leaders behave in opposition to what they know they need to do. Why? The intervening factors that lead individuals who know what it means to be an ethical leader, to act unethically, are widely documented. These factors can be grouped into three primary categories: psychological influencers, culture influencers, and external influencers. Each is examined separately here.

Psychological Influencers

The role of psychological processes in influencing ethical decisions is well-established in the literature, whether it is via biases (Tenbrunsel & Messick, 2004), defensive behaviors (Ashforth & Lee, 1990), or framing (Jones, 1991). What research tell us is that how individuals behave is powerfully impacted by the psychological factors.

Reframing a behavior that might sound despicable under its common name so that it is euphemistically referred to as something more innocuous, sparks more instances of the despicable behavior. For example, bullying activity renamed as playful banter encourages more bullying behaviors, as does financial fraud that is instead referred to as creative accounting. Failing to call something what it is, whether for political reasons or to blur one's own behavior, serves to increase the incidence of that unethical behavior (Bandura, 1999).

As Milgram (1963) and Zimbardo (Haney, Banks, & Zimbardo, 1973) acutely demonstrated, roughly 95% of individuals will comply with the directive of someone in authority, even if the directive is considered unethical. Much as the Nuremberg defense attempted to excuse those under Hitler's rule by stating they were simply following orders, individuals are held individually accountable even if they succumb to the powerful forces of authority (Heydecker, Leeb, & Downie, 1962).

Does absolute power corrupt absolutely? Not so, according to researchers (e.g., Jurkiewicz & Brown, 2000). But the degree to which a leader with power defines their cognitive schema as a person of influence, high standing, and power can increase the hypocrisy (Batson & Thompson, 2001) they exhibit toward employees, increasing unethical behaviors up and down the hierarchy. They tend to judge subordinate's ethical more harshly, and their own more gently, allowing them to act unethically yet disciplining subordinates for following the model they set (Galinsky, 2010).

It would be inaccurate to suggest that the factors leading to lapses in ethical leadership are a function of leadership ethics or psychological processing alone. Because there are always many actors influencing organizational decisions (Rosenfeld, Giacalone, & Riordan, 2002), leaders are subject to the influences of others who have vested interests in their decisions (Schlenker, 1980). Indeed, what is often unrecognized is that because ethics are not a physical reality but a social reality (Halle, 1965), the perception of what is ethical can be socially constructed. Thus, what is evident is that via a series of both protective and acquisitive self-presentational styles (Arkin, 1981), stakeholders (e.g., followers, other leaders, and the public at large) can manipulate information to reframe questionable ethical activities so as to make them appear more ethical for the leader (Lutz, 1983; Michaels, 2008). Similarly, these individuals can also reframe ethical activities to appear otherwise deleterious to the organization (to financial or public relations outcomes) if these activities are seen as being dysfunctional to the stakeholder's personal best interests. In either condition, the leader's perceptions can be manipulated so as to distort her judgment and undermine the efficacy of her ethical decision (Giacalone & Payne, 1995).

But the impact of psychological processes unplanned or driven by the desire to achieve any particular outcome. As the work of Baumeister and

Tierney (2012), has elucidated, individuals who are stressed, hungry, and/ or tired are much more likely to violate ethical standards they would not under the opposite circumstances. He posits that the more energy it takes to keep awake, calm, or suppress hunger, the less energy an employee has to resist temptation; effectively, he claims individuals have a limited amount of willpower and once it is expended, there is not left to moderate the impulse to compromise one's ethics (Mead, Baumeister, Gino, Schweitzer, & Ariely, 2009).

Leaders who encourage an employee to overlook an ethical standard or rule by stating it's a single instance that will bond the two together more closely, a phenomenon known as the "foot in the door" technique, can more easily use the employee to engage in greater and more frequent ethical violations (Freedman & Fraser, 1966). Such behavior can be used with intentionality to get the employee to do those things the leader does not want to be held accountable for, and for which s/he can then fire the employee and absolve themselves of any blame (Cialdini et al., 1975).

The Pygmalion and Golem effects (Kierein & Gold, 2000) are the terms used for research findings that assert the way an individual is perceived by their leader predisposes the individual to act in that way. Thus, if the leader's boss perceives him/her as ethical, then the leader is highly likely to behave in accord with that perception (the Pygmalion Effect). Conversely, if boss believes their subordinate to be unethical, then the leader will adjust his or her behaviors to be in line with that expectation (the Golem Effect).

Cultural Influencers

The influence of culture on ethical decision making, both from national (Williams, 2011) and organizational standpoint (Lozano, 1998), has been demonstrated in a variety of studies. Of interest here are the organization's cultural influences.

The Broken Window Theory, applied to many areas including urban studies, group behavior, and sociology, also applies to the ethical behavior of leaders and other organizational employees. If a leader sees another peer or boss engage in an unethical act and that act is not addressed nor is there a punishment, it provides an assumed license that this is acceptable within the organization's culture. One unethical deed can be followed by another similar in nature, then another, spreading throughout an organization (Keizer, Lindenberg, & Steg, 2008). Such unethical behaviors also escalate over time, from comparatively petty ethical transgressions to major ethical and legal violations (Mills, 1958). Such behavior is commonly referred to as an escalation of commitment.

A recent study wherein employees of multiple organizations were asked if their respective leaders engaged in any of thirty-two unethical behaviors, demonstrated that those who reported such behaviors from their leaders were more likely to act unethically themselves (Bandura, 1997). Unethical leader behaviors provide an unspoken roadmap for how subordinates understand they should behave if they, too, want to be promoted up the hierarchy.

An ethical culture whose shared system of values and beliefs includes norms of unethicality, such as padding expense accounts, using company time for personal activities, harassment, or theft, to name but a few, sets the standard for all employees' understanding of how they should behave (Kallgren, Reno, & Cialdini, 2003). A leader, or any employee, might come into an organization with an ethical framework that would define such behaviors as unethical, but is likely to bend his or her ethics to fit in with the general culture (Fisman & Miguel, 2007; Barr & Serra, 2006).

The relationship between organizational rules and unethical behavior is curvilinear; as the number of rules increases beyond a certain tipping point, unethical behavior will also increase. Rules are generally instituted to prevent ethical performance, and at a minimal level they can have that effect. But as the number of rules increases feelings of mistrust and fear of making mistakes increases, and individuals tend to violate ethical standards in protest (Hammock & Brehm, 1966).

Setting unrealistic and unattainable goals for employees increases instances of fraud in an organization; the higher the goal, the greater the amount of fraud (Larrick, Heath, & Wu, 2009). Unrealistic goals lead to decreased employee motivation and reduced productivity, and direct their activities elsewhere, generally into activities that thwart the organization that makes them feel poorly about themselves. Fraudulent activity can be viewed as an effective revenge by employees who perceive their organizations as unethical in setting performance measures they can never attain (Ajzen, 2002).

Organizations in which leaders behave loud and aggressively in the workplace, with regard to goals, competitors, or challenges to their authority, contribute to a culture where the ethical climate is one characterized by confrontation, belittling others, and intimidation (Fast & Chen, 2009). Such behavior leads to employees acting in a similar manner, to which leaders respond in an increasingly hostile manner, completing a downward spiral in organizational unethicality.

Organization's with a culture that ridicules indecisiveness and communicates that it is a sign of weakness, facilitates an environment that encourages unethical behaviors (Weenig & Midden, 1991). Employees unsure of the leader's priorities or preferences, and discouraged from asking, will act to attempt to please the leader, and set aside rationality and ethicality to do so. Especially in regard to ethical dilemmas, where a leader's influence is most crucial, an employee without direction and unwilling to suffer the negative consequences of not knowing all the answers, will respond from their limited frame of reference, most often putting the organization at risk (Janis & Mann, 1977).

External Influencers

Clearly, external forces are always operating on both leaders and followers, helping to both define and refine the parameters of ethical decisions. Whether it is by intent or by default, members of organizations always look at the realities of others' decision making, whether it be the ethical parameters used by colleagues, competitors, political and spiritual leaders, or decision makers in different business domains. Equally critical are those physical realities of the organization that create the impetus to behave in particular ways. And it is these realities that shape what organizational players will do with whatever decision confronts them.

While an organization's external reputation may be one of positivity and good will, such a mask induces employees within the organization to act more unethically than those organizations without such an external visage. Believing the goodwill created by the external impression, employees succumb to the belief that all they do is good, even when behaving unethically, and they tend to underestimate the chances they will get caught engaging in such violations (Isen & Patrick, 1983). It is important for top leaders in such an organization to communicate clearly the negative consequences of ethical violations, and to caution that the external perception must emanate from internal behavior, rather than be used as a veneer to cover misbehavior (Loewenstein, Weber, Hsee, & Welch, 2001).

Individuals believe, by and large, that they are more ethical, intelligent, funnier, caring, etc. than others; self-flattery is more common than not. Without leaders encouraging employees to view their actions and their organizations within a broader social and professional context, biases develop which allow employees to engage in delusional behaviors, including those that excuse unethical behavior as the norm (Zimbardo, 2007). This "ethical mirage," as Tenbrunsel, Diekmann, Wade-Benzoni, and Bazerman (2010) terms it, perpetuates escalating levels of unethical conduct. Requiring employees to reflect upon the impact of their decisions in a community context, and to compare their behavior with reported norms, can squelch this insular and misleading tendency.

Organizations that position themselves as in a competitive race against other organizations promote cheating and other unethical behaviors among employees (Schwieren & Weichselbaumer, 2010). Winning becomes everything in such an environment, and all means to the end are excused as necessary to achieve the coveted goal. Those with least skill and ability in the organization will respond to a competitive environment with the greatest zeal for winning and, concomitantly, engage in the most egregious unethical behaviors and do so more often (Schweitzer, Ordonez, & Douma, 2004). Time pressures have the same effect on employees, whether externally or internally imposed, with the greater the pressure to perform in the shortest amount of time leading to the highest incidence of unethical behavior (Batson et al, 1978).

The physical environment of an organization can facilitate unethical behavior. For instance, organizations with the highest number of malpractice and fraud-related lawsuits have buildings with reflective glass on the exterior (Berkowitz and LePage, 1967). Offices decorated with sales charts and financial data, rather than balanced with personal or team-related objects, have a greater proportion of employees who focus on the ends and disregard the means (Kaptein, 2013). Leader offices which are decorated with objects or weaponry have departments and organizations that exhibit higher levels of personal conflict, anger, and violent behavior (Lohmann, Arriaga, & Goodfriend, 2003).

The organization's dress code, whether communicated directly or subconsciously, can influence individuals to act unethically. Attire that expresses uniformity with a larger group tends to allow individuals to diffuse responsibility for their own ethical transgressions onto the group as whole, blaming such acts on the role one is enacting rather than owning the behavior as a personal choice (Bickman, 1974). If the attire expresses force, unassailability, superiority, or authoritarianism to those outside the group or organization, otherwise ethical individuals can engage in unethical behaviors as those exhibited by the uniformed for fear of retribution.

Organizations that exhibit obvious wealth in their buildings' furnishings and decorations have employees significantly more likely to engage in unethical behaviors than those that are less ostentatious (Gino & Pierce, 2009). Such excess evokes feelings of injustice in employees at nearly all hierarchical levels, as well as in clients or vendors who visit. Increased cheating, theft, and fraud result from these feelings, which translate into hostility, neglect, and indignation. Individuals in this situation can rationalize their unethicality with thoughts that such an organization can afford to lose some resources, and that in helping to equalize the inequity their unethical acts embody higher ideals (Vohs, Mead, & Goode, 2008).

The scent in an organization affects ethical behavior. If the building or department smells stuffy, like dust or mold, chemicals, food smells, or poor employee grooming, employees at all hierarchical levels are significantly more likely to act unethically (Liljenquist, Zhong, & Galinsky, 2010). Replacing such odors with the scent of lemon or lime, baby oil or powder, cinnamon, vanilla, pine-scented cleaners, or fresh herbs increases ethicality. It is believed that scents have deeply embedded associations, and those that remind individuals of wholesomeness and cleanliness establish a tone that resonates with ethicality, and that those which do not suggest to the employee that attention to detail is unnecessary, and that expectations of performance are low (Holland, Hendriks, & Aarts, 2005).

MEASURING ETHICAL BEHAVIOR

The literature is conclusive that individuals are unable to accurately assess their own ethicality; in fact, 90% of leaders rate themselves as well above others in this regard (Zimbardo, 2007). But we know from further research that the majority of leaders are a negative influence on their subordinates' and organizations' ethicality (Giacalone & Jurkiewicz, 2003; Jurkiewicz, 2003; Jurkiewicz & Nichols, 2002; Jurkiewicz & Thompson, 1999). Given this, how is a leader's effect on the ethicality of an organization to be accurately measured? Two different tools are suggested here.

The Leader Ethicality Checklist (see Table 1.1), is an inductive tool used to assess if the leader's behaviors are ethical, and if they are advancing the

TABLE 1.1 Leader Ethicality Checklist	
Transparency	Would you be embarrassed to discover a decision you made became a headline in your local newspaper? Would you feel confident in justifying your actions or decisions to your employees, colleagues, subordinates, shareholders, and the public?
Universalizability	Would you want to be a member of the group that is directly impacted by your decisions? Do you want to be treated as you treat others?
Justice	Are the dignity and freedom of others secured by this decision? Is the basic humanity of the affected individuals enhanced? Are their substantive opportunities broadened by your efforts?
Rights	Are the rights, happiness, and prosperity of minorities and lower-status people given full consideration? Does this decision prevent benefits only those with privilege but without merit?
Egoism	Is an opportunity for personal gain clouding your judgment? Would you make the same decision again regardless of the benefit you may receive from the outcome?
Principles	Is this decision or action consistent with your espoused principles? Is it consistent with the highest values to which your organization should aspire? Does it violate the spirit of any organizational codes, policies, or laws?
Utility	Does the action or decision lead to the greatest good for the greatest number or the least harm for the fewest? How essential is the benefit to society as a whole? Can any inescapable damaging effects be mitigated?
Social Contract	Does the action or decision facilitate the social contract, the bond of common purpose, and encourage pride in the individuals affected by these outcomes, both internal and external to the organization?

Source: Adapted from Jurkiewicz & Giacalone, 2015.

ethical climate of the organization as a whole. The greater the number of questions in the Checklist that can be answered in the affirmative, the stronger the evidence for leader ethicality. Conversely, if the responses are primarily negative, it suggests the leader is not acting ethically and that the organization is not performing as effectively or efficiently as it could, and that the incidence of low morale, turnover, ill health, violence, distrust, and organizational neglect, among other things, is significantly more likely (Jurkiewicz & Giacalone, 2015).

The Indicators of Organizational Ethicality tool (see Table 1.2) can be used in consort with the Leader Ethicality Checklist to ensure both a micro and macro view of leader ethicality, one by assessing the leader directly, the other by assessing the organizational practices, policies, and processes that the leader has established and fostered at the organizational level. The Indicators of Organizational Ethicality tool incorporates information points that supercede self-reports and encompass employee, shareholder, stakeholder, and community feedback. An organization that exhibited a majority of these factors could, with confidence, be termed an ethically competent organization (Jurkiewicz & Giacalone, 2015). It avoids the traps inherent in requesting self-reports from leaders as this

---

TABLE 1.2   Indicators of Organizational Ethicality

- Stakeholder and employee surveys support the belief that they are treated respectfully and valued
- Communication is straight-forward and clear in accessible and transparent language; employees, stakeholders, and shareholders feel honestly informed, gossip and rumor are minimal
- Meets or exceeds legal requirements
- Demonstrates through policies, practices, and programs the values the organization espouses
- Addresses hypothetical and actual ethical dilemmas regularly in meetings and training sessions
- Responds to claims of wrongdoing with respect, in a timely manner, and with transparency
- Resources and opportunities are distributed equitably, inside and outside the organization
- All employees at all hierarchical levels are held to the same standards of moral conduct, there is an absence of favoritism
- The culture is defined as openly transparent in policy and practice
- Actively rewards ethical behavior and punishes unethical behavior fairly across all organizational members
- Implements systems to prevent or minimize destructive behaviors
- Exhibits a culture of trust and commitment
- Low employee turnover and absenteeism, minimal sick days, attracts many qualified applicants for advertised positions
- Employees feel empowered and supported in taking risks and in the value they bring
- Training, promotions, and awards are tied to ethical performance
- Respects and encourages a variety of opinions and viewpoints
- An ethics crisis management plan with accountability at the highest levels is widely accessible

Source: Adapted from Jurkiewicz & Giacalone, 2015.

has proven unreliable. It is not possible that an ethical organization can be led by an unethical leader, nor that an unethical organization would have an ethical leader. Thus, using both measures can close the loop of assessment on leader ethicality.

CONCLUSION

Why bother to be so concerned with ethics at all? With all the suggestions provided here, an astute, pragmatic reader may wonder what understanding would motivate organizational leaders to want to invest the time and resources toward more ethical ends. The answer is simple: Unethical behaviors have substantive and undeniable positive impact.

Unethical behavior in organizations is damaging to individuals and to society (e.g., Chua & Rahman, 2011; Promislo et al., 2012; Jurkiewicz, 2012), with a multitude of macro and micro level negative impacts on organizations ranging from higher healthcare costs, greater levels of turnover, recruiting difficulties (Promislo, Giacalone, & Jurkiewicz, 2012), financial impacts (Orlitzky, Schmidt, & Rynes, 2003) constrained economic development (e.g., Blackburn et al., 2006), societal economic decline (Aguilera & Vadera, 2008; Argandona, 2003; Blackburn & Forgues-Puccio, 2010; Lindgreen, 2004; Matsumura & Shin, 2005; see also Zahra et al., 2005), and environmental damage (e.g., Barker, 2011; Cole, 2007; Kurzman, 1987; Patel, 2010).

And at the micro level, the consequences are no less concerning, ranging from psychological and physical stress (Mikkelsen & Einarsen, 2001), insomnia (Thomas, Bardwell, Ancoli-Israel, & Dimsdale, 2006; Elovainio et al., 2003), employee theft (Greenberg, 2002), unhealthy behaviors (Kaprio et al., 2000), substance abuse (Landrine & Klonoff, 1996), depression (Sheridan, 2006), and PTSD (post traumatic stress disorder; Bowling and Beehr, 2006; Mikkelsen and Einarsen, 2002).

Issues of ethics and social responsibility violations are, after all, not simply about academic discussions and political positioning for organizations—they are about real people, real lives, and substantive damage. They are about people hurt physically, psychologically, and financially, about lives lost, and about the future that we leave our children and grandchildren. Every disparity between knowing what is right and doing it leaves humanity in a state of affairs that is at best less optimal and at worse, heading closer to a cataclysm.

Focusing upon ethical impacts is time well-spent for our organization's leaders.

REFERENCES

Aguilera, R. V., & Vadera, A. K. (2008). The dark side of authority: Antecedents, mechanisms, and outcomes of organizational corruption. *Journal of Business Ethics, 77*(4), 431–449.

Ajzen, I. (2002). Perceived behavioral control, self-efficacy, locus of control, and the theory of planned behavior. *Journal of Applied Social Psychology, 32*(4), 665–683.

Andreoli, N., & Lefkowitz, J. (2009). Individual and organizational antecedents of misconduct in organizations. *Journal of Business Ethics, 85*(3), 309–332.

Argandona, A. (2003). Private-to-private corruption. *Journal of Business Ethics, 47*, 253–267.

Arkin, R. M. (1981). Self-presentational styles. In J. T. Tedeschi (Ed.), *Impression management theory and social psychological research* (pp. 311–333). New York, NY: Academic Press.

Ashforth, B. E., & Lee, R. T. (1990). Defensive behavior in organizations: A preliminary model. *Human Relations, 43*, 621–648.

Babin, B. J., Boles, J. S., & Robin, D. P. (2000). Representing the perceived ethical work climate among marketing employees. *Journal of the Academy of Marketing Science, 28*(3), 345–358.

Bandura, A. (1997). *Social learning theory.* Englewood Cliffs, NJ: Prentice Hall.

Bandura, A. (1999). Moral disengagement in the perpetration of inhumanities. *Personality and Social Psychology Review, 3*(3), 193–209.

Barker, K. (2011). Spillionaires: Profiteering in the Wake of the BP Oil Spill. *Business Ethics.* Retrieved from http://business-ethics.com/20 11/04/13/1612%E2%80%98spillionaires%E2%80%99-profiteering -and-mismangement-in-the-wake-of-the-BP-oil-spil

Barr, A., & Serra, D. (2006). *Culture and corruption.* London, England: University of Oxford Press.

Batson, C. D., & Thompson, E. R. (2001). Why don't moral people act morally? Motivational considerations. *Current Directions in Psychological Science, 10*(2), 54–57.

Batson, C. D., Cochran, P. J., Biederman, M. F., Blosser, J. L., Ryan, M. J., & Vogt, B. (1978). Failure to help when in a hurry: Callousness or conflict? *Personality and Social Psychology Bulletin, 4*(1), 97–101.

Baumeister, R. F., & Tierney, J. (2012). *Willpower: Rediscovering the greatest human strength.* New York, NY: Penguin Books.

Berkowitz, L., & LePage, A. (1967). Weapons as aggression-eliciting stimuli. *Journal of Personality and Social Psychology, 7*, 202–207.

Bickman, L. (1974). The social power of a uniform. *Journal of Applied Social Psychology, 4*, 47–61.

Blackburn, K., Bose, N., & Haque, E. (2006). The incidence and persistence of corruption in economic development. *Journal of Economic Development and Control, 30*, 2447–2467.

Blackburn, K., & Forgues-Puccio, G. F. (2010). Financial liberalization, bureaucratic corruption and economic development. *Journal of International Money and Finance, 29*, 1321–1339.

Bowling, N. A., & Beehr, T. A. (2006). Workplace harassment from the victim's perspective: A theoretical model and meta-analysis. *Journal of Applied Psychology, 91,* 998–1012.

Frances, C. & Rahman, A. (2011). Institutional Pressures and Ethical Reckoning by Business Corporations. *Journal of Business Ethics,* 98(2), pp. 307–329.

Cialdini, R. B., Vincent, J. E., Lewis, S. K., Catalan, J., Wheeler, D., & Darby, B. L. (1975). Reciprocal concessions procedure for inducing compliance: The door-in-the-face technique. *Journal of Personality and Social Psychology, 31*(2), 206–215.

Cole, M. A. (2007). Corruption, income, and the environment: An empirical analysis. *Ecological Economics, 62,* 637–647.

Cooper, T. L. (2006). *The responsible administrator.* San Francisco, CA: John Wiley & Sons.

Darley, J. (1996). How organizations socialize individuals into evil-doing. In D. Messick & A. Tenbrunsel (Eds.), *Codes of conduct: Behavioral research into business ethics* (pp. 13–43). New York, NY: Russell Sage Foundation.

Elovainio, M., Kivimaki, M., Vahtera, J., Keltikangas-Jarvinen, L., & Virtanen, M. (2003). Sleeping problems and health behaviors as mediators between organizational justice and health. *Health Psychology, 22*(3), 287–293.

Fast, N. J., & Chen, S. (2009). When the boss feels inadequate: Power, incompetence, and aggression. *Psychological Science, 20*(11), 1406–1413.

Fisman, R., & Miguel, E. (2007). Corruption, norms, and legal enforcement: Evidence from diplomatic parking tickets. *Journal of Political Economy, 115*(6), 1020–1048.

Freedman, J. L., & Fraser, S. C. (1966). Compliance with pressure: The foot-in-the-door technique. *Journal of Personality and Social Psychology, 4,* 195–203.

Galinsky, A. D. (2010). Power increases hypocrisy: Moralizing in reasoning, immorality in behavior. *Psychological Science, 21,* 737–744.

Giacalone, R. A., & Jurkiewicz, C. L. (2003). Workplace spirituality: On the need for measurement. *Journal of Organizational Change Management, 16*(4), 396–399.

Giacalone, R. A., & Payne, S. L. (1995). Evaluation of employee rule violations: The impact of impression management effects in historical context. *Journal of Business Ethics, 14*(6), 477–487.

Giacalone, R. A., & Promislo, M. D. (2010). Unethical and Unwell: Decrements in Well-Being and Unethical Activity at Work. *Journal of Business Ethics, 91,* 275–297.

Gino, F., & Pierce, L. (2009). The abundance effect: Unethical behavior in the presence of wealth. *Organizational Behavior and Human Decision Processes, 109*(2), 142–155.

Greenberg, J. (2002). Who stole the money, and when? Individual and situational determinants of employee theft. *Organizational Behavior & Human Decision Processes, 89,* 985–1003.

Halle, L. J. (1965). *The society of man.* New York, NY: Harper & Row.

Hammock, T., & Brehm, J. W. (1966). The attractiveness of choice alternatives when freedom to choose is eliminated by a social agent. *Journal of Personality, 34*(4), 546–554.

Haney, C., Banks, W. C., & Zimbardo, P. G. (1973). Interpersonal dynamics in a simulated prison. *International Journal of Criminology and Penology, 1,* 69–97.

Hejka-Ekins, A. (1988). Teaching ethics in public administration. *Public Administration Review, 48*(5), 885–891.

Heydecker, J. J., Leeb, J., & Downie, R. A. (1962). *The Nuremberg trial: A History of Nazi Germany as revealed through the testimony at Nuremberg.* New York, NY: World.

Holland, R. W., Hendriks, M., & Aarts, H. (2005). Smells like clean spirit: Nonconscious effects of scent on cognition and behavior. *Psychological Science, 16*(9), 689–693.

Isen, A. M., & Patrick, R. (1983). The effect of positive feelings on risk taking: When the chips are down. *Organizational Behavior and Human Performance, 31*(2), 194–202.

Janis, I., & Mann, L. (1977). *Decision making.* New York, NY: Free Press.

Jaramillo, F., Mulki, J., & Solomon, P. (2006). The role of ethical climate on salesperson's role stress, job attitudes, turnover intention, and job performance. *Journal of Personal Selling and Sales Management, 26*(3), 271–282.

Jones, T. M. (1991). Ethical decision making by individuals in organizations: An issue-contingent model. *Academy of Management Review, 16*(2), 366–395.

Jurkiewicz, C. L. (2000). The trouble with ethics: Results from a national survey of healthcare executives. *HEC Forum, 12*(2), 101–123.

Jurkiewicz, C. L. (2002a). The influence of pedagogical style on students' level of ethical reasoning. *Journal of Public Affairs Education, 8*(4), 263–274.

Jurkiewicz, C. L. (2002b). The phantom code of ethics and public sector reform. *Journal of Public Affairs and Issues, 6*(3), 1–19.

Jurkiewicz, C. L. (2003). Ethics governance structures. In J. Rubin (Ed.), *Encyclopedia of public administration and public policy, 1st Edition.* New York, NY: Marcel Dekker.

Jurkiewicz, C. L. (2012). *The foundations of organizational evil.* Armonk, NY: M.E Sharpe.

Jurkiewicz, C. L., & Brown, R. G. (2000). Power corrupts absolutely . . . not. *Public Integrity, 2*(3), 195–210.

Jurkiewicz, C. L. & Giacalone, R. A. (2002). Learning through teaching: Demonstrating ethical applications through a training session and manual development exercise." *Journal of Public Affairs Education, 8*(1), 57–70.

Jurkiewicz, C. L., & Giacalone, R. A. (2015). How will we know it when we see it? Conceptualizing the ethical organization. *Public Organization Review, 15*(2), 1–12.

Jurkiewicz, C. L. & Giacalone, R. A. (2016). Organizational determinants of ethical dysfunctionality. *Journal of Business Ethics, 136*, 1–12.

Jurkiewicz, C. L. & Grossman, D. (2012). Evil at work. In *The foundations of organizational evil.* Armonk, NY: M.E Sharpe.

Jurkiewicz, C. L., & Nichols, K. L. (2002). Ethics education in the MPA curriculum: What difference does it make? *Journal of Public Affairs Education, 8*(2), 103–114.

Jurkiewicz, C. L., & Thompson, C. R. (1999). An empirical inquiry into the ethical standards of health care administrators. *Public Integrity, 1*(1), 41–53.

Kallgren, C. A., Reno, R. R., & Cialdini, R. B. (2003). A focus theory of normative conduct: When norms do and do not affect behavior. *Personality and Social Psychology Bulletin, 26*(8), 1002–1012.

Kaprio, J., Kujala, U. M., Koskenvuo, M., & Sarna, S. 2000. Physical activity and other risk factors in male twin-pairs discordant for coronary heart disease. *Atherosclerosis, 150,* 193–200.

Kaptein, M. (2013). *Workplace morality: Behavioral ethics in organizations.* Bingley, England: Emerald Group.

Keizer, K., Lindenberg, S., & Steg, L. (2008). The spreading of disorder. *Science, 322,* 1681–1685.

Kennedy, S. S., & Malatesta, D. (2010). Safeguarding the public trust: Can administrative ethics be taught? *Journal of Public Affairs Education, 16*(2), 161–180.

Kierein, N. M., & Gold, M. A. (2000). Pygmalion in work organizations: A meta-analysis. *Journal of organizational behavior, 21*(8), 913–928.

Kohlberg, L. (1976). Moral stages and moralization: The cognitive-developmental approach. In T. Lickona (Ed.), *Moral development and behavior.* New York, NY: Holt, Rinehart, & Winston.

Kohlberg, L. (1981). *The philosophy of moral development.* New York, NY: Harper & Row.

Kohlberg, L. 1986. A Current Statement on Some Theoretical Issues. In S. Modigal and C. Modigal (Eds.), *Lawrence Kohlberg: Consensus and controversy* (pp. 485–546). Philadelphia, PA: Falmer.

Kurzman, D. (1987). *A killing wind: Inside union carbide and the Bhopal catastrophe.* New York, NY: McGraw-Hill.

Landrine, H., & Klonoff, E. A. 1996. The schedule of racist events: A measure of racial discrimination and a study of its negative physical and mental health consequences. *Journal of Black Psychology, 22,* 144–168.

Larrick, R. P., Heath, C., & Wu, G. (2009). Goal-induced risk taking in negotiation and decision making. *Social Cognition, 27*(3), 342–364.

Liljenquist, K., Zhong, C., & Galinsky, A. D. (2010). The smell of virtue. *Psychological Science, 21*(3), 381–383.

Lindgreen, A. (2004). Corruption and unethical behavior: Report on a set of danish guidelines. *Journal of Business Ethics, 51,* 31–39.

Loewenstein, G. F., Weber, E. U., Hsee, C. K., & Welch, N. (2001). Risk as feelings. *Psychological Bulletin, 127*(2), 267–286.

Lohmann, A., Arriaga, X. B., & Goodfriend, W. (2003). Close relationships and placemaking: Do objects in a couple's home reflect couplehood? *Personal Relationships, 10*(3), 437–450.

Lozano, J. M. (1998). Ethics and corporate culture. *Ethical Perspectives, 5*(1), 53–70.

Lutz, W. D. (1983). Corporate doublespeak: Making bad news look good. *Business and Society Review, 44,* 19–22.

Matsumura, E. M., & Shin, J. Y. (2005). Corporate governance reform and CEO compensation: Intended and unintended consequences. *Journal of Business Ethics, 62,* 101–113.

Mead, N. L., Baumeister, R. F., Gino, F., Schweitzer, M. E., & Ariely, D. (2009). Too tired to tell the truth: Self-control resource depletion and dishonesty. *Journal of Experimental Social Psychology, 45*(3), 594–597.

Menzel, D. C. (2016). *Ethics management for public and nonprofit managers: Leading and building organizations of integrity* (3rd ed.). New York, NY: Routledge.

Michaels, D. (2008). *Doubt is their product: How industry's assault on science threatens your health.* New York, NY: Oxford University Press.

Mikkelsen, E. G., & Einarsen, S. (2001). Bullying in Danish work-life: Prevalence and health correlates. *European Journal of Work and Organizational Psychology, 10*(4), 393–413.

Mikkelsen, E. G., & Einarsen, S. (2002). Basic assumptions and symptoms of post-traumatic stress among victims of bullying at work. *European Journal of Work and Organizational Psychology, 11*(1), 87–111.

Milgram, S. (1963). Behavioral study of obedience. *Journal of Abnormal Psychology, 67*, 371–378.

Mills, J. (1958). Changes in moral attitudes following temptation. *Journal of Personality, 26*(4), 517–531.

Mulki, J. P., Jaramillo, J. F., & Locander, W. B. (2008). Effect of ethical climate on turnover intention: Linking attitudinal and stress theory. *Journal of Business Ethics, 78*(4), 559–574.

Norman, A. D., Richards, H. C., & Bear, G. G. (1998). Moral reasoning and religious belief: Does content influence structure? *Journal of Moral Education, 27*(1), 89–98.

Orlitzky, M., Schmidt, F. L., Rynes, S. L. (2003). Corporate social and financial performance: A meta-analysis. *Organization Studies, 24*(3), 403–441

Patel, R. (2010). We Have Yet to See The Biggest Costs of the BP Spill. *The Nation.* Retrieved from http://www.thenation.com/article/153908/we-have-not-yet-see-biggest-costs-bp-spill.

Promislo, M. D., Giacalone, R. A., & Jurkiewicz, C. L. (2012). Ethical impact theory (EIT): Unethical work behavior and well-being. In R. A. Giacalone & M. D. Promislo (Authors), *Handbook of unethical work behavior: Implications for individual well-being.* Armonk, NY: M.E. Sharpe.

Rasmussen, J. (2010). Language and the most sublime in Kant's third critique. *Journal of Aesthetics and Art Criticism, 68*(2), 155–166.

Rosenfeld, P., Giacalone, R. A., & Riordan, C. A. (2002). *Impression management: building and enhancing reputations at work.* London, England: Thomson Learning.

Schlenker, B. R. (1980). *Impression management: The self-concept, social identity, and interpersonal relations.* Monterey, CA: Brooks/Cole.

Schminke, M., Ambrose, M. L., & Neubaum, D. O. (2005). The effect of moral development on ethical climate and employee attitudes. *Organizational Behavior and Human Decision Processes, 97*, 135–151

Schweitzer, M. E., Ordonez, L., & Douma, B. (2004). Goal setting as a motivator of unethical behavior. *Academy of Management Journal, 47*(3), 422–432.

Schwieren, C., & Weichselbaumer, D. (2010). Does competition enhance performance or cheating? *Journal of Economic Psychology, 31*(3), 241–253.

Sheridan, L. P. (2006). Islamophobia pre- and post-September 11th, 2001. *Journal of Interpersonal Violence, 21*, 317–336.

Sims, R. L., & Kroeck, K. G. (1994). The influence of ethical fit on employee satisfaction, commitment and turnover. *Journal of Business Ethics, 13*(12), 939–947.

Singhapakdi, A., & Vitell, S. J. (2007). Institutionalization of ethics and its consequences: A survey of marketing professionals. *Journal of the Academy of Marketing Science, 35*(2), 284–294.

Stewart, R. W., Volpone, S., Avery, D., & McKay, P. (2011). You support diversity, but are you ethical? Examining the interactive effects of diversity and ethical climate perceptions on turnover intentions. *Journal of Business Ethics, 100*(4), 581–593.

Thomas, K. S., Bardwell, W. A., Ancoli-Israel, S., & Dimsdale, J. E. (2006). The toll of ethnic discrimination on sleep architecture and fatigue. *Health Psychology, 25*, 635–642.

Tenbrunsel, A. E., & Messick, D. M. (2004). Ethical fading: The role of self-deception in unethical behavior. *Social Justice Research, 17*(2), 223–236.

Tenbrunsel, A. E., Diekmann, K. A., Wade-Benzoni, K. A., & Bazerman, M. H. (2010). The ethical mirage: A temporal explanation as to why we are not as ethical as we think we are. *Research in Organizational Behavior, 30*, 153–173.

Valentine, S. (2014). *Organizational ethics and stakeholder well-being in the business environment.* Charlotte, NC: Information Age.

Valentine, S., & Barnett, T. (2002). Ethics codes and sales professionals' perceptions of their organizations' ethical values. *Journal of Business Ethics, 40*(3), 191–2000.

Valentine, S., Godkin, L., Fleischman, G. M., & Kidwell, R. (2011). Corporate ethical values, group creativity, job satisfaction and turnover intention: The impact of work context on work response. *Journal of Business Ethics, 98*(3), 353–372.

Valentine, S., Godkin, L., & Lucero, M. (2002). Ethical context, organizational commitment, and person-organization fit. *Journal of Business Ethics, 41*(4), 349–360.

Viswesvaran, C., Deshpande, S. P., & Joseph, J. (1998). Job satisfaction as a function of top management support for ethical behavior: A study of Indian managers. *Journal of Business Ethics, 17*(4), 365–371.

Vohs, K. D., Mead, N. L., & Goode, M. R. (2008). Merely activating the concept of money changes personal and interpersonal Behavior. *Current Directions in Psychological Science, 17*(3), 208–212.

Weenig, M. W., & Midden, C. J. (1991). Communication network influences on information diffusion and persuasion. *Journal of Personality and Social Psychology, 61*(5), 734–742.

Williams, S. L. (2011). Engaging values in international business practice. *Business Horizons, 54*(4), 315–324.

Zahra, S. A., Priem, R. L., & Rasheed, A. M. A. (2005). The antecedents and consequences of top management fraud. *Journal of Management, 31*, 803–828.

Zimbardo, P. G. (2007). *The lucifer effect: Understanding how good people turn evil.* New York, NY: Random House.

CHAPTER 2

PUBLIC VIRTUE AND THE ETHICAL DIMENSIONS OF LEADING

J. Patrick Dobel

This paper presents a normative account of ethical leading as an agent centered form of public virtue. Public virtue involves an individual using focused reflection and judgment that emerge from a disciplined pattern of self-awareness. Self-aware leaders concentrate intentional thought through four dimensions of public action. These four dimensions grow from the personal responsibility entailed by the ethical consequences `of leading. Individual leaders structure their reflection in a way that creates mental frame models that shape intentional cognitive, emotional and perceptual actions and judgment. The paper integrates traditional understandings of virtue and action with modern cognitive understandings of how the mind and mental frames work and this integration provides a cognitive process that helps individuals practice virtue in judgment and action. The paper will examine the four dimensions that shape virtuous reflection and examine their understanding by looking at two masked but real life case studies.

The mental frame approach to virtuous leading postulates the individual as a responsible agent of action. The individual practices the discipline of virtuous

Radical Thoughts on Ethical Leadership, pages 21–46
Copyright © 2017 by Information Age Publishing

reflection by shaping their understanding and perception of situations through cognitive preparation and learning. This practice results in persons carrying cognitive frames in their minds. The frames guide them to concentrate attention and perception by attending to each dimension of responsible public leading. These frames provide the cognitive and emotional underpinnings of what traditional virtue theory calls habit or practice. Modern cognitive psychology demonstrates that mental frames (I will use "frame" to cover cognitive models or schema) are engraved in neural processes. These connected processes permit efficient and timely perception and assessment of situations. This type of cognitive integration of mental frames underlies the daily and alert deployment of judgment in professional and organizational life.

This approach provides greater reflective content to traditional conceptions of virtue. It does so by focusing upon the cognitive dimension of virtue. The virtue relied upon in leading grows from habits of thought that are connected to stable character traits and trained perception. These attributes are operationalized through a modern psychological frame understanding of judgment. Operational virtue, then, is a chosen, practiced and integrated cognitive, emotional and physical activity expressed as trained habits of judgment and action (Aristotle, 1999, 2013; Cooper, 1975; Cooper, 1987, 2012; Sherman, 1989). This approach to virtue as an intellectual and character frame supports the approaches that see virtue as reflecting judgment imbedded in a practice which defines its goods such as public leading (MacIntyre, 2007; Cooper, 1987).

Integrity relies upon virtue and both depend upon constrained judgment for intentional purpose that generates the will to act. This ethical approach is deepened in the case of leading because intentional leading results in ethical consequences in the world and people. Because leading has ethical consequences in the world, leading implicates a person in ethical responsibility for the quality of his or her values, reflection and judgment. This responsibility produces obligations to respect the mental process of the cognitive frame. Public leading without addressing these frames results in ethical negligence.

Individuals can lead from anywhere at any time. The paper uses a simple and expansive definition of leading. Leading occurs when individuals seek to help others achieve a common purpose. Leading happens when a person's intentional presence changes the conditions of life or human behavior from what would have occurred had the person not been present. In simple terms, individuals make a difference (Bass, 2008; Van Wart, 2012; Senge et al., 2005, Senge, 2006; Bolman, 2011). Being present in an intentional way can involve formal authorized action or self initiated informal activity. Individuals can act from the periphery or center of authority. This approach to leading can scale from dyads to helping individuals create a group to a senior organizational position. An individual's presence can lead to participatory or distributed leading or more directive forms. Such leading can deploy different modes such as coaching, authority, deliberative or coercive depending upon a situation (Goleman, 2000) This latitudinarian approach encompasses a wide array of leading styles but depends upon persons being intentionally present and seeking to make a difference in conditions and people through responsible decisions (Van Wart, 2012). Organizationally this means persons act in a manner consistent with the values and responsibilities of his or her position. In a formal position, individuals promise to address issues identified by values and mission and to build a policy or institution sustained by support and resources. This virtue approach nests comfortably with institutional leading, and the paper focuses heavily upon leading in an institutional context.[1]

Leading with public virtue depends upon a mental frame to judge. This framework should consist of an integrated cognitive model that individuals can adopt, practice and integrate into a habituated and intentional frame of judgment. The frame works as practiced cognitive activity where individuals recall information from memory, apply models, rules or analogies to make sense of information, deploy reasons, and develop actions to fit the situation (Klein, 1988; LeDoux, 2002; Sherman, 1989). The ethical worth resides in the ability of the cognitive frame to scan and identify ethically relevant aspects of a challenge and call up relevant and fitting ethical actions to address the issue based upon past practice and present learning. The paper lays out the frame and discusses each dimension in some detail to point to the wide range of aspects that take on ethical importance for public leading. (Damasio, 1999, 2012; Klein, 1988, 2008; Fairhurst, 1996; Bolman, 2011; Senge, 2006; Schon, 1984).

FRAME FOR JUDGMENT

The mental frame to structure public virtue involves four dimensions of reference and attention: (a) self and self-awareness, (b) defining the meaning of challenges, (c) building an institution or policy, and (d) developing power and resources.

Self	Challenge
Self-Awareness	Meaning of Incident/Issue
Building	**Power**
Long Term	Long Term
Institution & Policy	Resources & Support

These dimensions identify areas of cognition, perception, emotion to which a person should attend to be responsible to the internal logic of public virtue.

The practice of leading using this virtue frame asks a person self-consciously to pause and bring attention to each dimension as an ethical obligation. This attention leads individuals to scan the environment, weigh and integrate knowledge in a dimension and link them with perceptions and consequences in interrelated dimensions. Calibrated together they guide reflection and decision flowing from public virtue.

This frame driven approach avoids the stark dilemmas posed in political ethics between realists and idealists. It anticipates the claims of Machiavelli or Sun Tzu that "moral" public action can lead to ethically unacceptable outcomes because of political opposition and uncertainty in execution by attaching ethical significance to engaging meaning and power (Machiavelli, 1992; Sun Tzu, 2002). These four dimensions guide a leader to be aware of his or her values and commitments but entail an obligation to attend to the political and operational complexity of every moment. The framework can help leaders operationalize public virtue in judgment and achieve durable and ethically defensible policy and institutions. This ethical approach does not see ethics as deductions from principles or algorithms; rather ethical leading requires constant adjustments to the political context to pursue a purpose. Virtue based ethics linked to self-awareness and character enables leaders to endure through challenges and persist to achieve a goal and create shared commitments while addressing constraints, opposition, and noncooperation.

CASES

This study will explore two real life cases of public leading to illustrate how the proposed frame of public virtue deploys in practice and to show how the frame can scale from internal personnel incidents to institutional challenges at the agency level. The cases have been masked.

Judith Perez is an experienced manager facing a tough problem in a regional social service agency. Perez ran a major division of the agency that worked with at risk youth and families. She had twenty years of experience and had run the division for five years. She headed diversity efforts in her agency for years, often being a path breaker for minority hires. Early in her career she had been a protagonist in a union law-suit on institutional diversity climate issues.

She had worked hard to create a diverse force and provide culturally aware and impactful service. The division's target populations came from a wide array of backgrounds and under Perez's lead the division prided itself on its ability to engage an array of populations. The division had earned several awards in the last two years.

One day a staff member burst into a meeting to let Perez know that a major incident had flared between staff. Thomas Nguyen was a ten year veteran IT employee, a second generation Vietnamese American. Nguyen was valued for his technical skill and careful work. Quiet, shy, and not socially adept, he tended to have little sense of social space in his interactions. Most workers had gotten used to his interpersonal style and worked well with him. Richard Aleaga had served in another unit for two years and was a recent transfer into Perez's division. A recent college graduate Aleaga took great pride in his Pacific Islander heritage.

When Perez arrived at the IT unit, several upset staff informed her that Aleaga had verbally assaulted Nguyen. Aleaga then had lunged at Nguyen and screamed, "You cannot insult me like that; you cannot challenge me like that!" Two men had to restrain Aleaga. Nguyen was terrified and had no idea what had happened. Within hours both individuals had contacted union representatives, and both wanted to consult with the Human Rights office.

In the second case a fire in a major city broke out in an apartment subsidized by the city housing authority. The fire tragically resulted in the deaths of five East African immigrants, and the fire department response was plagued with problems. The equipment on the first engine to arrive broke. (Engine 81 was a reserve engine used while the regular engine had scheduled maintenance.) This caused a several minute delay before firefighters could put water on the fire. The second responding engine was slowed down when it had to stop to move a hose that fell off. The engine from the closest fire station could not respond because it had been called to help an elderly patient in an assisted living facility get back in bed. Some assisted living facilities used 911 to bring fire departments to address falls to avoid liability issues.

The local media and neighbors had quickly gathered around the fire and witnessed the problems. After the incident, the local media ran a series of high profile stories about the failures in execution. The mayor and city council members were called upon to comment on the incident. Local immigrant groups expressed outrage, and the East African community demonstrated outpourings of grief and anger. Some activists claimed the death of the Ethiopian immigrants grew from the fire department's lack of concern for new immigrants.

The paper will look at the two cases as challenges that required leaders to recursively reflect and act considering the four dimensions.[2]

SELF: KEEPING SELF-AWARENESS

Western ethics depends upon the claim that human beings possess a self—a coherent account of his or her life that a person can use to guide cognition, emotion, and perception to decide and execute action. This self is linked to the capacity for integrity that connects beliefs, values, will, and the physical and emotional foundations of character. The self is capable of intentional action based upon reflection using reasons and weighting of values and outcomes. This self can exercise will to act against internal emotional or cognitive resistance or external obstacles.

Humans vest identity in conceptions of self and self-regulate action upon self-understanding. Ethics and law depend upon this idea of a contingent but coherent self-understanding capable of guiding action. Often several possible selves will vie for dominance when a person deliberates, and the decision-making self will settle into one frame (Pinker, 1999). The "selves" often involve different professional or role frames a person can assume. Persons can choose to adopt a role or frame appropriate to the obligations and demands of a situation. Self-reflection permits persons to stand back from the array of roles and choose one to invest their selfhood in. An operational frame relies upon selecting values to guide commitments and gives content to integrity. This integrity permits individuals to make promises that align personal values to a purpose of helping people achieve a common goal. This includes promises to assume positions of authority. The key lies in the choice of the person to commit to values and purposes beyond their self-interests but joined to the welfare of others. A personal self builds on temperaments and practiced frames that shape character to decide, act, and persist when facing obstacles.

A leader who has developed integrated frames creates a coherent set of references and processes that operationalize virtue and integrity. With practice, and learning, individuals forge stable mental models or frames that permit them to make successful judgments to achieve purposes (Sherman, 1989; Klein, 1998; Cooper, 1975; Beiner, 1983; MacIntyre, 2007). The frame gains traction through trained perception that scans the world and recognizes patterns that point to proper action. Pattern recognition is one of the human mind's supreme accomplishments, and public virtue infuses pattern recognition with alertness to identify ethical significance (Klein, 2008). Individuals can also self-manage organizational identities to further goals and align their actions with their aspirational self (Dutton, 2010). These frames express engraved neural patterns that integrate perception, memory, cognition and emotions.

From the Delphic Oracle to Socrates and Sun Tzu knowing oneself or having self-awareness is a linchpin for successful ethics and leading. Research shows that self-awareness is critical to effective and ethical leading for several reasons. An individual's self tends to vest in a single frame that works and organizes reality. Self-awareness permits a person to become consciously aware of this preferred frame through which the self is acting. Stepping back to second order reflection permits a person to get cognitive and emotional distance from this frame of reference. This enables individuals to consider other frames to supplement their preferred or default frame.

The deeper moral commitments of the self enable these multiple frames to co-exist within the person's integrity. Self-awareness helps persons avoid the dangers of frame lock and translating all information into their frame's preferred cognitive models. He or she can then learn from a wider array of information, voices and points of view (Kouzes & Posner, 2006, 2011; Lakoff and Johnson, 2008).

Individuals are changed by action and their decision processes, values, perception and even energy levels can be subtly changed over time by the emotional and cognitive feedback loops of action (Cialdini, 2009). Self-awareness addresses these subtle erosions of self and addresses mental traps that arise from how self-understandings organize perception and decision. A person's commitment to a self-image can generate self-deception and distort information and interpretation of actions to protect a self-image. This form of self-deception leads individuals to ignore or reinterpret information that does not fit their preferred ethical self-understandings. Disconcerting information will be discounted or translated into the dominant mental frame. Decisions that individuals believe are wrong or troubling trigger emotional moral responses of guilt, shame, or discomfort. The mind on its own will seek to minimize this emotional discomfort and stress whether by reinterpreting the information or reconfiguring beliefs and perceptions to diminish the moral discomfort. This form of frame lock can become even more powerful under stress where individuals and teams default to their preferred frame even if it no longer fits the situation or recognizes new challenges (Janis, 1982; Janis & Mann, 1977). People can ignore, self-deceive or rationalize actions that may violate their values to fit their self-understanding and keep integrity intact even at the risk of self-deception (Baumeister, 1991; Bazerman, 2011; Cialdini, 2009; Fingarette, 2000). Being self-aware fights these temptations.

Self-awareness also helps avoid the traps of over-reliance on limited decision heuristics that accompany successful decision-making. Human beings have developed a wide range of effective heuristics to decide quickly. Decision heuristics such as overconfidence, status quo bias, anchoring, proximity traps, and affiliation or confirmation biases can fail under many conditions and reinforce frame lock. Heuristics such as priming or reciprocity can predispose behavior unless individuals make conscious efforts to counteract these default cognitive heuristics (Kahnaman, 2011; Bazerman, 2011; Cialdini, 2009; Beshears & Gino, 2015). Political history and modern cognitive psychology amply document the unconscious self-interested bias that distorts judgment in subtle ways such as conflict of interests (Stark, 2003; Bazerman, 2011; Moberg, 2006). Disciplined self-awareness of these issues, a good diverse leadership team, or critical advisors can avoid these heuristic traps.

Social context exerts powerful influence upon a person's self-image, information reception and strengthens self-deception or frame lock. Few individuals have the cognitive and moral strength to withstand continuous signals and pressure in their social context and will accommodate morally compromised action. Leaders seeking to keep self-awareness intact usually need groups of friends or advisors who help maintain cognitive and emotional distance and diverse points of view. Self-aware leaders need to build diverse teams who reinforce open deliberation or have advisors who can stand outside the political context to buoy independent self-awareness and judgment (Goldhamer, 1978; Garvin & Margolis, 2015).

Self-awareness possesses another critical aspect for leading. All leaders face diverse and shifting contexts that require adaptation of purpose and tactics (Bass, 2008; Van Wart, 2012). Persons can expand self-awareness and reinforce integrity by conceiving of themselves as existing in three dimensions of historically shaped political space. This awareness and stance towards life builds on the work of George Lakoff. In his foundational work on linguistics and meaning he argued that human beings possess a primordial cognitive orientation. Human beings exist as embodied and social, and people experience the world as spatial and directional—front, back, side, up, down. A human must attend to life and body in these terms to survive. This spatial orientation grounds meanings in language but also provides a stance that invites a 360° scanning of an environment (Lakoff & Johnson, 1999, 2008).

Cognitive psychology demonstrates how the human brain and mind continuously scan their environment and organize information in a way that makes sense to survive and pursue purposes. Perceptual information and coherence is screened through cognitive frames. The mind's pattern recognition and scanning organize information. The frame's information triage reveals strengths and weaknesses when frames rapidly cull information to make sense of the world and direct action. These very strengths mean that default frames can miss new information or translate anomalies into a preferred mental model.

Individuals can self-consciously adapt a stance that expands the mind's incessant scanning to focus on a 360° institutional environment. This aspect of self-awareness helps people hold their mind, body, emotions and perception open, alert, and attuned as they scan political environments. The positional leading the world of *above–across–below* may be identified with authorizers, funders, superiors or peers, contractors, partners or subordinates, staff, contractors, or clients. Stakeholders and actors inhabit all the quadrants of political space and often have normative claims on a leader's purpose such as opponents, allies, collaborators, or neutrals.

Persons who adopt a disciplined 360° stance experience life as a continuous flow of events—history. All events come encumbered with actors and forces that confront leaders in environments. Forces can be social, economic or political such as demographic changes or institutionally structured time. History also means political actors carry historically shaped understandings and interpret the present in light of past frames. Understanding the rich array of historical forces, meaning and expectation presented by any moment is a critical dimension of a leader's self-awareness.

Self-awareness of historical and political space alerts leaders to the realities of institutional life. Many institutions have decision forcing cycles such as budgets, elections, timelines, media cycles, hearings, or legal mandates. These construct institutionally informed time and urgency. Surprises such as scandals, disasters or unexpected events present new challenges and create windows for new contests over meaning and resources. Self-aware leading attends to all the dimensions of political space to situate individuals pursuing common purposes (Lynn, 1987). Figure 2.1 presents a way of mapping the major dimensions of political actors and forces.

A leader seeking to act with public virtue needs to use self-discipline to maintain the social conditions in their life that permit them to keep the capacity to step back from any situation and even frame. This ability to stand back as a self permits individuals to avoid being captured by cognitive traps and fit the most appropriate frame to the situation as well as

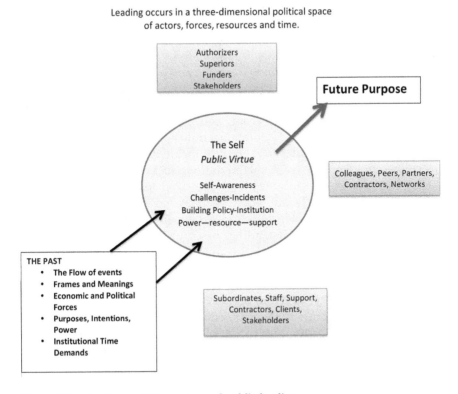

Figure 2.1 Context and dimensions of public leading.

being aware of the range of actors and forces and beliefs that impact any moment in time.

CHALLENGE: TACKLING THE MEANING OF INCIDENTS

Leading unfolds as continuous decisions that cumulatively build patterns of expectations. These expectations can contribute to or undermine a leader's purpose. The unfolding and cumulative quality of consequences points to the second dimension—how the perceived meaning of an incident affects the leader's goals. These issues play out across multiple levels of power and authority. The influence of meaning on action and the wide array of actors and levels require ethical leaders to attend to how the "game" is being played in multiple arenas of power (Lynn, 1987).[3] Each incident becomes a challenge that can affect to the leader's policy or institutional goals.

An evolving institution or policy depends heavily upon a leader's ability to influence the meaning of actions. Influencing the meaning and how people "make sense" of things erects a critical factor that leaders should address to provide momentum and legitimacy to their goals (Lynn, 1987; Weick, 1988, 1995, 2000). Leaders are often presented with incidents; events that evoke conflict and affect the stakes of the actors involved in the incident. The incidents and conflict permeate organizational life and need to be addressed in a strategic way to ensure continuous learning and progress towards a leader's goals. Most impactful incidents will involve a contest to define its meaning, and few issues arrive with interpretations baked in. Leaders need to engage quotidian incidents with care to ensure consistency of interpretation to support their long-term policy or institutional outcomes.

Incidents occur in contexts where past incidents influence present expectations, and there are few small things when seeking to lead (Badaracco, 2002). Whatever the event and however small it might seem, some protagonists will have interpretations and agendas and will fight to control the meaning of the incident. Many individuals experiencing the event will be neutral and default to understandings based on history or their positions (Schein, 2009, 2010). Good leaders who scan the environment know that many agendas and interests will compete with or contradict their ethical direction. Any incidents even minor ones as misperceived jokes, provide opportunities to further or derail purposes.

Who defines the issue and the perception of what it means can influence internal political and cultural intensity of support or opposition to goals. This contest over meaning of events impacts possible allies to build culture or power bases and can affect bringing people together in a collaborative approach. Any success in shaping the meaning of incidents can contribute to small victories that build credibility and momentum towards the leader's legitimacy and goals. It also points forward to the next dimension of play-ing the long game to build common understandings or institutional cul-ture (Lynn, 1987; Schein, 2009, 2010; Bridges, 1986, 2009; Huxham, 2003). Leaders should attend to many daily issues with special focus on ones that can leverage or derail ethical goals.

The high leverage issues often create focal events or strategic windows for change. Sometimes they might offer a tipping point for a culture or po-litical alignment. A vital nudge at a crucial moment can alter cultural mean-ings or fashion new paths or boundaries for behavior. The incident might open a sense of urgency that can create receptivity to change. To the extent the incident opens a space to change direction or start a new institutional path, it opens up all the advantages of path dependency that can support a new direction (Greener, 2002). The key becomes recognizing openings and acting in ways to build shared understandings to support long-term goals (Gladwell, 2006; Bridges, 1986, 2009; Kotter, 1996).

In any incident people will jostle to control the meaning. Individuals and groups might use events to push different agendas or test the resolve of leaders. This testing occurs constantly as individuals probe for openings to push their own interpretation or ways to stop or delegitimize a leader. These possibilities generate a strong priority for leaders to gain a wider understanding of both what occurred and what the stakes are perceived to be. Ethical leading needs to work with a fullest possible understanding (Badaracco, 2002; Huxham, 2003). Individuals can then marshal action and meaning consistent with ethical goals.

The two cases provide some insight into how the first two dimensions can be deployed.

Judith Perez's agency is riven over the incident involving Thomas Nguy-en and Richard Aleaga. Many are outraged at the physical violence threat-ened by Aleaga and protective of Nguyen whom they value and respect. More than a few have commented upon the violence inherent in the local Pacific Islander street culture. Several individuals are concerned about how quickly the agency has divided over the issue, especially when the multi-ethnic staff serves both Vietnamese and Pacific Islander populations.

Both individuals are planning to meet with lawyers and have contacted the office of Human Rights. The union representatives are torn. They are deeply upset over workplace safety issues and have voiced concerns about insufficient training but reluctant to take sides between members. Perez has met regularly with union representatives, and both she and the union are struggling with how to balance their commitments to both individuals. The office of Human Rights has made initial inquiries, and Perez worries senior attorneys want to use this incident as a punitive lesson.

Senior management has urged her to address the issue quickly and avoid media coverage. Perez and senior agency officials have worked hard to build a respect driven culture and are proud that a common social mission unites many ethnic individuals into a shared purpose. With the press of different views Perez began to wonder if the culture has the resilience to sustain the controversy. She is especially concerned about the incident escalating to the media and multiple litigations.

Perez decided to work quickly to find out exactly what happened. She brought in a professional mediator the office has used with clients to conduct a quick investigation. Perez reassigned Aleaga to a different physical location with the same level of pay and responsibility. She asked the supervisors of both Nguyen and Aleaga to explain to them their rights under contract and civil service and put this on record.

She personally asked both individuals to hold off on their immediate pursuit of human rights complaints until she had a chance to investigate. She held these meetings with two staff present to protect the record. After the meetings she did not meet with anyone involved until the investigation was finished. She had to work hard to reassure her superiors telling them that the agency and people need a "pause," and Perez needed "good information" before she could act. Perez met with union representatives and obtained their approval of the mediator. The union representatives agreed to wait before initiating action.

The firefighter incident had resulted in more deaths than any fire in forty years in the city. It remained a front-page story for days, and a picture of a firefighter with an empty hose dominated coverage. An anonymous blogger from the fire department revealed details about the condition of the back up fire truck and claimed firefighters were concerned that assisted living homes wasted firefighter resources by calling in the department to deal with minor issues to protect nursing home liability.

Chief Roger Dean had driven to the scene when he heard about the missing children over his radio. On the way he notified the mayor of the unfolding tragedy. At the scene he took over media inquiries from the harried incident commander so the commander could concentrate on the fire and rescue. The chief consulted with Greta Newberger the department's chief of public affairs while driving and at the scene. He gave media interviews immediately because he felt the gravity of the situation warranted an immediate message to the public from the fire chief. The chief always began by acknowledging the tragedy and its impact on the family and the community. He and Newberger openly acknowledged that firefighters encountered problems fighting the fire, but despite a media demand for blame and punishment, the chief drew no premature conclusions and praised the firefighters at the scene for quick action.

After consulting with Newberger on the site, Chief Dean understood that Engine 81 would be a critical piece of evidence and that any investigation must be conducted openly with no hint of bias. He ordered Engine 81 be towed to the city garage and sequestered. A third party expert was commissioned to investigate the engine's preparedness.

Chief Dean directed each of the 72 firefighters to immediately write an account of what they witnessed and did at the fire. He wanted to make sure that the department was able to answer questions in the event of a lawsuit, and he wanted the reports while memories were fresh. The mayor and the chair of the city council's public safety committee came to the fire scene that afternoon. They showed empathy with the victims' families and demonstrated involvement in this high profile incident. The media peppered all the individuals with questions aimed to elicit blame or controversy.

The days after the fire the East African immigrant community witnessed a huge outpouring of grief. The local Ethiopian community center overflowed with emotionally wrought people, and firefighters had to be called to treat distraught mourners. Police officers were dispatched to manage traffic caused by the crowd. East African custom called for community members to mourn for seven days, and it was clear that there was not room to contain the growing crowd for a week in the local community center.

Chief Roger Dean believed that the media was treating the fire department unfairly and was quite proud of how the firefighters had creatively addressed the equipment failures and fought the fire expeditiously and courageously. However, he pulled together a small group of senior chiefs and Newberger to think through the issues and publically address them in a timely and comprehensive manner. In particular he needed time to get all the information and he understood the anger that was unfolding in ethnic groups especially the growing East African community.

The morning after the fire, the chief and some of the mayor's staff met with community elders and relatives of the family to offer condolences and answer questions. The meeting was awkward and tense because of language barriers and the palpable grief in the room, but the chief believed the gesture was important. In the following days hostile neighbors and media looking for more stories confronted firefighters responding to alarms in the area.

In all his meetings and public statements the chief lead with concern about the tragedy even as he praised his firefighters. He and Newberger worked very hard not to be defensive, but actively acknowledged the sadness and anger of the community. The chief persuaded the mayor to open a much larger city facility for the community to publically mourn for seven days and have the funeral. The city provided police and medical support.

Various activists and ethnic group community leaders complained bitterly about the response time. Others attacked the fire department and city government for their failure to reach new immigrants. The alternative press and local bloggers picked up this theme and pushed it hard. Anonymous fire department bloggers continued to cite incidents of over use by the nursing homes and point to what they regarded as faulty back-up equipment.

The normal agency after-incident fire report was finished in four days, and Chief Dean and Newberger ensured that it was released with a full press conference. The fire had started in a closet where a foam-sleeping pad came into contact with a light fixture. Based on evidence from the investigation, the victims could have survived the accidental fire if they had taken different actions. Instead of getting the family out of the apartment and calling 911 when the smoke alarm went off, a family member pulled the smoldering pad out of a closet, and opened all of the doors and windows on the first floor to clear the smoke. Wind, carrying oxygen, caused the pad to burst into flames, and the fire spread quickly throughout the apartment. Upstairs a woman had taken the four children into the bathroom and locked the door and shut the windows.

The mayor wanted quick action but reluctantly worked with the fire chief to extend outreach and express both public concern for the tragedy and support for the department's professionalism. While some press grumbled about special treatment given to the mourners given use of city property, the executive and the fire department kept up outreach and began to speak often of improving outreach and prevention in the immigrant communities. The mayor had recently proposed cuts to the fire department as part of efforts to address a large deficit. In the aftermath of the tragedy city council members and community activists wondered about the need to address equipment shortfalls that the council had avoided for years. In private the mayor wanted the fire department to move quickly to get the issue off the front pages.

The chief and Newberger worked to change the focus to outreach and fire prevention, but this took time. The chief responded to the incident report with a request to the fire marshall to analyze the costs of retrofitting all subsidized housing with sprinkler systems. Newberger cleared the chief's schedule to conduct many public community meetings with elders and immigrant communities. The meetings were often raucous and angry, but Newberger and the chief listened and responded as they could while consistently asking for help in developing new ways to reach communities and address fire prevention. The department had traditionally relied upon school education to get fire safety information to these communities. Over time the meetings evolved into more specific efforts to meet with existing immigrant community associations to discuss how to get the word on prevention out. Even with impatient political leaders, activists and media, the fire department slowly shifted the dialogue to how to improve outreach and prevention.

INSTITUTION AND POLICY:
BUILDING TOWARDS A CULTURE

The third dimension leaders should integrate in public virtue reflection covers attention to the shared beliefs and connections across people and institutions needed to achieve a durable policy or institution. The ethical importance flows from the reality that no goals will be achieved and endure unless leaders put in place the policy and institutional buttressing necessary to implement them. This purpose informs the immediate effort to influence the interpretation of unfolding incidents. Responses to events set precedents for future actions and shape expectations. These responses can set boundaries for future actions and point to new paths of behavior as well as tackling to the inevitable testing that entrenched and skeptical groups try. Leaders need small victories to probe the environment and test for support or opposition. They build momentum, credibility, and can establish a new set of meaning to support the ethical culture (Daly, 2006).

Reflective action in this dimension aims to generate stable frame formation among individuals, groups, and institutions to support a culture of quality performance of goals. Leader's actions impart signals, precedents, expectations, boundaries, incentives, and establishes reputations and future possibilities (Schein, 2010). Success in the long run involves resetting expectations, reconnecting individual's actions with purpose, building trust in the purpose and leader as well as trust in each other (Huxham, 2003). Intentional actions shaped by consistent purpose and attention to the context and culture will accumulate impact over time and can lead to changed conditions, beliefs, and behaviors that give life to policy and institutions. These are fundamental to ethical success of purposes.

Leaders' actions convey information and signal to people the resoluteness, purpose, or competence of the leader or team. This signaling addresses not just the present but engages past interpretation and practice and gives rise to future expectations. The triad of signal, precedent, and expectations become focal dimensions for leaders to address. The strength of impact is reinforced when leaders attend to actions and when they measure actions and outcomes (Weick, 1995, 2000; Schein, 2010).

The leader's signals need to broadcast in 360° political space to authorizers, competitors, subordinates, or partners. Although this model depends heavily upon a person centered self and virtue, however, lone individuals can seldom withstand consistent pressure from the context, culture, and peers over a long period of time. The attribution error means people assign too much responsibility to an individual's character and ignore how institutional and culture pressures shape a person's behavior (Ross & Nisbett, 2011). To build up a reliable institutional purpose or policy implementation leaders must work to shape the meaning of incidents to build a political context and institutional culture that supports reliable behavior connected to the purpose. Unless actively managed, the impact of peer pressure and authority over time can erode both self-confidence and autonomy and lead people to become acclimated to dangerous or ethically problematic behavior. The institutionalization of deviance can result in massive institutional failure and wrongdoing. This means shaping the environment and culture become ethical imperatives, and leaders cannot rely solely upon individual behavior or virtue to achieve goals (Vaughn, 1997; Mischel, 1979; Ross, 2011; Zimbardo, 2007).

Self-awareness and a leadership team's attention can generate learning cultures where leaders and individuals discover unexpected or dangerous results. Adapting and learning becomes anchored in this approach to leading in multiple dimensions because the purposes and values must adapt to mistakes and new occurrences to give operational shape to purpose even as environments change (Bass, 2008). Leading for the long term will often involve adaptive actions that will depend upon slowing down time, learning and engaging a wide array of actors and stakeholders and careful cumulative exercise of power and cooperation. Seeking actions that grow from collaboration may take even more time to weave together a complex and durable outcome. Leaders need to devote constant vigilance to context and culture to organize collective action.

Actions influenced by focusing on this dimension can involve setting positive expectations about new forms of supported behavior. It may also breaking older cultural habits or historical inertia of an institution. Recalibrating culture involves setting new boundaries on behavior and moving problematic individuals out of the organization (Greener, 2002; Schein, 2009, 2010). Incidents often reveal deeper institutional dysfunctions or cultural challenges. To the extent leaders struggle to address cultural issues or respond to changes in the environment, then new boundaries have to be drawn even as new forms of positive action are patterned and supported. This approach means "unfreezing" existing norms and behavioral patterns as well as taking advantage of windows of urgency to create new organizational possibilities. Focusing upon the enduring impact on behavior, environment, and performance helps the leader shape the long-term ethical behavior of the organization (Schein, 2009, 2010). Boundary management poses unique dangers because people will carefully watch how boundaries are managed and how people are let go. When people are moved out or let go, these incidents ripple throughout organization and can create counter narratives that others use to discredit the leader and his or her goals. Leaders need to pay special attention to the fairness, care, and transparency of managing boundaries and moving people out because such actions set powerful precedents and reveal deep ethical concerns about fairness and impartiality. Building a culture or policy involves both linking an ethical narrative to the aspirations of individuals but also addressing people's interests and integrating them into long-term goals. The process of changing cultures reinforces the importance of seeing critical incidents as potential tipping points or strategic windows to shift agendas and belief systems. A new culture can arise from developing new attractors and behaviors sustained over time that transition from older norms and frames (Bridges, 1986, 2009; Kotter, 1996).

This dimensions requires relentless discipline in response to incidents and actions over time. The leader needs relentless self-awareness of their purpose and frames and how to adapt them to small daily incidents and meaning with a strategic focus upon the long term policy and institution values they are working towards. Culture accrues over time and practice as does learning. Leaders' actions set precedents that feed different narratives of support or opposition. The long game supported by sustained leadership modeling action builds incentives and paths to support a culture. This performance constructs new, shared frames sustained by cognitive practice over time.

POWER: BUILDING RESOURCES AND SUPPORT

The last dimension that carries critical ethical import in public virtue reflection involves the obligation to build the power, support, and resource bases for resilient policy or institution achievement (Lynn, 1987; Badaracco, 2002). This is the fourth dimension of the proposed public virtue frame for leading. The approach involves a recursive loop where individuals think through each dimension and test it against the other three and gradually come to a balanced judgment that incorporates all four dimensions. This approach incorporates both transactional and transformational approaches and is comfortable with integrating interest and ethical purpose as normal in leadership interactions (Bass & Riggio, 2006; Avioli, 1999; Badaracco, 2002). Some contemporary approaches emphasize a follower-oriented approach to leading to escape overemphasis upon a "heroic" model. This and other approaches often align with a heavy and sanguine focus upon collaboration that downplays individual efforts and intractable conflict (Lawler, 2008; Lemay, 2009).

This frame, however, remains resolutely person centered since persons, alone, work together with other persons to accomplish actions. Even in worlds of distributed leading or networked power, leaders will face opposition, conflict, and concerted effort to derail initiatives or interpret incidents in different ways. This opposition does not imply evil or ignorance but emerges as a normal facet of how humans of good will and institutions with different missions will differ over goals. Conflict can compound because at any nexus of a network or across partners, individuals on both sides become the critical mediators of common purpose. Individuals work to address the inevitable disagreements and misinterpretations that arise (Huxham, 2003; O'Leary, 2009). Any approach to leading cannot easily assume that distributive leading or preferences for collaboration or network solutions will not require individual initiative and responsibility to address opposition and power (Bass, 2006; Van Wart, 2012).

Attention to building power and resource bases for resilient performance begins with continuous self-awareness and a consistent focus upon attending to a person's own political capital and reputation (Badaracco, 2002; Daly and Watkins, 2006). These inhere to the person and can be developed and carried across different domains. Individual reputation become foundations of trust, partnership, or coalitions that individuals develop to achieve policy and institutional goals. This combination of political capital and reputation also inform credibility and trust in any negotiations.

In shared or diffuse power worlds, leaders need conscientious awareness of the range of actors and forces inhabiting a political environment. Scanning the environment to map relevant actors is an obligation of public virtue reflection. This reflection opens up inclusion and ethical recognition of significant actors. Understanding the actors and forces in political space identifies actors who can be engaged as collaborators, allies or opponents but also who should be included to address equity. Attending to sustainable power can focus leaders on building support networks and attending to weak and latent connections which provide a web of support, information, and resilience that can be called upon when needed (Grant, 2013; Gladwell, 2006; Crosby & Bryson, 2005).

Not attending to these actors and forces is a form of negligence because effective institutional or policy performance depends on political support and maintaining resources such as revenue, budgets, and expertise. Each funding cycle, election or regime change provides repeat chances for opponents to undermine a leader's institution or policy. Building and protecting resource bases means leaders have to attend to this institutional reality.

The power dimension also concentrates on creating strong cultures of performance that build on bases of educated and committed support within an organization. This can involve long term efforts to win over senior leaders or supervisors or change recruiting or reward standards. Deep change in normative behavior and performance means leaders need long term allies at multiple levels of power and support (Lynn, 1987). The culture evolves as "shared mental frames" to operationalize ethical standards of performance (Schein, 2009; Senge, 2006). This work establishes norms that endure when leaders change. It requires leaders work in a protracted manner to build support and resources for the culture. This dimension of leading can result in a range of distributed and committed leaders inhabiting multiple levels of authority and power to continue the evolving purpose.

This type of leading requires consistent self-awareness in the leader and leadership team to recur to the values, mission, and character that sustain them. This recurrence is doubly important because the existence of oppositional power and resource constraints will require compromises and changes. Changing conditions will necessitate regular adaptations that constitute both compromises with power but also learning. Likewise connections with collaborators or allies involve a never-ending adaptations to cultivate common commitments even as distance in networks and local conditions constrain beliefs and actions. Sometimes keeping momentum alive or minimizing mortal harm to the institution becomes the best that can be achieved. This last dimension to building support, legitimacy, and resources that possess political resilience. Figure 2.2 lays out a checklist to

Self-awareness	Incident—Challenge

• Self-mastery—self-discipline
• Self-reflection linked to integrity
• Know one's values—purpose
• Know one's character
• Basis of promises & accountability
• Know one's frames of judgment
• Aware of self narrative
• Fit frames/roles to values
• Fit values & frame to situation
• Avoid self-deception
• Avoid frame lock
• Avoid heuristic traps
• Avoid groupthink
• Build diverse team
• Friends-external support for integrity
• Map historical context
	• Leading as continuous decisions
	• Daily events matter
	• Each incident cast in multiple ways
	• History affects meanings
	• Default frames define incident
	• Address incident in light of purpose
	• Actors conflict over interpretation
	• Focal points of conflict—actors with different agendas
	• Incident as:
	    Agenda setting moments
	    Windows of opportunity
	    Build long term authority
	• Leader sets precedent & energy
	• Expectations built culture over time
	• Long term purpose

Build policy—institution	Build power—resource base
• Self aware of purpose--mission • Connect law, mandate & purpose • Map 360 degree environment • Build resilient capacity • Set expectations, boundaries & norms • Shape authority and peer culture • Link culture & competence • Adapt purpose to environment • Engage levels of environment • Play long game	• Keep awareness of purpose • Prepare for world of opposition or collaboration—allies • Map & address opposition/allies • Deploy influence for purposes • Attend to Reputation/credibility • Connect partners and allies • Build up resources-expertise • Manage media • Budget support • Culture support • Distributed leader cadre • Address disagreements and seek common ground and values across partners & collaboration

Figure 2.2 Four dimensions of public virtue.

identify the key point of each of the four dimensions of the Public Virtue frame to guide a leader's thinking.

Judith Perez and her senior staff sought solutions to the crisis that would both reframe the issues and rebuild support for the mission. At the core they needed to buy time to gather information, engage protagonists, and come up with their own solution. The agency continued to fracture and arguments flared in the hallway. After the mediator reported to Perez on what appeared to have happened, Perez and her team worked closely with the union representatives to develop a shared picture of what happened. She negotiated with the Human Rights department to wait until she could respond. Informal contacts with office friends of the two helped persuade them to delay grievance filing.

The mediator's report gave Perez and her team a more complex picture. Thomas Nguyen often stared into space or at fellow workers as he worked or talked with people. He seldom read the personal reaction of coworkers to this. His coworkers and supervisors understood he processed information in a different way. His supervisor had worked with him about reading emotional signals. For Richard Aleaga, however, his Pacific Islander identify had been influenced by staredowns as a form of confrontation. In traditional society staring could be an attempt to capture souls, but in street life it was about tests of power and respect among young males.

Perez believed the incident illustrated the very issues her agency grappled with every day and wanted to model to everyone how to address these issues on the inside. She preferred no punitive action, and the union agreed but wanted serious training to deal with workplace violence. Perez and his supervisor worked with Aleaga to understand the cognitive style of Nguyen and arrange a private apology. Aleaga's manager found a Pacific Islander from another division to meet periodically with Aleaga as a mentor. The agency integrated this experience into their next training session. They also incorporated issues of how to respond to different cognitive processing styles into their orientation. Human Rights chose not to act when neither person pursued their complaints.

Perez emphasized how volatile this relatively minor incident became. She worked hard to slow down the process and avoid escalation into litigation. She spent time keeping each major institutional actor updated and worked carefully with union representatives. At the same time she had to reassure impatient senior managers that the issue was being addressed. She believed union support was crucial to maintain for the long-term culture she wanted; the division's relation with Human Rights was strained because the agency wanted to move but could not without a formal grievance. Her decision to address the issue largely informally with mentoring and an apology also led to some opposition from people who felt the "violence" merited harsher action. Perez accepted that criticism and pointed out that the agency protocol emphasized working with clients at the most informal level. She believed the incident was a chance to reaffirm the mission and model consistency within the agency as well as strengthen the range of orientation teaching.

The open-ended but dual strategies devised by Chief Dean and Newberger revealed many of the same concerns about shifting culture and building support. They began serious efforts to shift the agenda and initiated proposals when the reports were completed. An outside technical review concluded that the replacement engine had been well maintained and been tested four days before the fire. All replacement engines were tested and found up to standards. The report did highlight the age of the engines. The incident study discovered the deaths had occurred very quickly because of the small space, closed windows and fire speed.

When the city council and mayor did not respond to the fire marshall's recommendation for sprinklers, the media aggressively pushed for concrete changes. After meeting with the chief, the mayor quietly pulled back the cuts to the department, and Chief Dean announced a phased replacement of older fire equipment as well as new resources for hiring and community outreach. He framed the campaign around prevention. The mayor's office announced a citywide effort to review fleet management and maintenance procedures. City lawyers began intense dialogues with the community about how traditional forms of restitution could be made.

Newberger believed the timing of outreach efforts was critical because the tragedy presented a short window to educate people. The chief continued his community meetings often bringing captains or assistant chiefs to gain their ownership of outreach. The chief and most senior leaders concluded that the traditional reliance upon school education was insufficient. The department continued to face mistrust and opposition across some community activists but worked hard with established community groups and elders to find respected community individuals to be champions of fire education. These persons were trained in basic fire prevention using visual training aids. The individuals received a stipend and used the information to build outreach into the community even meeting in homes with gathered families. The department encouraged the champions to bring firefighters to these meetings to reinforce the education and build commitment within the department.

The chief and senior fire department staff used new funds to expand a highly publicized hiring campaign aimed at increasing diversity in the department. The fire department found itself newly connected in mutual relations with a wide array of neighborhoods and groups. The fallout from the tragedy continued for several years around legal liability concerns that ranged from mattresses to fire hoses. Relations with the assisted living homes had to be addressed in ongoing negotiations to both smooth their anger over the emails but also address the resource cost to the department. Some activists considered the outreach efforts "fake" or irrelevant, but the department and local community leaders believe significant success had been made.

Chief Dean believed that the tragedy required major changes in the department's commitment to prevention and outreach. To gain trust from the communities meant engaging people's anger and frustration for a much longer period of time than many politicians preferred. The chief worked to defend the beleaguered line firefighters but worked constantly to get firefighters more invested in prevention. In addition after the mayor and council refused to mandate sprinkling systems in all subsided housing, the chief and leadership team leveraged that action into serious investments in needed equipment upgrade and hiring and outreach. They discussed afterwards how hard it had been to slow down time and not respond to the vituperation of the media or demand for quick and uninformed action. The senior management team devoted hours to listen and work with communities to reframe the political debate to support prevention and outreach.

CONCLUSION

This paper argues that leading with public virtue involves using a frame of judgment to focus reflection and perception. The frame identifies the ethically relevant aspects of leading that flow from the goals and consequences of taking responsibility to lead in public life. The frame lays out four dimensions that a leader seeking to act with public virtue should account for in their decision-making. These dimensions become obligations of public virtue to which a leader should attend or risk ethical negligence. This frame grows from a very simple understanding of leading as being present in a way that changes the expected impact upon people and conditions. As presented the frame can accommodate diverse approaches to leading as well as a wide array of tactical styles of leading. The dimensions scale to cover a wide array of situations with special emphasis upon leading in institutions. The mental frame and dimensions help individuals exercise public virtue as a disciplined guide to think decide and act in a fast and knowledgeable manner.

The mental frame of public virtue depends upon individuals possessing the self-awareness and discipline to attend to the four dimensions: self and self-awareness, the meaning of incidents and challenges, building an institution or policy, and achieving power and resources to sustain goals. The level of self-awareness covers not only one's value commitments and the threats of self-deception or flawed decision making but expands to an awareness of 360° understanding of political space. Practice and awareness permits one's body, mind, and judgment to exquisitely map the world, recall past experiences, and contribute to judgment by learning and adapting

(Damasio, 1999, 2012; Bazerman, 2011; Klein, 1998, 2009). Individuals can practice deploying the frame to focus their decision-making and actions.

This approach to public virtue understands leading as intentional presence to change the expected outcomes if a person had not intentionally chosen to be present. Leading involves action that entails ethical consequences and imposes a responsibility to perform reflectively. This approach sees leading as an activity that is agnostic about transactional or transformative methods as well as authority or participative. It scales from dyads to collections of individuals to institutions. Realistically, this approach nests most comfortably with individuals seeking to lead in institutional settings. The frame requires self-awareness and adopting a way of thinking and to train one self to focus and guide a person's attention and energy. This frame requires cognitive, emotional, and perceptual discipline consistent with a virtue based ethics that integrates a wide range of values, principles and mandates, as well as obligations based upon a person's promise to abide by the mandates of the position. As a form of human virtue the frame can be learned, used, and adapted to the historical mutability of leading for public purpose.

NOTES

1. The focus on institutions makes sense given that most individuals seeking to make a difference in public life will be involved in government or nonprofit institutions or living at the intersection of them in a world of governance. In the United States in 2015 an estimated 32 million individuals participate in government and nonprofit organizations.
2. The names and places in the cases have been masked to protect confidentiality.
3. The dimensions laid out as well as the emphasis upon seeing the world in 360 degrees where the political actors and forces are addressed above, below, equal and back and front of the actor with purpose owe much to the initial formulations of Laurence Lynn (1987) about how public leaders must play a complex game at multiple levels to succeed.

REFERENCES

Aristotle. (1999). *Nicomachean ethics 2nd Ed.* (T. Irwin, Trans.). Indianapolis, IN: Hackett.

Aristotle. (2013). *Eudemian ethics* (P. Simpson, Trans.). New Brunswick, NJ: Transaction..

Avolio, B. J., Bass, B. M., & Jung, D. I. (1999). Re-examining the components of transformational and transactional leadership using the multifactor leadership. *Journal of Occupational and Organizational Psychology, 72*(4), 441–462.

Badaracco, J. (2002). *Leading quietly.* Cambridge, MA: Harvard Business School Press.

Bass, B. M. (2008). *The bass handbook of leadership: Theory, research, & managerial applications.* New York, NY: Free Press.

Bass, B. M., & Riggio, R. E. (2006). *Transformational leadership.* New York, NY: NY: Psychology Press.

Baumeister, R. F. (1991). *Meanings of life.* New York, NY: Guilford Press.

Bazerman, M. H., & Tenbrunsel, A. E. (2011) *Blind spots: Why we fail to do what's right and what to do about it.* Princeton, NJ: Princeton University Press.

Beiner, R. (1983, 2010). *Political Judgment.* London, England: Methuen.

Beshears, J., & Gino, F. (2015). Leaders as decision architects. *Harvard Business Review,* May, 52–62.

Bolman, L. G., & Deal, T. E. (2011). *Reframing organizations: Artistry, choice and leadership.* New York, NY: John Wiley & Sons.

Bridges, W. (1986). Managing organizational transitions. *Organizational dynamics, 15*(1), 24–33.

Bridges, W. (2009). *Managing transitions: Making the most of change.* New York, NY: Da Capo Press.

Cialdini, R. B. (2009). *Influence: Science and practice* (5th ed). Boston, MA: Pearson.

Cooper, J. M. (1975). *Reason and human good in Aristotle.* Cambridge, MA. Harvard University Press.

Cooper, T. L. (1987). Hierarchy, virtue and the practice of public administration: A perspective for normative ethics. *Public Administration Review, 47*(4), 320–328.

Cooper, T. L. (2012). *The responsible administrator: An approach to ethics for the administrative role* (6th. ed). San Francisco, CA: Jossey-Bass.

Crosby, B., & Bryson J. (2005). *Leadership for the common good: Tackling public problems in a shared power world.* San Francisco, CA: Jossey Bass.

Daly, P. H., & Watkins, M. (2006). *The first ninety days in government: Critical success strategies for new public managers at all levels.* Cambridge, MA: Harvard Business Review Press.

Damasio, A. (1999). *The feeling of what happens: Body and emotion in the making of consciousness.* New York, NY: Harcourt Brace.

Damasio, A. (2012). *Self comes to mind: Constructing the conscious brain.* New York, NY: Vintage.

Fairhurst, G. T., & Sarr, R. A. (1996). *The art of framing: Managing the language of leadership.* San Francisco, CA: Jossey-Bass.

Fingarette, H. (2000). *Self-deception: With a new chapter.* Berkeley, CA: University of California Press.

Garvin, D. A., & Margolis, J. D. (2015). The art of giving and receiving advice. *Harvard Business Review,* January–February, 60–71.

Gladwell, M. (2006). *The tipping point: How little things can make a big difference.* Boston, MA: Little, Brown.

Goleman, D. (2000). Leadership that gets results. *Harvard Business Review,* March–April, 78–90.

Goldhamer, H. (1978). *The advisor.* New York, NY: Elsevier.

Grant, A. (2013). *Give and take: A revolutionary approach to success.* New York, NY: Viking.

Greener, I. (2002).Theorising path-dependency: How does history come to matter in organisations? *Management Decision, 40*(6), 614–619.

Huxham, C. (2003). Theorizing collaboration practice. *Public management review, 5*(3), 401–423.

Janis, I. L. (1982). *Groupthink: Psychological studies of policy decisions and fiascoes.* Boston, MA: Houghton Mifflin.

Janis, I. L., & Mann, L. (1977). *Decision making: A psychological analysis of conflict, choice, and commitment.* New York, NY: Free Press.

Kahneman, D. (2011). *Thinking fast and slow.* New York, NY: Farrar, Strauss, and Giroux.

Klein, G. A. (1998). *Sources of power: How people make decisions.* Cambridge, MA. MIT Press.

Klein, G. A. (2008). Naturalistic decision making. *Human factors: The journal of the human factors and ergonomics society, 50*(3), 456–460.

Klein, G. A. (2009). *Streetlights and shadows: Searching for the keys to adaptive decision making.* Cambridge, MA. MIT Press.

Kotter, J. P. (1996). *Leading change.* Cambridge, MA: Harvard Business Press.

Kouzes, J. M., & Posner, B. Z. (2006). *The leadership challenge* (Vol. 3). New York, NY: John Wiley & Sons.

Kouzes, J. M., & Posner, B. Z. (2011). *Credibility: How leaders gain and lose it, why people demand it* (Vol. 244). New York, NY: John Wiley & Sons.

Lakoff, G., & Johnson, M. (1999). *Philosophy in the flesh: The embodied mind and its challenge to western thought.* New York, NY: Basic books.

Lakoff, G., & Johnson, M. (2008). *Metaphors we live by.* Chicago, IL: University of Chicago press.

Lawler, J. (2008). Individualization and public sector leadership. *Public administration, 86*(1), 21–34.

LeDoux, J. (2002). *The synaptic brain: How our brains become who we are.* New York, NY: Penguin.

Lemay, L. (2009). The practice of collective and strategic leadership in the public sector. *Innovation Journal, 14*(1), 1–19.

Lynn, L. E. (1987). *Managing public policy.* Boston, MA: Little Brown.

Machiavelli, N. (1992). *The Prince* (R. M. Adams, Trans.). New York, NY: Norton Critical Edition.

MacIntyre, A. C. (2007). *After virtue: A study in moral theory (3rd ed).* Notre Dame, IN: Notre Dame University Press.

Mischel, W. (1979). On the interface of cognition and personality: Beyond the person–situation debate. *American Psychologist, 34*(9), 740.

Moberg, D. J. (2006). Ethics blind spots in organizations: How systematic errors in person perception undermine moral agency. *Organization Studies, 27*(3), 413–428.

O'Leary, R., & Bingham, L. B. (Eds.). (2009). *The collaborative public manager: New ideas for the twenty-first century.* Washington, DC: Georgetown University Press.

Pinker, S. (1999). *How the mind works.* New York, NY: W. W. Norton.

Ross, L., & Nisbett, R. E. (2011). *The person and the situation: Perspectives of social psychology.* New York, NY: NY: Pinter & Martin.

Schein, E. H. (2009). *The corporate culture survival guide (JB warren Bennis series)*. San Francisco, CA: Jossey-Bass.

Schein, E. H. (2010). *Organizational culture and leadership*. New York, NY: NY: John Wiley & Sons, NY.

Sherman, N. (1989). *The fabric of character: Aristotle's theory of virtue*. Oxford, England: Clarendon Press.

Senge, P. M., Scharmer, C. O., Jaworski, J., & Flowers, B. S. (2005). *Presence: An exploration of profound change in people, organizations, and society*. New York, NY: Doubleday

Senge, P. (2006). *The fifth discipline: The art and practice of the learning organization*. New York, NY: Doubleday.

Schon, D. (1984). *The reflective practitioner: How professionals think in action*. New York, NY; Basic Books.

Stark, A. (2003). *Conflict of interest in American public life*. Cambridge, MA: Harvard University Press.

Sun-tzu. (2002). *The art of war*. In J. Minford (Trans.). New York, NY: Penguin.

Van Wart, M. (2012). *Leadership in public organizations: An introduction*. New York, NY: M. E. Sharpe.

Vaughan, D. (1997). *The Challenger launch decision: Risky technology, culture, and deviance at NASA*. Chicago, IL: University of Chicago Press.

Weick, K. E. (1988). Enacted sensemaking in crisis situations. *Journal of management studies, 25*(4), 305–317.

Weick, K. E. (1995). *Sensemaking in organizations* (Foundations for organizational science). Thousands Oaks, CA: SAGE.

Weick, K. E. (2000). Emergent change as a universal in organizations. *Breaking the code of change*, 223–241.

Zimbardo, P. (2007). *The Lucifer effect: Understanding how good people turn evil*. New York, NY: Random House.

CHAPTER 3

SHAMANS, MEMES, AND ETHICAL LEADERSHIP

The Transformational Role of Shamanic Leadership in Healing the World

Sandra Waddock
Boston College

ABSTRACT

In traditional cultures, shamans are leaders within their communities. As medicine women and men, shamans focus on healing individuals and cultural mythologies on which communities make sense of their world. Shamans are dedicated to making their world a better place, an important aspect of ethical leadership. This chapter explores how shamanism can enhance today's ethical leaders—business shamans. A shamanic orientation can help leaders work towards profitability *and* a better world and argues that the world needs many more people in leadership and management to explicitly assume the healing mantle of the shaman.

When we think of leaders with our modern sensibilities, just about the last thing that comes to mind is the shaman. Yet in traditional cultures,

Radical Thoughts on Ethical Leadership, pages 47–67
Copyright © 2017 by Information Age Publishing
All rights of reproduction in any form reserved.

shamans are clearly among the leaders within their communities. As medicine women and men, they are focused on healing individuals and the cultural mythologies on which the community relies to make sense of their world. Shamans, that is, are dedicated to making their world a better place, arguably the core task of ethics writ large, and an important aspect of ethical leadership. This chapter explores how the fundamentals of shamanism can enrich and enhance today's ethical leaders, whether in business (where we might call them business shamans), politics, or other walks of life. A shamanic orientation can help leaders work towards not just profitability and other forms of success for their firms but also and importantly, a better world. Further, I will make the case that the world needs many more people in leadership positions of all sorts to explicitly assume the healing mantle of the shaman, in this case the business shaman (also, edgewalkers, Neal, 2006), to cope with the many problems facing our troubled world.

This chapter focuses on shamans in the modern context without ritualistic trappings or belief systems. Traditional shamans primarily focus at the individual and community levels, while modern leaders as shamans work within organizations of various types as well as in the broader society using a wide range of capacities. In developing these ideas, I draw from wide reading about shamanism and two books in which I explore the ways that people make a difference in the world, *Intellectual Shamans: Management Academics Making a Difference* (Waddock, 2015), and *The Difference Makers: How Social and Institutional Entrepreneurs Built the Corporate Responsibility Movement* (Waddock, 2008). *Intellectual Shamans* explores the ways leading academics in management are shamanic and here that thinking extends to leaders in other domains, particularly business. *The Difference Makers* explores how individuals work in the interstices between organizations and institutions to create change that helps improve the world. Business leaders can arguably do much the same in the contexts of their businesses and in the ways that those businesses interact with their stakeholders and the greater world around them.

To be clear, I am not arguing that today's leaders should return to the occult, mystical, or ritualistic practices of the traditional shaman, and particularly not to the dark practices of the sorcerer (the shaman who uses his/her power for negative or selfish purposes). Rather, the argument is that many more of today's leaders can and need to tap into the healing that understanding of connectedness, relationship, and reframed cultural mythologies that shamans work with to bring about healing in our troubled world. Shamans have three core tasks, healing, connecting, and sensemaking, which they use to bring about the changes needed in their worlds, arguably much as business shamans do in today's world and its institutions. The mantle of the shaman is accessible to people if they are willing to take the risks and step away from expectations and conventions within their contexts, to become fully who they must be, fulfilling their unique higher purpose in life, and putting their effort towards building a better, more constructive, values-based world using their particular gifts of healing, connecting, and sensemaking.

OVERVIEW AND BACKGROUND

Little has been written in the management literature on shamans, with the exception of two papers by Peter Frost and Carolyn Egri, who focus on organizational development practitioners as shamans, and synthesize a great deal of literature, and my own recent book on *Intellectual Shamans*. As noted, shamans in traditional cultures are the medicine men and women who work on both individual patients and the community. Typically, shamans are well-known, respected, even revered figures central to the life and wellbeing of their local people and communities. Whether they are found in modern society or more traditional cultures, shamans have three central tasks: healing, connecting, and sensemaking (Waddock, 2015; Frost & Egri, 1994; Egri & Frost, 1991).

Not all leaders are shamans, since shamans have certain qualities and functions that they perform. The key function is a healing orientation, that is, shamans (unlike their destructive counterparts—sorcerers) are fundamentally healers. In the case of business shamans, they are leaders who want their enterprises to, for example, deliver useful and needed products or services, where participants can make real contributions and find wellbeing. Or they are business leaders who use their power to help enhance the world outside their organizations.

A healing orientation alone is not sufficient to classify someone as a shaman. Shamans are also connectors, who cross a variety of realms or boundaries to gather information (e.g., Frost & Egri, 1994), work with others, and create new relationships, insights, and ideas that link across boundaries for healing purposes. Further, they are sensemakers, who help others to understand their world in new ways that make life better not just for humans but for other living creatures as well.

Business leaders as shamans, like intellectual shamans, are what scholar James P. Walsh calls people of light, that is, they seem to have an inner light that seems to draw others to them (see Waddock, 2015). They have and use their particular powers and gifts to do the healing work of the shaman, rather than for more inward or self-interested purposes. They are, that is, oriented toward helping others or helping the world and its enterprises and institutions become better—more healed. Recognizing that they are working in the modern context without the psycho-magical rituals and trappings of traditional shamans, today's business shamans would most likely not even recognize themselves as shamans.

Healing

Shamanic healing involves the integration of mind, body, heart, and spirit, first for the shaman and then for others (King, 2009; cf. Wilber, Patten, Leonard & Morelli, 2008) and its translation into healing work of some sort. Tending towards holistic thinking, the shaman avoids the fragmentation of much western and modern thought, especially the separation of mind and body by taking a holistic, integrated perspective on the world, on people and their relationships to the world, and to each other. She or he sees the whole, not just the parts—the whole organization, the way the enterprise interacts with others or society, the linkages between businesses and nature, for example. This holistic orientation helps avoid what stakeholder scholar Ed Freeman (1994) calls the separation thesis—the idea that ethics can be separated from actions and decisions.

Healing the patient, the community, the organization, and especially the relationships among them (King, 2009) and with nature, at whatever level of analysis is relevant, is the central shamanic task. For leaders in business enterprises that means working in organizations, and sometimes more broadly in societies, rather than working with individual patients as traditional shamans do, although effective leaders certainly work with and influence individuals. Indeed, one mark of a good leader is that people feel that they do their best for her or him, transcending whatever problems they might have to do their best work for that leader.

"Healer, heal yourself" is something often said to psycho-therapists, physicians, and nurses. It is equally true that shamans first need to heal themselves before they can heal others, their organizations, or communities. It is hard to be an effective shaman, to do good in the world and be a change agent for the better, that is, do healing work, while suffering from physical, emotional, spiritual, or psychological ills. It is equally hard to be a shaman when ego gets in the way or one is caught up in the frenzy of power and greed that seems to beset too many so-called leaders today. In many shamanic traditions, the would-be shaman undergoes some sort of trauma to be "reborn" as a healthy person. Sometimes the healing or rebirth experience is a physical near-death experience; other times, the rebirth takes place while in the trance state or other "imaginal" realm. Some shamans become apprentices and go through various initiations. Others are simply "called" to shamanism and the healing that is involved.

The idea of the "imaginal" is an important underpinning to understanding shamanism in the modern context, because it allows the shaman to experience "real" things through the imagination, as when the shaman "journeys" to other realms to experience new insights and gather information for healing purposes. The word imaginal was invented by Henri Corbin to make a distinction between the imaginary and the experienced realm of everyday reality. Corbin and Horine (1976) wanted to provide a concept that suggested a greater degree of realism and vividness than the purely imaginary while recognizing that the images seen cannot necessarily be found in everyday reality. The *imago*, which means image of god or in more modern manifestations an idealized image of another individual, can be found between experienced or everyday reality and pure imagination. The trance state in which the imaginal—real-seeming experiences—can be found can be induced by meditative techniques, or it can be induced via drugs, drumming, dancing, singing, chanting, deprivation experiences, intense exercise (e.g., the runner's high), hard work, or other extreme conditions. Similarly, modern business shamans transcend the narrowness of shareholder wealth maximization, growth at all costs, and similar strictures on how business is practiced, by focusing holistically and realistically on broader purposes, relationships, and understanding of their organization's impacts and "imagining" ways for their enterprises to perform and behave better for stakeholders, societies, and nature.

Connecting

The connecting function of the shaman involves crossing into different realms to gather information that is needed and bring it back to the community (patient) that needs it. Connecting, or what Frost & Egri (1994) call "mediating realities" for traditional shamans, is a boundary-spanning function. Connecting involves traditional shamans going to different spiritual realms and speaking with guides or spirits. Done in trance states (induced by a variety of means), connecting exposes the traditional shaman to new information (derived, I speculate, from inner resources or the collective unconscious articulated by Jung) that can be used in the healing process. Business leaders today also need to experience multiple realms to be successful and to be able to fully understand the complexities of their tasks. They also need to understand that ethical aspects of decisions and actions by companies and their managers are not separable.

Boundary-spanning or connecting of all sorts has become an imperative for the business shaman, not just in partnership situations, but also in integrating across functional and disciplinary areas in companies, in bringing in stakeholder perspectives, different cultural and national perspectives, and in incorporating a wide range of ideas and issues into the ways in which products and services are developed, among others. Because the complexity of business has increased and because companies, particularly large and transnational companies, no longer operate successfully within restricted or limited domains, their leaders have to be comfortable crossing boundaries of all sorts that were less relevant in earlier days. For example, social and ecological pressures on companies today demand some degree of familiarity with the different societies within which the company operates—a boundary-spanning activity, as well as with the limits and resilience of natural resources on which the company depends. Further, companies increasingly are called upon to engage with a variety of stakeholders—who often have quite different perspectives than do corporate executives and who can be severe critics of the firm if their views are not fairly and equitably taken into consideration. One relevant definition of the shaman, from Serge Kahili King, is "a healer of relationships: between mind and body, between people, between people and circumstances, between humans and Nature, and between matter and spirit" (King, 2009, p. 14). This definition focuses both on the healing and connecting aspects of shamanism.

Within businesses, crossing boundaries or realms has become more important. Calls for integration across sub-units and functional areas within the firm, cross-disciplinary research and development that takes numerous perspectives into account, and incorporation of numerous stakeholders' perspectives are crucial elements of successful innovation today. Indeed, some corporate innovation these days is actually social innovation, because it integrates the company's business purposes with its numerous roles and impacts in societies. Cross sector collaborations have become common in many corporations as companies struggle to figure out how to enact positive roles in societies—and connectors—leaders who can bridge between sectors, disciplines, functions, and stakeholders—are essential to handling these growing complexities well.

Sensemaking

Sensemaking is a word coined by Karl Weick, who defines it as "[t]he ongoing retrospective development of plausible images that rationalize what people are doing" and "turning circumstances into a situation that is comprehended explicitly in words and that serves as a springboard to action" (Weick, Sutcliffe & Obstfeld, 2005, p. 409). Weick and colleagues argue that sensemaking occurs when there is a gap between the way the world is currently perceived and the way that perceivers expect (or perhaps want) it to be. The sensemaking process thus represents an attempt to improve and make sense of the world. For the shaman, that effort involves shifting the relevant cultural mythology, which is the reason that the patient is thought to be sick, to something more coherent or better (e.g., Dow, 1986). The role of sensemaker is thus as crucial to the shaman as that of healer and connector (e.g., Frost & Egri, 1994; Egri & Frost, 1991).

Indeed, often it is through the sensemaking role played by business shamans that we can recognize them. Sometimes called seers (but equally, feelers, sensors, knowers, visionaries, or interpreters), shamans are tellers of the truth as they see it—having gained insight and even wisdom from their journeys across different realms in the connecting role. In their sensemaking capacity, they function as meaning makers for others, often working at the level of memes, or foundational units of information, ideas, and culture, to shape or reshape them in ways that heal the cultural mythology that seems somehow broken.

Traditional shamans as sensemakers gain their insights from journeying in trance states induced in a variety of ways. In their journeys they imaginally speak with power animals and other spirits, who provide needed information and insights. Similarly, modern shamans can, through reflective practices such as meditation, mindfulness practice, yoga, qi gong, and other approaches that enhance mindfulness and that can put one into the trance state, or states such as amazing teamwork, exercising, and intensive concentration on something that challenges and engages and produces the state called "flow" (Csikszentmihalyi, 1991). Such states, I believe, permit access to what the great psychologist Karl Jung (1981) called the collective unconscious, and hence what he called "primordial images" of which human myths are constituted. Accessing these archetypes arguably releases deep wisdom that lies within each of us when we quiet down and search internally. Jung believed that these archetypes (e.g., the mother, the father, the self) within the collective unconscious were the material out of which myths and mythologies were formed, and which manifest through dreams and visions. Jung also believed that these archetypes and the wisdom that they convey are universally accessible to humans—and innate, that is, something that we are all born with. Having the courage to access these "imaginal" realms in the trance state is partly what distinguishes the shaman from others. I believe that transformational leaders, too, experience the deep questions about what it means to be human that are aroused in these experiences, bringing these questions to their leadership.

Egri & Frost (1991, p. 175) argued that understanding shamanic healing builds on a set of three principles that recognize: (a) multiple realities or worlds, (b) the interconnectedness and interdependence and holism of the world (a view that is consistent with what complexity science and physics now tell us), and (c) that "change is a process, not an outcome." These three aspects of shamanic healing are deeply intertwined with the idea of the shaman as sensemaker, which they term spiritual leader. When we think of business leaders in this sensemaking capacity as articulating the deeper purpose(s) of businesses rather than simply repeating the mantra of growth and profitability at all costs, this sensemaking role becomes clearer.

Shamans, in other words, clarify experienced reality for people, helping them to understand it in new and potentially more powerful (and healing) ways. Implicitly, the sensemaking function of the shaman is that of helping others to make sense of a confusing and often troubled world in ways that promote healing ideas, connections, and actions. Thus, business shamans can focus on purposes for their enterprises beyond growth or shareholder wealth—and thereby inspire others to work for a better world by setting out new memes—new ideas of what the role of the business is in the world. Business leaders accomplish much the same task through envisioning how the business relates to the world around it in constructive, positive, and ethical ways and helping people to understand their vision.

Shapeshifting

Shapeshifting, which is also part of shamanic traditions, involves transmuting oneself imaginally into something else—someone else, an animal, a part of nature, for example. Shapeshifting means experiencing the imaginal realm, for example, what it feels like to be a tree, another person, a rock, or whatever it is the shaman shapeshifts into imaginally. The experience can feel quite "real" when the shapeshifter lets his or her imagination go and allows the experience of the other being to enter the psyche. In Corbin's view (Corbin & Horine, 1976), the imaginal realm is as to the soul as the physical realm is to the body and the intellect/imagination to spirit.

Shapeshifting involves a very real capacity to "put ourselves into the other's position," whether the other is a stakeholder (e.g., an employee, a customer, a community member, an investor), a part of nature like a tree, or something that is not typically considered alive, like a lake or a rock. Because the imaginal allows us to see through the eyes of the other, whether the "other" is another person, a piece of technology, or a part of nature, it can provide interesting new insights and perspectives. Arguably, this capacity to shapeshift, which really means to embody the perspective of another being of some sort, is an attribute of the highly cognitively and morally-developed individual, one who has achieved a post-conventional level of consciousness (Kohlberg, 1973).This capacity as a post-conventional level of human development where the capacity to take on the perspective of others is evident is also associated with holistic thinking characteristic of the shaman, and the capacity to understand multiple paradigms and perspectives simultaneously (Kegan, 1982). Psychologist Robert Kegan (1994) has argued that unless leaders and managers can accomplish these tasks and progress to such post-conventional levels of development, they are likely to be "in over [their] heads."

The capacity to shapeshift permits a recognition of the inherent "otherness" and ultimately, the worthiness, of the person or object that we shapeshift into, allowing us to inherently recognize the other's dignity and worth, as well as to see their perspective on the world in wholly new ways. Too many of today's leaders lack these capabilities, which fundamentally reflect the capacity for empathy, perspective-taking, and systems thinking. Shapeshifting as shamanic practice can potentially help leaders develop this and other essential capabilities needed for business leaders to gain much needed wisdom for them and their enterprises to cope successfully in the world today.

Shamanic power, and there is power associated with the shaman, is decidedly spiritual in traditional cultures in the sense given by the physicist Fritjof Capra and his co-author Pier Luigi Luisi (2014, p. 276):

Spirituality is a much broader and more basic human experience than religion. It has two dimensions: one going inward or "upward," as it were; and the other going outward, embracing the world and our fellow human beings. Either of the two manifestations may or may not be accompanied by religion. (Capra & Luisi, 2014, p. 276)

It is in particularly the "outward" orientation toward the world and other people that is relevant in the context of ethical leadership. Such an orientation embraces spirituality as identifying with what Capra and Luisi (2014, p. 276) call the "mysteries of the cosmos," and "expressing through their lives higher ideals of a better humanity." Such a view of spirituality is entirely compatible with current scientific understandings of the world (Capra & Luisi, 2014). It may, however, conflict with some of the more negative practices sometimes associated with businesses, including pollution, environmental degradation, or technologies that are destructive of a harmonized relationship between human and nature. In this sense, the leader considered as shaman carries an ethical responsibility to treat other people and nature as integrally worthy, that is, as if it has dignity (Hicks, 2011a, b; see also, Waddock, 2016). By exploring deeper purposes, assumptions, and narratives that surround business practice, shamanic business leaders can begin to articulate purposes—and new practices—that help heal the troubled world.

The power of the shaman as leader, even if the leader is not explicitly spiritual, comes from understanding that insight, knowledge, creativity, and the capacity to help heal a situation comes from something beyond the individual leader and flows through her or him. In traditional contexts, the shaman would call on Spirit or multiple spirits for guidance and insight. Modern leaders as shamans draw upon personal or more universal sources of creativity, insight, and knowledge, for example, through meditative techniques and mindfulness practices of various sorts that allow access to what psychologist Carl Jung called the collective unconscious. They can also draw upon other sources, for example by expanding their awareness across traditional boundaries that others may not access (e.g., organizational or social boundaries, disciplinary boundaries, inspiration from different readings, people, or other sources).

Wisdom can be defined as the integration of moral imagination (the good), systems understanding (the true), and aesthetic sensibility (the beautiful) in the service of the greater good (Waddock, 2010, 2014). Business shamans move toward wisdom and away from self-interest. Too many of our business (and other) leaders today are blinded by self-interest and fail to even recognize the existence of a construct called the common good. But wisdom tells us that we need systems understanding—a reasonably realistic perspective on the system, which is the shaman's holistic perspective— if we are to begin to heal our world.

That our current system is experiencing human-induced climate change is accepted by some 98+ percent of actual climate scientists . . . and that it is rejected by far too many so-called leaders is a denial of system reality that comes about in part because leaders are benefiting from the system of business as usual and dealing with the sustainability crisis requires significant change in business and other practices. Such leaders have conveniently been influenced by an ideology (neoliberalism/neoclassical economics) that tells them that the system will benefit if they act in their own self-interest. It will not and does not, as the mounting evidence of the negative impact of externalities like CO_2 and other forms of pollution suggests. Further evidence is provided by acknowledge growth in the gap between rich and poor throughout the world, which as Diamond (2005) has pointed out is one of two major factors in civilizational collapse, along with pushing environmental resources beyond the limits at which they can support the civilization.

Wisdom also requires moral imagination—the ability to see the ethical implications and consequences of decisions, actions, and practices within the system (e.g., Werhane, 2002, 2008), that is the ethical issues associated with any given system. Werhane has noted that systems thinking (understanding) and moral imagination are related. This aspect of wisdom requires leaders to really understand how the decisions and actions undertaken on behalf of their companies affect different stakeholders and the natural environment. It relates to a definition of wisdom offered by management scholar Russell Ackoff (1999) that argues that wisdom is the ability to understand the consequences of decisions. Wisdom can thus be associated with the connecting capacity of the shaman—the ability to see across systems, boundaries, limits, realms, people(s), and lines that can impede holistic or systems understanding.

Aesthetic sensibility is a less commonly noted attribute of wisdom; it applies to a sense of the design of the system, organization, society, or other relevant entity of interest. Recent focus on design thinking in management and management education highlights the importance of giving aesthetic considerations attention. How the elements of a system relate to each other, how people are able to relate to each other—and to the system itself—represent important and too frequently overlooked aspects of well a system is functioning, which relates to its basic design. We can associate this latter capacity of aesthetic sensibility with the work of the sensemaker, making sense of the way things fit together and looking for the aesthetic aspects of the system's, the business's, the organization's, or the relationship's design.

Wise leaders—business shamans—take all three attributes of wisdom into account as they make decisions—and also focus their efforts on the realities of the world and the role(s) that their organizations can play in making that world a better place. For example, recognition of inequities, sustainability and climate change issues, and other fundamentally ethical considerations incorporates both a realistic understanding of the system, the moral imagination to see how the organization's initiatives affect the system's functioning and design.

POWER: SORCERERS, BULLIES, DIGNITY, AND WISE/ETHICAL LEADERS

Like most individuals in leadership capacities, shamans can use their power for good or for ill, or they can use it unthinkingly and unreflectively without regard for the consequences of their actions and decisions. In the case of traditional shamans, negative use of power or dark power is termed sorcery, where power is thought to come from evil spirits. Sorcery is the use of power for dangerous, mischievous, or selfish purposes rather than for the good of the community. While power can obviously be misused by any leader, there are clear implications that such use is not ethical. Because they claim to access spiritual realms to gather needed information and because they play central roles within their communities, traditional shamans, like many business leaders today, are powerful figures and even transformational leaders as they reframe their communities' problematic cultural mythologies (Dow, 1986). Their power is associated with their role as healers, for they are often considered the world's first priests, timekeepers, artists, psychological counselors, among many other professions that have positive connotations. But power is also associated with corruption and unethical behaviors and practices, as in Lord Acton's long-ago comment, "Power corrupts. Absolute power corrupts absolutely."

When we think of ethical leaders, we typically think about moral virtues—leaders of honesty, integrity, who are values-driven and use their power, as shamans do, for constructive ends. What is too infrequently taken into consideration is the day-to-day behavior of the leader, that is, the way the leader treats others, the enterprise, stakeholders, and, ultimately, the natural environment. It is the behavior of leaders towards others, the enterprise, its stakeholders, and ultimately its broader community (including the planet itself) that ultimately matters in thinking about ethical leadership. That is because shamanism is all about relationships, the quality and nature of those relationships is important. Leadership that develops, builds, and supports, leadership that is generative for other people, the enterprise, and the world, rather than leadership that destroys or harms these things is ethical leadership. Leadership that has a healing rather than destructive form is what I mean by ethical and, indeed, shamanic leadership. Such ethical leadership contrasts distinctly with the work of the sorcerer, who is all about self-interested or negative ends.

For years, business publications like *Fortune* and *Forbes* lionized "tough bosses" or tough leaders, leaders who lead through fear, intimidation and abuse of their subordinates and sometimes their peers. Such leaders, essentially bullies, have what *Fortune* magazine once called a "winning is everything" mentality. They are leaders who play "head games," and "do whatever works" without looking at the consequences of their behavior, and who act in ways that "transform underlings into quivering masses of Jell-O" (Dumaine, 1993), among other descriptors. Although the *New York Times* argued in 2005 that "in business, tough guys finish last" and that such leaders would "eventually be rejected" (Nocera, 2005), the idea that the behavior of such bullies gets results has not disappeared. *Business Insider* named 18 executives who "lead by fear" in 2012, using words like outbursts of rage, madman, ruthless, brusque and micromanaging, blunt and a "famously bad listener," terrifying, intimidating, brash, arrogant, volatile, and abrasive to describe them along with descriptions of violent acts that some have perpetrated (Nisen, 2012). The problem is that such leaders are thought to get results.

There is arguably a distinction that could be made between being demanding and being abusive, with abusive crossing the ethical line. Without executives being grounded in an ethical stance, as shamans are, and an orientation towards making the world better, that line is all too likely to be crossed. Lipman (2013), writing for *Harvard Business Review*, argues for what she calls "tough love," suggesting that empty praise be banished, and that expectations be set high with clearly articulated goals and goal-posts, but also that leaders should recognize that failure is not the same as defeat and should remember to say thank you. Business shamans, while they may be demanding bosses, understand these distinctions and avoid leadership that is actually destructive of the whole, of human spirit, and even of the much-touted maximization of shareholder wealth. Leadership that is not oriented towards the whole, that is, leadership that is abusive and narrowly construed cannot be ethical leadership. Nor is it shamanic.

There is a distinct contrast between these abusive and exploitive behaviors of leaders and the ways the shaman views the world around him or her. As discussed in depth elsewhere (Waddock, 2016), because shamans believe that there is spirit in everything—other people, of course, and also other living beings, but also Nature and all of her manifestations—they treat others, living beings, and nature as if it has dignity—inherent worth—and with considerable respect. Taking on the mantle of the shaman and this attitude that accords dignity to all would consequentially change the ways that leaders engage with other stakeholders, as well as the business practices that would make ethical sense. Exploitation, whether of people or nature's many manifestations, both living and inert, needs to be replaced by more respectful treatment aimed at enhancing vitality through practices and principles associated with restoration, renewal, and resilience. Abuse of others is unseemly and unethical, as are so-called efficiency measures that result in different types of abuses ranging from sweatshops to customer fraud to constant product churn that unnecessarily uses natural resources. Products that are inherently problematic and wasteful, for example, bottled water in many instances where public water is safe and potable, tobacco, diamonds mined using child or forced labor, and related practices that create inherent dignity violations (Hicks, 2011a, 2011b) would increasingly be seen as unseemly and unworthy of the leader.

The power of the shaman in traditional cultures is thought to derive from the shaman's interaction with spirits in realms beyond the day-to-day realm. These spirits provide useful and important information to the shaman, who then uses it in healing practices. If we think of meaning-making, having a strong sense of purpose and calling to our work, and a great desire to make the world a better place, then business shamans today can create a better secular story. That story is not necessarily imbued with the trappings of any particular tradition or set of spiritual beliefs, but involves vision for a better future, purpose, relationships, understanding of and connection to nature and its resources and limits, and other factors that bring meaning into organizational life.

REFLECTIONS ON EDUCATION
AND PRACTICE FOR BUSINESS SHAMANS

What would it take to develop business leaders into business shamans? In traditional cultures shamanic training is often an apprenticeship in which the future shaman learns from a more experienced individual. Some are oriented to shamanism through crisis, illness, vision questing, or sudden insight. Many of today's leaders are educated in MBA and management development programs, which are fraught with their own problems in creating ethical leaders (Giacalone, 2004, 2007; Giacalone & Thompson, 2006; 50+20, 2012; among many, for insights), and do not typically follow an apprenticeship model. Arguably, however, there are things that could be done to open up both students and practicing managers/leaders to a more shamanistic perspective.

Think for a minute about the ways in which shamans work (see Waddock, 2015a). They are oriented towards holistic or systemic thinking. They engage in relationships with others, with other living beings, and with nature. They are willing to take risks and, if necessary, be mavericks within their institutional contexts in order to "become fully who they are," (i.e., achieve their unique purpose and use whatever their particular gifts are to make the world better). What is fostered in many MBA and management development programs, as opposed to tapping such healing and service-oriented purposes, is an orientation towards analytical, self-interested behavior, with the concept of the purpose of business being to maximize wealth for one group of stakeholders, the shareholders, through practices of efficiency oriented toward constant growth. Aside from the obvious ecological, resource, and human costs of these approaches, they represent a far-from-shamanic perspective on the ethical role of the leader.

A more shamanic approach to leadership development would dive deeply into the purposes of businesses and come up with the ways in which they serve humanity, other living beings, and nature, that is, all living (and non-living) stakeholders (or "as if" stakeholders), rather than accepting current neoclassical economics dogma as given. In doing this exploration, leaders would be exposed to the ways in which businesses can serve humanity without destroying natural resources (i.e., play a healing role), and encouraged to think more holistically about the nature, purposes, and roles of businesses in society and nature (i.e., the connecting role).

Further, management education programs could solidly locate businesses in their ecological and broader institutional and societal contexts, not just their economic and financial contexts. Doing so would illustrate how businesses can and do contribute to a better world. In existing businesses, leaders could gather managers, employees, and key stakeholders together to discuss how the work of their enterprise contributes to the greater good—and eliminate those areas where it doesn't, even if there were implications for growth or profitability. Such conversations have one important function of developing holistic or systems thinking, by not separating business out from the rest of society and from nature, thereby helping to close the human-nature gap that currently dominates much of Western culture.

Holistic and systemic thinking can be fostered in other ways, as can the healing orientation, by deeply exposing leaders and future leaders to significant societal and ecological problems and fostering their capacities for good interpersonal relationships and a respect for nature. For example, exposing current and future leaders to people who are dissimilar from themselves, particularly disadvantaged people in a variety of settings, can help open their eyes to the real lives that other people live, rather than the lives in gated communities or wealthy enclaves where many leaders live. Experiences in and with nature alongside such experiences of different peoples can also be helpful in enhancing awareness or what Mirvis (2008) called consciousness raising among executives. Conversations in which people deeply share their lived experiences can also help develop shamanic consciousness, in which it becomes important to be able to take the perspectives shared by other people and, in a sense, step into their shoes in the shapeshifting sense, can enhance relational capabilities and sensitivities to the impacts of actions and decisions on others and on systems. Such conversations can help shamanic leaders call into question the real purposes of businesses and avoid overly narrow framings that suggest that wealth maximization is the only feasible goal.

Because shamans heal in part by making sense of broken cultural mythologies, teaching (future) leaders to become aware of the assumptions that shape their belief systems and those in their cultures, and helping them to see how the narratives or stories that we tell shape our beliefs can also be helpful. Many executives seem to blindly accept the given dominant narratives (e.g., about the purpose and functions of businesses), without questioning whether these narratives are realistic or even what their impact on the world is. By enhancing awareness that we exist within a context of cultural mythologies, based on memes (Waddock, 2015b) that shape attitudes, beliefs, and such stories, the leader can begin to shape new stories using the sensemaking capacity of the shaman. Understanding this important sensemaking function can also help leaders with their visioning capacity as they attempt to articulate how they see their enterprises going forward, generating meaningful purposes that attract other stakeholders engaged in the business.

One of the things that the shaman does is to "see" what needs to be seen, by opening up awareness, connecting across multiple boundaries and bringing together ideas, insights, and potential initiatives that others have not yet seen. Mindfulness practices of various sorts can enhance these capabilities and their capacity for thinking about ethical and responsibility issues, as demonstrated in an intriguing research study by Schneider, Zollo, and Manocha (2010). Meditation and related approaches to mindfulness can help engage what Csikszentmihalyi (1991) calls the sense of "flow," or being fully engaged in the moment in an activity. Flow, as he demonstrates, happens in numerous ways ranging from the runner's high to a team that is working in harmony to being fully engaged in work or hobbies that challenge. Engaging in mindfulness practices and activities that increase the potential for flow states has multiple benefits that help the shaman reach out in new ways without being reactive, abusive, or "tough." Such leaders can still be effective in working with others, dealing with communities and institutions, and gaining insights into appropriate uses of natural resources, using, as suggested elsewhere, principles of renewal, restoration, and resilience rather than today's markets of growth, efficiency, and profitability (Waddock, 2016).

In today's overly "busy" business environment, opportunities for reflection and becoming mindful are few—unless the leader and relevant teams take time to create spaces where these things become possible and are encouraged. Orientation towards mindfulness could conceivably begin in management education and development programs by actually having participants meditate or engage in other mindfulness techniques that include practices like yoga, tai qi, and some martial arts (among others), as well as engaging them in numerous types of individual and group reflection practices, where they are asked to be fully themselves, not simply serve the expectations of others. Such practices not only have the potential to enhance individual awareness of "others," systems, and nature when geared these different directions, but also can help people go deeper into themselves to find out what they are really all about—and how they can act to "become fully who they are," not simply following the dictates of parents, "society," or organizational expectations. The key is to have people explore deeper purposes for self, others, and enterprises rather than simply accepting whatever currently exists or what the current narratives are. Ethical leaders then become responsible for creating opportunities for themselves to live out their purposes, for others to do so in the contexts of their work, and for their businesses as a whole to do so.

REFLECTIONS ON RESEARCHING SHAMANIC BUSINESS LEADERS

Obviously, the view of the ethical business leader as shaman does not neatly fit into traditional research using business ethics frameworks. For one thing, if we take the shaman's view of dignity for all living and nonliving manifestations of nature, and the healing, connecting, and sensemaking functions of the shaman seriously, the ethical task becomes more profound than simply following rules, regulations, and laws, or even broader moral precepts. Ethics in this context becomes a matter of how one relates to others and the world around him or her, how one *is* in the world, and how business practices impact that world.

The researcher as intellectual shaman has an ethical task, too, and that task is to study and call out the normative implications of leader behaviors that may be abusive, threatening, or otherwise ethically problematic, including broader, more systemic practices that are typically simply accepted (e.g., "efficiency" measures that create abuses of various sorts). The same can be said of whole businesses' behaviors and impacts. Questions of ethics for the shaman have to do with how healthy the overall system is, with one's self and organization recognized as a part of that overall system. Storytelling (sensemaking) and narratives then become a vitally important way for scholars to think about these functions, and qualitative methodologies, perhaps supplemented with quantitative research that provides some set of "numbers" that give insight into overall effectiveness of leader and enterprise becomes ways to think about research.

If the healing, connecting, and sensemaking functions of the shaman provide a source of power that enables the shaman to influence the world, its narratives and stories, and business practices, then as I have argued repeatedly about corporate responsibility, is not about the "explicitly ethical" aspects of doing business as they are frequently understood, but much more robustly about the type, nature, and impacts of businesses and their leaders in doing whatever work it is that they do. The work of the leader as shaman needs to be considered holistically much as the work of the business in its societal and ecological contexts needs to be considered much more holistically than many journals might find attractive. That need points us towards qualitative, narrative-based, and deeply personal research journeys, perhaps supplemented with quantitative data to bring out key systemic issues, including how to appropriately use "big data" in understanding systemic issues.

Qualitative approaches that explore the felt experiences of stakeholders (and scholars themselves) as they relate to the businesses, the ways in which leaders themselves experience their interactions with others—and how those others experience the leaders, might become topics of investigation. Quantitative approaches that involve mapping networks of relationships at the individual, unit, business, and societal levels could help demonstrate the impacts that different businesses and their leaders have on whole societies. Studies might need to be done of products that question the nature, durability, quality, churn levels, and usefulness of products, particularly as they relate to the climate change and sustainability contexts, rather than simply trying to "grow" more sales. The real ethical questions for the shaman lie at the system level and in the cultural mythologies (Dow, 1986) around businesses, their purposes, their products and services, how they relate to various constituencies, and their impacts, pro and con, on people, communities, societies, and the ecological system.

Questions about how leaders behave in businesses, whether they act in the best interests of the system (considered, perhaps from a prisoner's dilemma perspective), how they affect various stakeholders, and what kinds of practices they engage in make narrative analysis, interview studies, in-depth cases, observational and ethnographic studies, potentially powerful research tools. Even if these types of studies are more difficult and time-consuming than quantitative studies, they have the most potential to provide the types of insights about ethical leadership that are needed. Even if such studies force scholars to return to lengthier formats for explication of their results (e.g., books and monographs), as opposed to article-length manuscripts, such studies can potentially provide significant insights.

The positive and negative impacts of companies and their outputs need to be taken seriously as ethical considerations so that we as scholars are not ignoring problematic impacts, while lauding the profitability and "success" of firms and their leaders. What, for example, are the societal implications of 24/7/365 availability to bosses? What are the implications of mass production of little needed goods in a resource- and sustainability-constrained context? How do organizations and their leaders need to change to cope with the actual environment and groups of real stakeholders that they now face—and that have constant access to social media, making transparency both vitally important—and a reality whether the leaders wish it or not? For scholars, paying attention to such issues also suggests another shift: becoming public intellectuals at least to the extent of translating important research insights into accessible (and short, probably blog-length) pieces that can easily be digested and understood.

CONCLUSION

Perhaps there are psychological reasons why it is convenient for many leaders (and many of us) to ignore the realities around us, climate change, growing disparity between the wealthy and ordinary people, the potential for social disruption, species extinction. But that does not speak of the wisdom or holism of a shamanic approach. Wisdom defined as above tells us that leaders need to be aware of and thinking about the moral consequences of their decisions—as Pope Francis' (2015) encyclical on climate change, *Laudato Si'*, dramatically urges. Wisdom tells leaders that they need to understand the system as it is for most people, not just for themselves—and that they need to get out beyond the circle of the privileged within which they live their lives and really experience how most hard-working (or would-be-working, given the global jobs crisis) people live, and then become actively engaged in healing a world that creates problems for so many. Wisdom, which is inherent in the shamanic path, tells leaders that they need to look at, and understand how the design of the system, its aesthetics, creates the conditions that now leave so many behind. Wisdom and shamanic traditions dictate that such leaders act on behalf of the whole, not just in their or even just their firm's self-interest.

That is, indeed, a radical perspective to put forward in our times, I suspect. To go against the dominant economic model, to act in the interests of the whole, when you are benefiting from what is. But it may be what is needed to change our world.

REFERENCES

50+20 (2012). The 50+20 agenda: Management education for the world. Retrieved on July 8, 2014 from http://50plus20.org/5020-agenda

Ackoff, R. L. (1999). On learning and the systems that facilitate it. *Reflections, 1*(1), 14–24.

Capra, F., & Luisi, P. L. (2014). *The systems view of life: A unifying vision.* Cambridge, England: Cambridge University Press.

Corbin, H., & Horine, R. (1976). *Mundus imaginalis, or, the imaginary and the imaginal.* Ipswich, England: Golgonooza Press.

Csikszentmihalyi, M. (1991). *Flow: The psychology of optimal experience* (Vol. 41). New York, NY: HarperPerennial.

Diamond, J. (2005). *Collapse: How Societies Choose to Fail or Succeed.* New York, NY: Penguin.

Dow, J. (1986). Universal aspects of symbolic healing: A theoretical synthesis. *American Anthropologist, 88*(1), 56–69.

Dumaine, B. (1993, October 18). America's toughest bosses. *Fortune.* Retrieved from http://archive.fortune.com/magazines/fortune/fortune_archive/1993/10/18/78470/index.htm

Egri, C. P., & Frost, P. J. (1991). Shamanism and change: Bringing back the magic in organizational transformation. *Research in organizational change and development, 5,* 175–221.

Francis, Holy Father (2015). Encyclical letter of *Laudato Si',* on care for our common home. Retrieved on July 7, 2015 from http://w2.vatican.va/content/francesco/en/encyclicals/documents/papa-francesco_20150524_enciclica-laudato-si.html.

Freeman, R. E. (1994). The politics of stakeholder theory: Some future directions. *Business Ethics Quarterly, 4*(04), 409–421.

Frost, P. J., & Egri, C. P. (1994). The shamanic perspective on organizational change and development. *Journal of Organizational Change Management, 7*(1), 7–23.

Giacalone, R. A. (2004). A transcendent business education for the 21st century. *Academy of Management Learning & Education, 3*(4), 415–420.

Giacalone, R. A. (2007). Taking a red pill to disempower unethical students: Creating ethical sentinels in business schools. *Academy of Management Learning & Education, 6*(4), 534–542.

Giacalone, R. A., & Thompson, K. R. (2006). Business ethics and social responsibility education: Shifting the worldview. *Academy of Management Learning & Education, 5*(3), 266–277.

Hicks, D. (2011a). *Dignity: The essential role it plays in resolving conflict.* New Haven, CT: Yale University Press.

Hicks, D. (2011b). Leading with dignity. *Leadership Excellence,* September, *28*(9), 6.

Jung, C. G. (1981). *The archetypes and the collective unconscious* (No. 20). Princeton, NJ: Princeton University Press.

Kegan, R. (1982). *The evolving self: Problem and process in human development.* Cambridge, MA: Harvard University Press.

Kegan, R. (1994). *In over our heads: The mental demands of modern life.* Cambridge, MA: Harvard University Press.

King, S. K. (2009). *Urban shaman.* New York, NY: Simon and Schuster.

Kohlberg, L. (1973). Stages and aging in moral development—Some speculation. *Gerontologists,* 1, 498–502.

Lipman, J. (2013, December 17). The fine art of tough love. *Harvard Business Review.* Retrieved from https://hbr.org/2013/12/the-fine-art-of-tough-love/

Mirvis, P. (2008). Executive development through consciousness-raising experiences. *Academy of Management Learning & Education, 7*(2), 173–188.

Neal, J. (2006). *Edgewalkers: People and organizations that take risks, build bridges, and break new ground.* Westport, CT: Greenwood Publishing Group.

Nisen, M. (2012, September 12). 18 executives who lead by fear. *Business Insider.* Retrieved from http://www.businessinsider.com/18-executives-who-lead-by-fear-2012-9#

Nocera, J. (2005, June 18). In business, tough guys finish last. *New York Times.* Retrieved from http://www.nytimes.com/2005/06/18/business/18nocera.html?n=Top%2FNews%2FBusiness%2FColumns%2FJoseph%20Nocera&_r=0

Schneider, S. C., Zollo, M., & Manocha, R. (2010). Developing socially responsible behaviour in managers. *Journal of Corporate Citizenship,* (39), 21–40.

Waddock, S. (2010). Finding wisdom within—The role of seeing and reflective practice in developing moral imagination, aesthetic sensibility, and systems understanding. *Journal of Business Ethics Education,* 7, 177–196.

Waddock, S. (2014). Wisdom and responsible leadership: Aesthetic sensibility, moral imagination, and systems thinking. In D. Koehn and D. Elm (Eds.), *Aesthetics and business ethics, Issues in business ethics,* Vol. 41 (pp. 129–147). The Netherlands: Springer.

Waddock, S. (2015a). *Intellectual shamans: Management academics making a difference.* Cambridge, England: Cambridge University Press.

Waddock, S. (2015b). Reflections: Intellectual Shamans, Sensemaking, and Memes in Large System Change. *Journal of Change Management, 15*(4), 259–273.

Waddock, S. (2016). Generative businesses fostering vitality: Rethinking businesses' relationship to the world. Boston College Working paper, Boston, MA.

Weick, K. E., Sutcliffe, K. M., & Obstfeld, D. (2005). Organizing and the process of sensemaking. *Organization science, 16*(4), 409–421.

Werhane, P. H. (2002). Moral imagination and systems thinking. *Journal of Business Ethics, 38,* 33–42.

Werhane, P. H. (2008). Mental models, moral imagination and system thinking in the age of globalization. *Journal of Business Ethics, 78,* 463–474.

Wilber, K., Patten, T., Leonard, A., & Morelli, M. (2008). *Integral life practice: A 21st century blueprint for physical health, emotional balance, mental clarity and spiritual awakening.* Boston, MA: Integral Books.

CHAPTER 4

THE RESTORATIVE POTENTIAL OF DISCOVERY LEADERSHIP

Corporate Responsibility as Values-Informed Participating Consciousness

Diane L. Swanson
Kansas State University

ABSTRACT

This chapter describes some dissociations common to the modern era and explores their relevance to business and society. My thesis is that the possibilities for corporate responsibility have been thwarted by a myopic mindset that tends to divide mind from matter, subjects from objects, self from others, facts from values, means from ends, and humans from nature. I propose an *associative* mindset for *discovery leadership* aimed at ameliorating such perceptual schisms, so that a sense of connectivity and shared participation that once marked human consciousness can be restored and harnessed in a quest for *values-informed corporate responsibility*.

Radical Thoughts on Ethical Leadership, pages 69–95
Copyright © 2017 by Information Age Publishing
All rights of reproduction in any form reserved.

INTRODUCTION

Many years ago, I was intrigued by Morris Berman's (1981, 1989) thesis that the human mind was transformed by a profound loss of meaning that accompanied the Scientific Revolution. In Berman's view, the story of the mind in the modern era has been one of progressive dissociation, because modern consciousness does not recognize elements of mind or spirit in the objects surrounding it. Instead, this mindset tends to dissociate mind from matter, subjects from objects, self from others, facts from values, means from ends, and humans from nature. Perhaps the most well-known expression of this dissociation is René Descartes' work, which dualistically demarcates mind from matter (Sullivan, 1949, p. 134). Given this lingering habit of thought, Berman (1981, p. 16) holds that most humans no longer feel a strong sense of belonging in the world. Instead, non-participating consciousness based on the aforementioned dissociations distinguishes the modern period. Max Weber (1958), borrowing from Friedrich Schiller, refers to this state of affairs as the "disenchantment of the world." I argue that this sense of non-participating consciousness has run its course, especially given the pathologies posed for business and society in general and corporate responsibility in particular.

Along these lines, this chapter describes some pathologies of dissociation and their relevance to business organizations. My thesis is that the potential for corporate responsibility has been thwarted by an executive mindset that tends to dissociate mind from matter, subjects from objects, self from others, facts from values, means from ends, and humans from nature. As such, dissociative leaders help create and reinforce *non-participating consciousness* in business and society. More specifically, these leaders forge relationships with stakeholders that are defined more by separation and alienation than by a shared awareness that corporations are part of a larger society, which they should serve. I propose that a necessary condition for alleviating this malady is *discovery leadership*[1] based on an *associative* mindset that forgoes the perceptual schisms of dissociation, so that some degree of connectivity and participation that once marked human consciousness may be restored in a *values-informed business and society relationship*.

To preview, the discovery leader realizes the potential to enact corporate responsibility by creating values-informed consciousness among employees and other stakeholders. More specifically, he or she strives to activate those values in organizational culture that facilitate corporate responsibility (see Swanson, 1999, 2008, 2014). As employees and other stakeholders become conscious of the executive's commitment to such values, a collective quest to participate in the greater good becomes possible. This actualization of *values-informed participating consciousness* within organizations and between organizations and their external stakeholders speaks to the radical essence and restorative potential of discovery leadership. I conclude with some implications for research, practice, and education.

SOME PATHOLOGIES OF DISSOCIATIVE
NON-PARTICIPATING CONSCIOUSNESS

Berman's thesis about the state of mind in the modern era is too complex to cover extensively here, especially since it is shaped by longstanding scholarship in many fields, including psychology, art, anthropology, sociology, systems theory, and the history and philosophy of science.[2] Given this breath of scholarship, my modest aim is to highlight some pathologies of dissociation that affect the business and society relationship and propose a mindset for corporate leaders that can help alleviate them. Before doing so, it is important to recall Berman's assertion that dissociation, a product of the Scientific Revolution of the sixteenth and seventeenth centuries, creates artificial dichotomies between mind and matter, subjects and objects, self and others, facts and values, means and ends, and humans and nature. In contrast, humans prior to the Scientific Revolution did not perceive such rigid distinctions. Berman holds that a profound loss of meaning resulted from the shift from participating consciousness in the earlier period to non-participating consciousness later. This loss of meaning occurred because humans no longer experienced an innate feeling of belonging in the world. Instead, the dissociative mindset of non-participating consciousness isolates the self from all else while holding values-based understandings of material conditions at bay. For this reason, dissociative non-participating consciousness enforces a mechanical philosophy that reduces everything beyond the self to a static object for the self to control or manipulate (Laing, 1959).

Berman's (1981, p. 16) claim that non-participating consciousness perceives nature as dead and subject to exploitation recalls the Cartesian duality of mind and matter. Moreover, since everything is seen as an object for the self to control, dissociation provides a rationale for dehumanizing and manipulating others instead of recognizing and respecting their innate dignity. This mindset can prompt a sense of alienation, futility, and even an acceptance of the blatant violence associated with modern methods of mass administration (see Jacoby, 1975). Indeed, Adams and Balfour (1998, p. 6) hold that contemporary administrative systems based on this mindset are capable of large-scale evil behavior, and they point to the Holocaust as a prime example (see also Brecht, 1944). Such behavior is consistent with the separation of instrumental reasoning from substantive rationality that is characteristic of dissociation. In the first case, instrumental reasoning, similar to technical rationality, can be used to pursue narrow goals that are not defined by normative standards, such as ethical values.[3] In contrast, substantive rationality involves the ability to understand the purposeful nature of the whole system in which a particular task is embedded (Mannheim, 1940). The separation of means from ends that distinguishes dissociation precludes such comprehension. To illustrate, a person can use a hammer to destroy or build something. To choose between these options depends on the purpose of the project. This requires a mindset capable of integrating instrumental reasoning with substantive rationality.

Until the modern era, reason was conceived of as a process that saw instrumental techniques as serving substantive goals (Adams & Balfour, 1998, p. 38). However, given dissociative tendencies, it is easy for the contemporary mindset to default to instrumental reasoning that is amoral (reasoning devoid of ethical values) or immoral (reasoning that intentionally violates ethical values; see Carroll & Buchholtz, 2015, p. 199). Administrative systems governed by this pattern of thought are prone to antisocial behavior (Jackall, 1988), especially since the separation of instrumental reasoning from substantive rationality justifies the bifurcation of means and ends, respectively. We will return to this matter later. For now, it is important to note that dissociation separates instrumental means from normative ends, instead of seeing both on a continuum within larger systems of ongoing processes. Such amorality can be destructive, especially when carried out by administrative systems that justify ends by any means used to reach them.

Dissociative nonparticipating consciousness gives rise to addictive tendencies. As reported by Bateson (1972), the dissociative mindset is prone to addiction because it does not recognize or respond to information relevant to the whole system. In other words, a mindset mired in dichotomies cannot comprehend the relational nature of reality in which everything is connected to everything else. As Berman (1981, p. 273) explains, nonparticipating consciousness will continue to pollute a lake because the resulting chain reaction of harm to the social and natural environments will not be considered in decision making. Hence, dissociation fuels an escalating commitment to narrow decision parameters, regardless of their consequences. This corresponds to the cybernetic definition of addiction as a compulsive pursuit of rewarding stimuli that ignores attendant outcomes (Bateson, 1985, p. 320).

This addiction is ironic because, although dissociation promotes the perception that everything outside oneself can be controlled, individuals who dissociate find it difficult to regulate their own addictive tendencies (Laing, 1959). Put differently, their illusion of control traps them in a lack of control. Moreover, given their state of nonparticipating consciousness, dissociative individuals in their self-imposed isolation become alienated from the social and natural worlds that they have objectified (see Berman, 1981; Jacoby, 1975). This state of mind suggests another irony: it is not the social and natural worlds that are dead but rather the authentic self (Marcuse, 1964, p. 9). We shall return to the cozy relationship between dissociation and irony. For now, it is important to emphasize that alienated, inauthentic selves focused on amoral or immoral instrumentalism are not capable of sharing a collective consciousness of a greater good that is other- and nature-inclusive. Hence, dissociative consciousness contributes to cultural disintegration because it discourages social cohesion around a shared commitment to the greater good. Dissociation also contributes to environmental degradation because it legitimates exploiting the natural environment instead of preserving and protecting it.

To summarize, several related pathologies are implied by the dissociative mindset, starting with a loss of meaning inherent to non-participating consciousness. Additionally, dissociation contributes to the dehumanization and manipulation of others, organizational violence, amorality or immorality in decision making, addictive tendencies, an illusion of control, an artificial isolation of the self, alienation, a sense of futility, and a loss of self-authenticity. Given cultural disintegration and environmental degradation, corporations that embody dissociation will inevitably harm their social and natural environments. The next section elaborates on this proposition.

THE RELEVANCE OF DISSOCIATIVE PATHOLOGIES TO BUSINESS AND SOCIETY

Berman (1981, p. 132) holds that the dissociative mindset uses science and technology to promote a hostile attitude toward the environment that challenges the very notion of what it means to be human in the world. He concludes that some kind of change will need to take place in our systems, including an alternative mental framework for capitalism, if humanity is to engage in some form of participating consciousness again. Otherwise, the pathologies of disassociation may be our downfall, given the predilection for narrow instrumental reasoning that was embedded in capitalism as it emerged in the wake of the Scientific Revolution (see Adorno, 1991, pp. 98–99). This myopic instrumentalism portends organizational systems that are prone to anti-social, anti-environmental behavior. In a business and society context, dissociation is profoundly irrational: it means that business organizations will neither protect nor preserve the very host environments that sustain them.

Enabling Economic Mythology

In reality, there is no schism between business and society. Business organizations are not freestanding entities. Instead, they are embedded in human communities and natural environments that involve complex dependencies and interactions (Frederick, 1998). In essence, the relationship between business firms and their social and natural environments is symbiotic (Waddock & Rasche, 2013, p. 300). Despite this reality, a particularly influential theory of economics has been used to justify a dissociative role for business. The influence of this theory is longstanding, taken-for-granted, and rarely confronted. Specifically, a contemporary articulation of neoclassical economics has promoted the myth that business operates outside of a community of shared values and aspirations (Etzioni, 1988; see also Lorsch & Khurana, 2010). Consistent with this contrivance, standard economics has also been invoked to legitimate a freestanding self that does not need to consider other-regarding values in decision making. (Aram, 1993; Etzioni, 1998; Swanson, 1996). It is a short step from legitimizing such freedom for self to justifying the freedom for corporations to ignore their social responsibilities, a line of thought described next.

Besides artificially separating the self from others and elevating unfettered freedom for the former, standard economics is Newtonian. That is, its logic predicts that mechanical forces of supply and demand fueled by narrow self-interest will, in the long run, tend to produce equilibria states that represent the greatest good under conditions of competition (Etzioni, 1988; Hausman & McPherson, 1996). Because this portrayal gives unconscious market forces more credence than conscious human choices, it has kept a coherent view of responsible business leadership from taking hold in theory and practice. Instead, standard economic theory has been used to conflate *freedom for individuals in markets* to *freedom for managers in corporations* (Swanson, 2014). This conflation diverts attention from the power managers have to misuse the bureaucratic means at their disposal (see Frederick, 1995; Perrow, 1986; Swanson, 1996). A perspective that elevates managers' freedom while ignoring their instrumental power obfuscates the responsibilities they have for their actions. In brief, it legitimates amoral management.

Doubtlessly, this legitimation of amorality was popularized by Milton Friedman's (1962, 1970) interpretation of neoclassical economics by which he concluded that corporate managers should not be moral agents. He reached this conclusion by appealing to the belief that market forces guided by individual self-interest would inevitably produce the best outcomes for society. Pursuant to this view, there is no need for business leaders to strive to create socially responsible outcomes, especially since Adam Smith's metaphor of the invisible hand has long been conjured to buttress the belief that unfettered market forces will bring about the greatest good. However, this metaphor is more an article of faith than reality (Stiglitz, 2001; see also Ghoshal, 2005, p. 79). Worse, it can be entreated to excuse corporations for harming their social and natural environments (see Galbraith, 1996; Matthews, 2014). If not for this line of thought, society might force corporations to accept full responsibility for their negative spillover effects.

The model of discovery leadership, covered later, substitutes an executive mindset that *consciously* pursues corporate responsibility for faith that *unconscious* market forces will bring about the greatest good.

Harmful Organizational Dynamics

Standard economics is not immune from the irony of dissociative logic. Instead of resulting in equilibria states benefitting society, unwavering faith in automated market forces can be a Trojan horse for harming society, as suggested above. Consider that the business sector manifests cycles of growth fueled by the attitude that more is better than less and bigger is better than smaller. By this standard, the recurrent cycles of corporate mergers and acquisitions that fail by any standards can be seen as an addiction to greed, growth, and empire building exhibited by amoral executives (see Roll, 1986; Swanson, 1996). This likelihood recalls Bateson (1972) and Berman's (1981) descriptions of runaway systems, in that economic behavior based on amoral addiction cannot be self-correcting, as persistent Enron-like scandals seem to demonstrate. Moreover, the harm caused by this behavior includes a decline in social well-being that accompanies unemployment and economic instability (Silverstein, 2013; Swanson, 1992). An economic perspective that justifies this predicament by appealing to the prerogatives of amoral self-interest and faith in self-regulating markets should be rejected in favor of a new paradigm. To paraphrase Albert Einstein, the same mindset that caused a problem cannot be part of its solution.

It bears repeating that organizations that dissociate from their host environments will neither preserve nor protect those environments. This fuels cultural disintegration in the sense that stakeholders will feel alienated from organizations that harm them. To rationalize this state of affairs, executive managers can point to their prerogatives to pursue narrow self- or firm-interest, since economic mythology depicts markets as self-correcting in the long run. This rationalization diverts attention from the fact that many executives are paid exorbitant salaries when their decisions are destructive by any standards (Lorsch & Khurana, 2010; Stewart, 2011). It also ignores the damage to society and the natural environment that accrues while the illusive long run market adjustments are pending. Many scholars have interpreted the famous quote by economist John Maynard Keynes, "In the long run, we are all dead," (Keynes, 1923, p. 74) to mean that it is pointless to wait for markets to self-correct instead of searching for solutions to economic dilemmas (Lekachman, 1976).

Simply put, dissociation is dangerous in practice. This danger is exacerbated when employees bracket or ignore their values in order to carry out questionable directives from their superiors (see Beenen & Pinto, 2009;

Schwartz, 1991). Because the chain of command facilitates this dissociation, organizations are fertile grounds for amoral and immoral behavior
that is difficult to address (Jackall, 1988; Morrison & Milliken, 2000). Employee silence contributes to this difficulty, since it decreases an organization's ability to confront problems and learn from the experience (Schein,
2010; Swanson, 2014; Wickens, 1995). To compound matters, employees
can experience alienation from work devoid of moral purpose (Jackall,
1988; Schwartz, 1991). That society at large can be alienated from amoral
or immoral organizations is suggested by persistently low public confidence
in the business sector (see Jones, 2015). It appears that dissociation creates
alienation in business and society.

Economic mythology keeps the public from understanding what needs
to be done to turn the situation around. Unfortunately, business education
is complicit in perpetuating this ignorance.

Complicit Business Education

The contemporary interpretation of neoclassical economics does not recognize the cultural disintegration and environmental degradation implied
by its logic. Business schools mirror this myopia, given that amoral self-interest is a staple of their curricula (Ghoshal, 2005, p. 76). Not surprisingly,
therefore, corporate responsibility and business ethics courses are relatively
scarce in business schools, even though they represent longstanding fields
of study. The most recent statistic verified by the Association to Advance
Collegiate Schools of Business (AACSB), the agency that accredits business
schools, is that only one-third of these schools offer an ethics course, and
presumably fewer require one (Willen, 2004). This statistic comports with
Evans and Weiss's (2008, p. 45) survey of business school deans who reported that only 25% of MBA programs require an ethics course. This statistic is
unremarkable. Business schools have long functioned as vehicles for amoral economic theory and its offshoot positive agency theory that privileges
shareholder wealth more than broader social concerns (Lan & Heracleous,
2010, p. 301). Even in the aftermath of Enron-like scandals and a sharp
decline in public confidence in the business sector, many business schools
axed their lone ethic course or resisted adding one to their curricula (Kelly,
2002; Swanson, 2004).

This resistance keeps normative coursework from taking hold in business schools, especially that which is behaviorally-based (see Rynes, Trank,
Lawson, & Ilies, 2003). The narrow-mindedness is self-perpetuating: Doctoral students who are not exposed to normative coursework are ill-pre-
pared to deliver it when they join business school faculties. This is not to
deny the existence of behaviorally-based normative business scholarship,

some of which manifests as a course or two in a minority of business schools. *However, this scholarship functions in the context of a dissociative worldview that is uncomfortable with it.* This discomfort persists when business students join the workforce after being inculcated with a mentality that justifies corporate freedom from responsibility. That this status quo passes for sound business education recalls Kuhn's (1962, p. 77) assertion that scientists rarely renounce a paradigm that has led them into a crisis (see also Frederick, 2008; Mitroff & Swanson, 2004; Swanson & Fisher, 2008). In like manner, business education has not confronted the economic mythology that is used to rationalize cultural disintegration and environmental degradation.

Given the stakes for business and society, a mindset that incorporates normative reasoning is needed to replace habitual, unreflective thought patterns (see Giacalone & Thompson, 2006; Hartman & Werhane, 2013, p. 41). Discovery leadership is offered as an embodiment of the former.

DISCOVERY LEADERSHIP AS PART OF THE CURE

Although the model of discovery leadership has been proposed elsewhere (Swanson, 1999, 2008, 2014), it is reformulated here to redress dissociative pathologies. Because the reformulated model is designed to help restore a sense of values-informed participating consciousness in a social realm, specifically in the business and society relationship, it represents a radical approach to leadership. Yet the time is ripe for it. The aforementioned ironies suggest that dissociation has run its course as a habit of thought, similar to Popper's (1945) assertion that the internal contradictions of absolutist ideologies morph into oppressively unproductive views of society. This is the case for economic mythology that justifies business's freedom *from* responsibility and, in doing so, deters society from insisting that corporate conduct improve. This harkens to Ghoshal's (2005, p. 86) declaration that nothing is as dangerous as bad theory. Since the premise of bad economic theory is dissociation, a perspective on socially responsible business leadership cannot be based on it.

That said, discovery leadership is not a call to return a pre-modern mindset. Nor does it represent a blanket condemnation of the instrumental or technical rationality that was emphasized in the wake of the Scientific Revolution. Indeed, as will be shown, discovery leadership is predicated on decision making that blends instrumental reasoning with substantive rationality. This integrative approach comports with the scientific method, which itself is a process of discovery that has allowed the human mind to expand and accommodate levels of abstraction that were not possible prior to its ascent (Swanson, in press). Or, as Sullivan (1949, p. 48) put it, the web of reason that constitutes modern science has made it possible for the human mind to break through some mental barriers. Analogously, the responsible executive must abandon dissociation to discover ways to lead in a socially responsible manner. The necessary condition for such leadership is the adoption of an associative mindset based on four essential realizations, presented next.

Realizing an Associative Mindset

In contrast to the myopia of dissociation, the associative mindset understands connectivity, starting with realization #1.

Realization #1: *Business organizations have symbiotic relationships with their social and natural environments.*

An associative mindset realizes that economic goal-seeking occurs in and depends on a firm's social and ecological contexts (Frederick, 1995; Porter & Kramer, 2006; Waddock, 2009). Accordingly, the triple bottom line framework proposed by Elkington (1994) is based on the awareness that accounting solely for profit ignores the impacts that business has on people and the planet. For instance, a mining firm can show a profit after causing thousands of human deaths from pollutants that also harm the natural environment. Given symbiosis, the true value of business is to generate profit while also sustaining and improving the social and natural environment. This triple bottom line goal of pursuing positive economic, social, and environmental performance simultaneously is the substantive or normative purpose of business that gives it institutional legitimacy, as indicated by realization #2.

Realization #2: *The responsible business leader pursues a balanced enactment of economic, social, and environmental goals.*

In agreement with this realization, the responsible executive will use technical means to direct a firm to enact triple bottom line responsibilities. In the process, amoral instrumentalism is discarded in favor of using technology to carry out a substantive purpose. This realization comports with Swanson's (1995, 2014) reformulated principle of responsibility, which holds that business organizations are institutional *tools* for enacting economic, social, and environmental goals.[4] This principle is informed by Frederick's (1995, pp. 157–162) description of mutualistic economizing, which takes place when organizations engage in projects that benefit their bottom lines while also permitting exchange conditions that benefit the social or natural environment (Frederick, 1995). For instance, an insurance company might work with a nonprofit organization to expand affordable housing in a local community. This partnership could potentially increase insurance sales and reap reputational advantages while bolstering home ownership and public well-being in the process (Swanson, 2014). Porter and Kramer (2006) recount such practices as creating shared value from the symbiotic relationship between competitive advancement and social progress.

Mutualistic economizing can also occur when corporations strengthen ties to community by making charitable contributions to nonprofit organizations that support social or environmental goals. Porter and Kramer (2002), refer to this practice as strategic philanthropy, asserting that:

> There is no inherent contradiction between improving competitive context and making a sincere commitment to bettering society. Indeed, as we've seen, the more closely a company's philanthropy is linked to its competitive context, the greater the company's contribution to society will be. (p. 16)

Not that a singular project will necessarily fulfill economic, social, and environmental responsibilities concurrently. Nevertheless, according to realization #2, responsible executives will strive to create a portfolio of projects that optimizes their firms' beneficial triple bottom line impacts. This quest to provide shared value recalls why an associative mindset is necessary for socially responsible leadership. It is an antidote to the dissociation that leads to cultural disintegration and environmental degradation, especially if the executive understands the role of values in organizational decision processes.

Realization #3: *The responsible business leader discovers how to embed (a) value information and (b) personal and organizational values that facilitate triple bottom line performance in organizational decision processes.*

Realization #3 attends the comprehension that business firms are legitimate if they fulfill their triple bottom line purpose. The corollary is that the responsible executive needs to facilitate the kind of value information and personal and organizational values that make positive triple bottom line impacts possible. This key aspect of discovery leadership is elaborated upon in the next section.

Finally, because complexity and continuous change are integral to the co-evolving, symbiotic relationship between business and society (see Frederick, 1998, pp. 359–360), realization #4 is that corporate responsibility must be an ongoing process of discovery, which brings organizational learning into focus.

Realization #4: *The responsible business leader directs employees to learn continually about the firm's economic, social, and environmental impacts and stakeholders' expectations and assessments of them.*

Leading Value Discovery Processes

These four essential realizations suggest that the executive who adopts an associative mindset will perceive a business organization as a means-end continuum of value processes, as depicted in Figure 4.1.

Commensurate with this model, the discovery leader will strive to use organizational *means* to enact corporate responsibility as an *end* in sight. In relation to realization #3, this requires understanding how value information gets incorporated into decision processes. Using Weick's (1969, 1995) perspective, this incorporation involves selection, retention, and enactment. *Selection* involves the filtering of data by decision makers so that the equivocality or lack of clarity regarding information is reduced. *Retention* determines what information decision makers can recall for further use. Finally, *enactment* refers to the processing of information by organizational participants that ultimately creates the environment to which their organization adapts. Correspondingly, values can be *selected* and *retained* in decision processes to *enact* the environmental imperatives to which an organization responds.

Figure 4.1 shows this dynamic as a culmination of decision processes involving the (a) executive office, (b) formal organization, (c) informal organization, and (d) office of external affairs management. In agreement with realization #4, the discovery leader will direct the office of external affairs to detect information about economic, social, and environmental issues relevant to the firm's performance. Two-way arrows in Figure 4.1 indicate that this information, including stakeholder expectations and assessments of performance, should be transmitted to the executive and employees in the formal and informal organization to be selected and retained in decision processes. In this way, decisions can be infused with information that is typically expressed by stakeholders as their value expectations. For example, *safety* is a value to consumers, *transparency* is a value to shareholders, *compliance* is a value to regulators, and the *well-being of the natural environment* is a value to citizens in their communities. The executive governed by an associative mindset will direct the office of external affairs to discover the specific nature of these expectations and their relevance to triple bottom line performance, à la realization #4.

Although culture includes both the formal and informal organization, these two aspects are shown separately in Figure 4.1 to underscore the importance of selecting and retaining value information along the chain of command in ways that countervail the tendency for hierarchy to facilitate

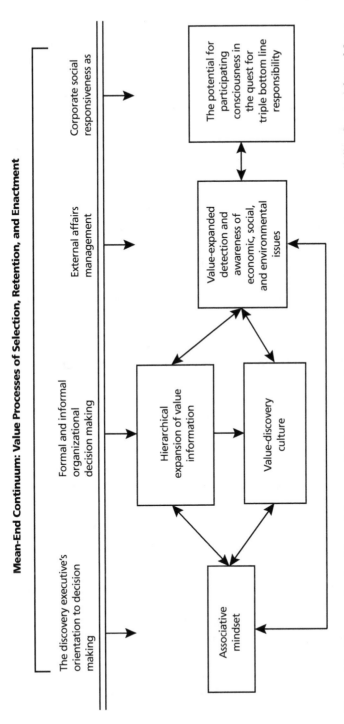

Figure 4.1 Discovery leadership and the potential for participating consciousness in corporate responsibility. *Source:* Adapted from Swanson, 1999, 2008, 2014; reproduced with permission.

dissociative amoral management. In terms of realization #3, the responsible executive will encourage a hierarchical expansion of value information by insisting that data about stakeholder expectations be codified in formal reports that are distributed widely. If managers are officially rewarded for attending to this information, and if other employees capable of following suit are hired, retained, and also rewarded, then a value-discovery culture is possible, as indicated by the arrow from hierarchy to culture in Figure 4.1. Executives should also encourage value-discovery in the informal organization. This could include unofficially mentoring employees to encourage their value-awareness. The responsible executive could also make it possible for informal gatherings, communication, and networking about stakeholder value expectations to occur, perhaps by using social media.

The associative executive has the potential to create and maintain a value-discovery culture if he or she finds the means to insure that relevant value information gets detected, selected, retained, and transmitted throughout the organization without getting distorted, ignored, or lost. Realization #3 indicates that the discovery leader can also leverage the potential for corporate responsibility by striving to embed *constructive* values in the culture.

Embedding *Constructive* Values in Organizational Culture

The responsible executive must do more than facilitate the transmission of value information via formal and informal decision processes. Suggested at the top of Figure 4.1, she or he must also understand the personal and organizational values that make the enactment of corporate responsibility possible. Candidates for such *constructive* values on the individual level include *broadmindedness, courage, helpfulness, honesty, imagination,* and *responsibility.*[5] These values may be embedded in the culture if the executive directs department heads and human resource management specialists to hire and reward employees who exhibit them. Candidates for constructive values on the organizational level include *cooperation, communication, compliance, teamwork, quality, learning, innovation, productivity, safety, transparency,* and *trust.* The discovery executive will view departments as unique incubators for developing and leveraging such value proficiencies. For instance, *transparency* and *compliance* should be especially cultivated in accounting and finance, *innovation* and *quality* should be emphasized in engineering, and *safety* should be a particularly strong standard in production.

The discovery executive's special proficiency is that he or she is adept at finding and leveraging the permutations of individual and organizational values that facilitate beneficial triple bottom line impacts.

Creating the Potential for Values-Informed Participating Consciousness

The detection of value information by the office of external affairs accords with the nature of normal science, which relies on empirical evidence, observations, and experiments (Kuhn, 1962, p. 27). The experimental nature of corporate responsibility involves comparing actual triple bottom line results to desired results and making necessary adjustments. This comparison should be conducted by external affairs specialists and communicated to the executive and other employees for analysis and action. Realistically, this means that corporate responsibility is always an end in sight or work in progress. Hence, in terms of realization #4, the discovery executive discerns that feedback from external affairs (shown as two-way arrows in Figure 4.1) is a necessary condition for organizational learning. More pointedly, feedback about triple bottom line impacts can help the executive and other employees improve upon the means by which they pursue corporate responsibility. Such learning along the means-end continuum in Figure 4.1 may increase value awareness among employees if it is celebrated and rewarded by the executive. That is to say, the restorative potential of discovery leadership involves replacing unreflective amorality with conscious morality in organization life.

If organizations develop such values-informed consciousness, then their dissociative tendencies may be alleviated. Frederick (1995, pp. 14–20) summarizes the properties of values and valuation that make this possible. One, values are beliefs about preferred end states or conduct. As such, they have *cognitive, affective, and behavioral* dimensions (see also Rokeach, 1968, 1973). Two, values are *experiential* because they represent the meaning that humans assign to experience and the learning that occurs in the process (see also Williams, 1979). Three, values are relational in that they express an association that a person or group has to others or to the environment. Hence, they speak to the interconnectedness of all things and the continuity of human experience (see also Ayres, 1944, p. 43), which is the opposite of dissociation. Finally, valuation is the process by which means are appraised or judged for attaining the ends sought. Since goals attained become means to other ends, valuation is a means-ends process (see also Dewey, 1922; Kluckholn, 1951), described herein as a pragmatic process of discovery that redresses the bifurcation of means and ends that result from dissociation. Likewise, Figure 4.1 illustrates an organization as a means-end continuum in which values and facts are entwined in decision processes that are cognitive, affective, behavioral, experiential and, ultimately, relational. Accordingly, artificial dissociations are diminished. Rigid distinctions between mind and matter, subjects and objects, self and others, facts and values, means and ends, and humans and nature are no longer perceived.

Instead, mind as shared consciousness is understood to be embedded in human interactions with physical and natural systems, a conceptualization that comports with Bateson's (1972, 1985) cybernetic perspective.

When a firm attends to expectations of responsible conduct and communicates its responses to stakeholders via the office of external affairs, then it is possible for a sense of participating consciousness to develop between business and society as a shared interest in the greater good. Befitting this symbiotic interest, *corporate social responsiveness* can be understood as a conscious quest to enact triple bottom line outcomes, as shown in Figure 4.1. The discovery executive can amplify this consciousness among employees and between a firm and its external stakeholders by establishing appropriate boundary-spanning practices for external affairs managers. For example, employee engagement in community projects may create shared benefits that facilitate participating consciousness. In the process, employee alienation from work and society's alienation from business, both byproducts of dissociation, may be alleviated, since helping others can be meaningful and satisfying for both parties (see Schwartz & Sendor, 1999; Weinstein & Ryan, 2010). This prospect speaks to the discovery leader's potential to heal the rift between business and society. The stakes are no less than societal and environmental well-being.

CHARTING A WAY FORWARD

To summarize, discovery leadership is a theoretical perspective for helping to restore a sense of values-informed participating consciousness in contemporary life, specifically in the business and society relationship. Although the discovery model rejects the dissociations that accompanied the Scientific Revolution, it retains the attributes of normal science that attach importance to empirical evidence, observations, experiments, explorations, and continual learning. Normal science involves ongoing puzzle-solving efforts (Kuhn, 1962) that cannot be reduced to a bifurcation of means and ends. Instead, means and ends are non-dualistic in that *means* can facilitate the achievement of *goals* which, in turn, become *means* to other *goals* (Ayres, 1944; Dewey, 1922; Swanson, 1995; Wartick & Cochran, 1985). Similarly, the discovery leader should view triple bottom line responsibilities as *goals in sight* that require organizational puzzle solving efforts for determining the best *means* to pursue them. Corporate responsibility can then be comprehended as a means for achieving the greater good, a larger goal in sight.

In this context, discovery leadership can be seen as a necessary condition for creating values-informed participating consciousness between business and society. This dynamic, not the market's invisible hand, is key to understanding the frontier of possibilities for corporate responsibility.

Some Implications for Research and Practice

Discovery leadership has many implications for practice, some of which have already been identified. Of these, the discovery executive will try to embed *constructive values* in an organization's culture, keeping in mind that these values are those that can facilitate beneficial triple bottom line impacts. This involves directing human resource management specialists to screen employee applicants for unique *value proficiencies,* some of which were proposed earlier. For example, employees in accounting and finance should be adept at enacting *transparency* and *compliance* and employees in engineering should be proficient at working to achieve *innovation* and *quality.* Additionally, external affairs specialists must be skilled at building relationships with stakeholders that facilitate *trust, transparency,* and *engaged communication* (Browne, 2016). The discovery executive should ensure that such value proficiencies are reflected in performance evaluations, with the goal of rewarding and retaining employees who master them. This policy comports with Savitz's (2013, p. 132) recommendation that organizations intent on triple bottom line outcomes implement performance appraisal systems that help bring them about. Research informed by discovery leadership should identify the full range of triple bottom line value proficiencies needed in various parts of the organization and refine hiring and performance appraisals accordingly. Another implication for practice is that the discovery leader should hire human resource management specialists for the kind of *broadmindedness* that allows them to comprehend an organization as a system of interrelated decision processes that can be used to leverage employee value proficiencies for the enactment of social responsibility. Future research should refine methods of screening these specialists for this mindset.

Above all, boards of directors should filter executive candidates for discovery potential. This involves considering not only an executive's ability to attain firm profitability, but also his or her record in bringing about beneficial social and environmental performance. Various rankings, ratings, and benchmarking reports track such performance, including those published by CSRHUB (www.csrhub.com), the Reputation Institute (www.reputationinstitute.com), and MSCI ESG (www.msci.com/esg-ratings). The board nominating committee should use these reports to ascertain a candidate's record in triple bottom line performance and the compensation committee should structure pay incentives to reward positive performance going forward. Importantly, boards should also assess an executive's ability to be other-regarding. Otherwise, he or she will not grasp the necessity of directing external affairs specialists to respect stakeholders and engage them in relationships based on trust and transparency (see Frederick, 2012). In the lexicon of discovery, this form of engagement can help create and maintain values-informed participating consciousness between business and society, the reputational effects of which may be substantial. As reported by Browne (2016), a company's ability to engage stakeholders constructively is worth more than 20% in superior stock performance over the course of a decade (see also Orlitzky & Benjamin, 2001; Orlitzky & Swanson, 2012). Boards of directors striving for such results would be well advised to hire executives who have demonstrated an associative mindset that is other-regarding. A study of executives, discussed next, provides clues as to what this mindset entails.

A key aspect of discovery leadership is that an executive must be receptive to the role of values in organizational life. The opposite of this *value receptivity* is *value myopia,* which indicates a mindset that does not consider the role of values in decision making (Swanson, 1999, 2014). In a preliminary study of executive respondents, Orlitzky, Swanson, and Quartermaine (2006) examined the relationship between value myopia and executives' preference for highly stratified organizational pay structures. Specifically, this research team surveyed executives for (a) agreeableness, (b) value myopia, and (c) preference for pay dispersion, with agreeableness denoting the inclination to be cooperative, friendly, altruistic, tender-minded, and trusting (see Goldberg, 1993), value myopia representing the propensity to ignore, suppress, or deny the role of values in decision making (Swanson, 1999), and preference for pay dispersion indicating whether an egalitarian or top-heavy compensation structure is favored. The results of this study support the hypothesis that "agreeable executives" are less likely to exhibit value myopia and a preference for highly stratified or top-heavy organizational pay structures.

This finding suggests that boards should screen executive candidates for agreeableness, a proposition that is supported by three considerations. One, agreeableness indicates an ability to consider the interests of others (i.e., to be other-regarding). The discovery executive needs this ability in order to perceive the importance of factoring stakeholder value expectations into decisions. Two, significant disparities in pay may contribute to internal dynamics that pit employees against each other and discourage cooperation and trust among them (Beenen & Pinto, 2009; Cohen & Prusak, 2001; Pfeffer, 1998). By implication, executives who do not prefer highly stratified pay structures may be best suited to formulate pay policies based on ethical standards of distributive justice that may motivate employees to work collectively to pursue triple bottom line goals. This possibility is closely related to a third consideration: Research indicates that individuals who are more agreeable tend to prefer team-oriented cultures in which trust, support, and cooperation are valued more than individualism (Judge & Cable, 1997; O'Reilly, Chatman, & Caldwell, 1991). Given these considerations, agreeable executives may be predisposed to create and sustain the kind of employee cohesion that can be directed to enact corporate responsibility that is other-regarding. If so, agreeableness should be used to screen executives for discovery potential. Further research should investigate this possibility and also whether value receptivity is correlated with other factors, including gender, industrial background, and education. The point is to create a valid instrument for assessing discovery potential.

Another consideration for research and practice is that discovery dynamics do not preclude value tradeoffs, as when shareholders' desire for greater profits is seemingly at odds with the cost of retooling production for consumer or employee safety. A recent development in U.S. public policy portends changes in practice that may shed light on how executives can handle such tradeoffs. This recalls realization #2, which propounds that executives need to formulate balanced or *optimal* responses to stakeholder expectations of triple bottom line performance. The relatively new benefit corporation may provide clues for how this can be accomplished. As of this writing, the benefit corporation is chartered in 32 states as a legal structure for social entrepreneurs who want to enact triple bottom line goals for multiple stakeholders. The premise behind the legislation that created the benefit corporate charter, first passed in Maryland in 2010, is that organizations can pursue these goals simultaneously (Field, 2013). This assumption is not farfetched. Shareholders are increasingly aware that companies that deliver responsible social and environmental performance also reap financial advantages (www.benefitcorp.net; see also Orlitzky, Schmidt, & Rynes, 2003; Swanson & Orlitzky, in press). Benefit corporations present a unique opportunity to understand how executives can strive for a balanced approach to the triple bottom line when stakeholder interests appear to conflict. Research should also seek to understand conditions under which public policy should mandate that social or environmental goals take precedent over profit and vice versa After all, discovery leadership does not rule out a role for government regulation, although it may reduce the need for it among responsible firms (see Swanson, 2000, 2014).

A Role for Business Education

The business school curriculum tends to be myopic. It privileges economic doctrine that elevates narrow self-interest while equating freedom for self with freedom for corporations to ignore their social responsibilities. The advent of the benefit corporation and the exponential growth in the number of social entrepreneurs that helped bring it about (Pless, 2012) suggests that the public's interest in corporate responsibility has reached new heights. Business education, which has long lagged society's concern for corporate responsibility (Frederick, 2006, 2008), is especially out of step with the values of the millennial generation. This generation's demand for socially responsible business practices, backed by $2.45 trillion in spending power, has prompted big brands to incorporate corporate responsibility into their business models (Richards, 2015). Business schools ignore this state of affairs at peril of becoming irrelevant, especially in light of a 2007 Aspen study indicating a jump in the number of MBA students who believe that a primary responsibility for firms is to create value in the communities in which they operate (Aspen Institute, 2008).

What can business schools do to catch up to public expectations? For starters, every course in the business school curriculum should be redesigned around triple bottom line goals. For instance, marketing should emphasize consumer expectations of corporate responsibility and how firms can differentiate their brands accordingly. Operations management should focus on how to conduct audits of supply chains for triple bottom line impacts. Accounting should feature how triple bottom line reports can be generated and finance should incorporate the growing evidence of a positive relationship between corporate financial performance and corporate social performance and the role of executives and boards of directors in bringing it about. Additionally, human resource management courses should concentrate on the value proficiencies that employees in the triple bottom line organization need and attendant hiring and performance conventions. Presently, such topics tend to be covered as an afterthought, if they are covered at all. Hence, business students can graduate without knowing how to think systematically about corporate responsibility. An obvious solution to this problem is to require a standalone course in corporate responsibility that ties various topics together, akin to what is shown in Figure 4.1.

If students are not required to take such a course, they will be hard pressed to grasp the complex relationship between business and society and the values at stake. To further redress this deficiency, required complementary coursework should include leadership and organizational culture, social entrepreneurship, and business ethics, the latter being an important course for conveying the kind of other-regarding decision making essential to associative thinking. To reinforce discovery precepts, modules in the scientific method and systems thinking should also be mandated. The sooner they are, the sooner myopic business education can be eradicated. Ultimately, reforming the business curriculum around triple bottom line goals means purging amoral self-interest from coursework and elevating a role for other-regarding associative thinking.

Such reform will not be easy. The lure of unfettered self-interest is powerful. Business education will not discard this habit of thought easily. Indeed, even after a massive outbreak of corporate scandals at the beginning of the 21st century, the accrediting agency for business schools, the Association to Advance Collegiate Schools of Business, voted on new standards in 2004 that ruled out the requirement of even one ethics or corporate responsibility course as a condition of accreditation (Willen, 2004). This helps explain why only a minority of business schools require such a course (Swanson, 2004; see also Evans & Weiss, 2008). Indeed, in what appeared to be a blatant exercise in shortsightedness, many business schools axed their ethics or corporate responsibility course even while the news of Enron's demise was still in the media spotlight (Kelly, 2002). Arguably, such behavior does little to assuage the dismally low public opinion of big business (see Dugan, 2016). As the dangers of dissociation become more apparent, it may only be a matter of time before business schools are forced to reform their curricula. Meanwhile, discovery executives should not wait for them to catch up to reality. Discovery leaders must necessarily forge ahead of bad education. In time, business schools might take notice and include more of these leaders on their advisory boards and in their classrooms. This may provide the needed impetus for curricula changes based on discovery goals.

CONCLUSION

This chapter has described some pathologies of dissociation that affect the business and society relationship. Discovery leadership was proposed as a necessary condition for ameliorating these maladies and enacting the values that facilitate corporate responsibility. Implications for practice include hiring executives and other employees who are capable of participating in this mission. Implications for research include helping human resource management practitioners design methods that screen employees for this capability and performance appraisal systems that reward it. Finally, the business school curriculum should be revamped around the precepts of discovery leadership. Otherwise, business schools will continue to lag public expectations of responsible business education.

NOTES

1. Discovery leadership is an ideal type. According to Max Weber (1947), an ideal type is a simplified model that focuses attention on a phenomenon's distinctive features in order to highlight its logical implications systematically. The distinctive features of discovery leadership are the four realizations that constitute an associative mindset, covered later.
2. John Dewey (1922) is among those who have argued against dissociation by rejecting the subject/object dualism in epistemology, the human/environment dualism in metaphysics, and the self/society dualism in social and political theory (see also Ayres, 1944).

3. Although this chapter focuses on values, it recognizes the affinity between values and ethics. Hence the term "values" should be understood to mean "ethical values." The logic for this equivalence is as follows. Values are inherently normative because they represent beliefs about desirable end states and relationships. At the same time, these beliefs are expressed in terms of ethics, especially in the language of rights and justice. For example, consumers who *value* safety typically express this *belief* by referring to their *right* to safe products and *fair* or *just* compensation if products cause harm.

4. Swanson's (2014) reformulated principle of corporate responsibility is informed by Frederick's (1995) value theory, and also by extant models of corporate responsibility, including Sethi's (1975), Carroll's (1979), Frederick's (1987), and Wartick and Cochran's (1985), as codified by Wood (1991). Of these perspectives, Wartick and Cochran's description of corporate social responsiveness and corporate social responsibility as representing a means-end continuum is reflected in the illustration of value processes at the top of Figure 4.1.

5. Candidates for constructive individual values are drawn from Rokeach's (1973) survey of personally-held values. Candidates for constructive organizational values are selected from Frederick (1995), Schein (2010) and Swanson's (2014) research.

REFERENCES

Adams, G. B., & Balfour, D. L. (1998). *Unmasking administrative evil.* Thousand Oaks, CA: SAGE.

Adorno, T. (1991). *The culture industry.* London, England: Routledge Classics.

Aram, J. (1993). *Presumed superior.* Englewood Cliffs, NJ: Prentice Hall.

Aspen Institute. (2008). Where will they lead? MBA student attitudes about business & society. Retrieved from https://www.aspeninstitute.org/sites/default/files/content/docs/bsp/SAS_PRINT_FINAL.PDF

Ayres, C. (1944). *The theory of economic progress.* Chapel Hill, NC: University of North Carolina Press.

Bateson, G. (1972). *Steps to an ecology of mind.* New York, NY: Ballantine.

Bateson, G. (1985). *The cybernetics of self: A theory of alcoholism in steps to an ecology of mind.* New York, NY: Ballantine Books.

Beenen, G. & Pinto, J. (2009). Resisting organizational-level corruption: An interview with Sherron Watkins. *Academy of Management Learning & Education, 8,* 275–289.

Benefit corporation website. Retrieved from http://benefitcorp.net/policymakers/state-by-state-status

Berman, M. (1981). *The reenchantment of the world.* Ithaca, NY: Cornell University Press.

Berman, M. (1989). *Coming to our senses: Body and spirit in the hidden history of the west.* New York, NY: Simon & Schuster.

Brecht, A. (1944). *Prelude to silence.* New York, NY: Oxford University Press.

Browne, J. (2016, March 30). Here's a better way for companies to tackle big social problems. *Harvard Business Review.* Retrieved from https://hbr.org/2016/03/heres-a-better-way-for-companies-to-tackle-big-social-problems

Carroll, A. B. (1979). A three-dimensional conceptual model of corporate social performance. *Academy of Management Review, 4,* 497–506.

Carroll, A. B., & Buchholtz, A. K. (2015). *Business & society: Ethics, sustainability, and stakeholder management.* Stamford, CT: Cengage Learning.

Cohen, D., & Prusak, L. (2001). *How social capital makes organizations work.* Boston, MA: Harvard Business School Press.

Dewey, J. (1922). *Human nature and conduct.* New York, NY: Henry Holt and Company.

Dugan, A. (2015, July 6). Americans still more confident in small vs. big business. *Gallup.* Retrieved from http://www.gallup.com/poll/183989/americans-confident-small-big-business.aspx

Elkington, J. (1994). Towards the sustainable corporation: Win–win business strategies for sustainable development. *California Management Review, 36,* 90–100.

Etzioni, A. (1988). *The moral dimension: Toward a new economics.* New York, NY: The Free Press.

Evans, F. J., & Weiss, E. J. (2008). Views on the importance of ethics in business education: Survey results from AACSB deans, CEOs, and faculty. In D. L. Swanson & D. G. Fisher (Eds.), *Advancing Business Ethics Education* (pp. 43—66). Charlotte, NC: Information Age.

Field, A. (2013, January 25). First-ever study of Maryland benefit corps released. *Forbes.* Retrieved from http://www.forbes.com/sites/annefield/2013/01/25/first-ever-study-of-maryland-benefit-corps-released/#1e99b384517e

Frederick, W. C. (1987). Theories of corporate social performance. In S. P. Sethi & C. Falbe (Eds.), *Business and society: Dimensions of conflict and cooperation* (pp. 142–161). New York, NY: Lexington Books.

Frederick, W. C. (1995). *Values, nature, and culture in the American corporation.* New York, NY: Oxford University Press.

Frederick, W. C. (1998). Creatures, corporations, communities, chaos, complexity: A naturological view of the corporate social role. *Business & Society, 37,* 358–389.

Frederick, W. C. (2006). *Corporation, be good! The story of corporate social responsibility.* Indianapolis, IN: Dog Ear.

Frederick, W. C. (2008). The business schools' moral dilemma. In D. L. Swanson & D. G. Fisher (Eds.), *Advancing Business Ethics Education* (pp. 25–42). Charlotte, NC: Information Age.

Frederick, W. C. (2012). *Natural corporate management: From the big bang to Wall Street.* Sheffield, England: Greenleaf.

Friedman, M. (1962). *Capitalism and freedom.* Chicago, IL: University of Chicago Press.

Friedman, M. (1970, September 13). The social responsibility of business is to increase its profits. *New York Times Magazine, 33,* 122–126.

Galbraith, J. K. (1996). *The good society: The humane agenda.* New York, NY: Houghton Mifflin.

Ghoshal, S. (2005). Bad management theories are destroying good management practices. *Academy of Management Learning & Education, 4,* 75–91.

Giacalone, R. A., & Thompson, K. R. (2006). Business ethics and social responsibility education: Shifting the worldview. *Academy of Management Learning & Education, 5,* 266–277.

Goldberg, L. R. (1993). The structure of phenotypic personality traits. *American Psychologist, 48,* 26–34.

Hartman, L. P., & Werhane, P. H. (2013). Proposition: Shared value as an incomplete metal model. *Business Ethics Journal Review, 1,* 36–43.

Hausman, D. M., & McPherson, M. S. (1996). *Economic analysis and moral philosophy.* New York, NY: Cambridge University Press.

Jackall, R. (1988). *Moral mazes.* New York, NY: Oxford University Press.

Jacoby, R. (1975). *Social amnesia.* Boston, MA: Beacon Press.

Jones, J. M. (2015, June 15). Confidence in U.S. institutions still below historical norms. *Gallup.* Retrieved from http://www.gallup.com/poll/183593/confidence-institutions-below-historical-norms.aspx

Judge, T. A., & Cable, D. M. (1997). Applicant personality, organizational culture, and organization attraction. *Personnel Psychology, 50,* 359–394.

Kelly, M. (2002, November/December). It's a heckuva time to be dropping business ethics courses. *Business Ethics Magazine, 16,* 17–18.

Keynes, J. M. (1923). *A tract on monetary reform.* London, England: Macmillan.

Kluckholn, C. (1951). Values and value-orientations in the theory of action. In T. Parsons & E. A. Shils (Eds.), *Toward a general theory of action* (pp. 388–433). New York, NY: Harper & Row.

Kuhn, T. S. (1962). *The structure of scientific revolutions.* Chicago, IL: University of Chicago Press.

Laing, R. D. (1959). *The divided self.* London, England: Tavistock.

Lan, L. L., & Heracleous, L. (2010). Rethinking agency theory: The view from law. *Academy of Management Review, 35,* 294–314.

Lekachman, R. (1976). *Economists at bay: Why the experts will never solve your problems.* New York, NY: McGraw-Hill.

Lorsch, J., & Khurana, R. (2010, May–June). The pay problem: Time for a new paradigm for executive compensation. *Harvard Magazine.* Retrieved from http://harvardmagazine.com/2010/05/the-pay-problem

Mannheim, K. (1940). *Man and society in an age of reconstruction.* New York, NY: Harcourt, Brace and World.

Marcuse, H. (1964). *One dimensional man.* Boston, MA: Beacon Press.

Matthews, D. (2014, August 13). The "invisible hand" has an iron grip on America. Retrieved from http://fortune.com/2014/08/13/invisible-hand-american-economy

Mitroff, I., & Swanson, D. L. (2004). An open letter to the deans and faculties of American business schools: A call to action. *Academy of Management News, 35.*

Morrison, E. W., & Milliken, F. J. (2000). Organizational silence: A barrier to change and development in a pluralistic world. *Academy of Management Review, 25,* 706–731.

O'Reilly, C.A., Chatman, J. A., & Caldwell, D. (1991). People of organizational culture: A profile comparison approach to assessing person-organization fit. *Academy of Management Journal, 34,* 487–516.

Orlitzky, M., & Benjamin, J. D. (2001). Corporate social performance and firm risk: A meta-analytic review. *Business & Society, 40,* 369–396.

Orlitzky, M., Schmidt, F. L., & Rynes, S. L. (2003). Corporate social and financial performance: A meta-analysis. *Organizational Studies, 24,* 403–441.

Orlitzky, M., & Swanson, D. L. (2012). Assessing stakeholder satisfaction: Toward a supplemental measure of corporate social performance as reputation. *Corporate Reputation Review, 16,* 119–137.

Orlitzky, M., Swanson, D. L., & Quartermaine, L. K. (2006). Normative myopia, executives' personality, and preference for pay dispersion: Toward implications for corporate social performance. *Business & Society, 45,* 149–177.

Perrow, C. (1986). *Complex organizations: A critical essay.* New York, NY: McGraw-Hill.

Pfeffer, J. (1998). *The human equation: Building profits by putting people first.* Boston, MA: Harvard Business School Press.

Pless, N. M. (2012). Social entrepreneurship in theory and practice—an introduction. *Journal of Business Ethics, 111,* 317–320.

Popper, K. R. (1945). *The open society and its enemies.* Princeton, NJ: Princeton University Press.

Porter, M. E., & Kramer, M. R. (2002). The competitive advantage of corporate philanthropy. *Harvard Business Review, 80,* 5–16.

Porter, M. E., & Kramer, M. R. (2006). Strategy & society: The link between competitive advantage and corporate social responsibility. *Harvard Business Review, 84,* 78–92.

Richards, K. (2015, December 15). How agencies are meeting millennials' demand for socially responsible marketing: Doing some good is good for business. *Adweek.* Retrieved from http://www.adweek.com/news/advertising-branding/agencies-are-carving-out-niche-socially-responsible-marketing-168592

Rokeach, M. (1968). *Beliefs, attitudes, and values: A theory of organization and change.* San Francisco, CA: Jossey-Bass.

Rokeach, M. (1973). *The nature of human values.* New York, NY: Free Press.

Roll, R. (1986). The hubris hypothesis of corporate takeovers. *Journal of Business, 59,* 197–216.

Rynes, S. L., Trank, C. Q., Lawson, A. M., & Ilies, R. (2003). Behavioral coursework in business education: Growing evidence of a legitimacy crisis. *Academy of Management Learning & Education, 2,* 269–283.

Savitz, A. (2013). *Talent, transformation, and the triple bottom line.* San Francisco, CA: Jossey-Bass.

Schein, E. (2010). *Organizational culture and leadership* (4th ed.). San Francisco, CA: Jossey-Bass.

Schwartz, H. (1991). Narcissistic process and corporate decay: The case of General Motors. *Business Ethics Quarterly, 1,* 249–268.

Schwartz C. E., & Sendor M. (1999). Helping others helps oneself: Response shift effects in peer support. *Social Science & Medicine, 48, 1563*–1575.

Sethi, S. P. (1975). Dimensions of corporate social performance: An analytic framework. *California Management Review, 17,* 58–64.

Silverstein, L. (2013, May 14). Enron, ethics and today's corporate values. *Forbes.* Retrieved from http://www.forbes.com/sites/kensilverstein/2013/05/14/enron-ethics-and-todays-corporate-values

Stewart, J. B. (2011, September 30). Rewarding C.E.O.'s who fail. *New York Times.* Retrieved from http://www.nytimes.com/2011/10/01/business/lets-stop-rewarding-failed-ceos-common-sense.html?_r=0

Stiglitz, J. E. (2001, December 8). Information and the change in the paradigm in economics. Prize Lecture at Columbia Business School. Retrieved from http://www.nobelprize.org/nobel_prizes/economic-sciences/laureates/2001/stiglitz-lecture.pdf

Sullivan, J. W. N. (1949). *Limitations of science: A creative scientist's approach to the unknown.* New York, NY: Mentor Books.

Swanson, D. L. (1992). Dysfunctional conglomerates: An explanation provided by linking ontological individualism to social relations within an open systems context. *Behavioral Science, 37,* 139–152.

Swanson, D. L. (1995). Addressing a theoretical problem by reorienting the corporate social performance model. *Academy of Management Review, 20,* 43–64.

Swanson, D. L. (1996). Neoclassical economic theory, executive control, and organizational outcomes. *Human Relations, 49,* 735–756.

Swanson, D. L. (1999). Toward an integrative theory of business and society: A research strategy for corporate social performance. *Academy of Management Review, 24,* 506–521.

Swanson, D. L. (2000). Codetermination: A business and government partnership in procedural safety for ecological sustainability. *Systems Research and Behavioral Science, 17,* 527–542.

Swanson, D. L. (2004). The buck stops here: Why universities must reclaim business ethics education. *The Journal of Academic Ethics, 2,* 43–61.

Swanson, D. L. (2008). Top managers as drivers for corporate social responsibility. In A. Crane, A. McWilliams, D. Matten, J. Moon, & D. Siegel (Eds.), *The Oxford handbook of corporate social responsibility* (pp. 47–62). New York, NY: Oxford University Press.

Swanson, D. L. (2014). *Embedding CSR into corporate culture: Challenging the executive mind.* Basingstoke, England: Palgrave Macmillan.

Swanson, D. L. (in press). CSR discovery leadership: Society, science, and shared value consciousness. London, England: Palgrave Macmillan.

Swanson, D. L., & Orlitzky M. (in press). Leading the triple bottom line: A corporate social responsibility approach. In D. S. Ones, N. Anderson, C. Viswesvaran, & H. K. Sinangil (Eds.), *Handbook of industrial, work, and organizational psychology* (2nd edition). Thousand Oaks, CA: SAGE.

Swanson, D. L., & Fisher, D. G. (2008). Business ethics education: If we don't know where we're going, any road will take us there. In D. L. Swanson & D. G. Fisher (Eds.), *Advancing business ethics education* (pp. 1–23). Charlotte, NC: Information Age.

Waddock, S. (2009). *Leading corporate citizens: Vision, values, value added.* New York, NY: McGraw-Hill Irwin.

Waddock, S., & Rasche, A. (2013). *Building the responsible enterprise: Where vision and values add value.* Stanford, CA: Stanford University Press.

Wartick, S. L., & Cochran, P. L. (1985). The evolution of the corporate social performance model. *Academy of Management Review, 10,* 758–769.

Weber, M. (1947). *The theory of social and economic organization* (A. H. Henderson & T. Parsons, Trans.). New York, NY: Oxford University Press. (Original work published 1922).

Weber, M. (1958). *The Protestant ethic and the spirit of capitalism.* New York, NY: Scribner.

Weick, K. E. (1969). *The social psychology of organizing.* Reading, MA: Addison-Wesley.

Weick, K. E. (1995). *Sensemaking in organizations.* Thousand Oaks, CA: SAGE.

Wickens, P. D. (1995). *The ascendant organization: Combining commitment and control for long-term, sustainable business success.* New York, NY: St. Martin's Press.

Weinstein, N., & Ryan, R. M. (2010). When helping helps: Autonomous motivation for prosocial behavior and its influence on well-being for the helper and recipient. *Journal of Personality and Social Psychology, 98,* 222–244.

Willen, L. (2004, March 8). Kellogg denies guilt as B-Schools evade alumni lapses. *Bloomberg Press Wire.*

Williams, R. (1979). A sociological perspective. In M. Rokeach (Ed.), *Understanding human values* (pp. 15–46). New York, NY: Free Press.

Wood, D. J. (1991). Corporate social performance revisited. *Academy of Management Review, 16,* 691–718.

CHAPTER 5

CHALLENGES OF DECISION-MAKING FOR ETHICAL LEADERS IN DEVELOPING STATES

W. N. Webb
University of South Africa

Corruption prevention measures could broadly be divided into two main themes: a compliance based approach and a values based approach. Whereas the compliance-based approach focuses on the imposition of external control and compliance with policies and rules, the value-based approach focuses on the development of integrity and requires individuals to internalize ethical values. The value-based approach identifies the less formal aspects of ethics management including *inter alia* communicating moral expectations with employees, visibly punishing offenders, providing ethics training, and appraising ethics performance of employees by making it a stand-alone key performance area. With a value-based approach to ethics management, senior officials are expected to demonstrate commitment to their own ethical conduct. This integrity (or values) based approach is

Radical Thoughts on Ethical Leadership, pages 97–112
Copyright © 2017 by Information Age Publishing
97

rooted in self-governance; rather than simply compliance with acts, policies, and procedures (Lawton, Rayner, & Lasthuizen, 2013, p. 162).

In this chapter, the author sets out to identify the main attributes of ethical leadership, the context within which ethical leadership is applied, and the extent to which such leadership could bring about enhanced measures of integrity management. For Menzel (2015, p. 316) ethical leadership serves to build trusts and confidence in government, but for Lawton and Paez (2014) it serves to enhance employee attitudes and effectiveness.

Research on ethical leadership has been inattentive to the organizational context; assuming that "one size fits all"; even in different cultures and societies (Lawton et al., 2013, p. 167). In this chapter it is suggested that the development state context often introduces complexity in ethical leadership and provides for a myriad of unpredictable variables that public officials should consider when they become aware of moral dilemmas and practice moral judgments.

A SOUTH AFRICAN CASE STUDY
ON POOR ETHICAL LEADERSHIP

Schwella (2013, pp. 65–90) cites various qualities of bad leadership including being cynical, corrupt, and untrustworthy. Bad leaders in his view are blinded by their self-interest and are unable to distinguish between right and wrong. These leaders ignore incompetence, cronyism, and corruption. In his investigation into poor leadership at the South African police service, Schwella reflects on the leadership qualities of Mr. Jackie Selebi—the National Commissioner of this institution who also became the President of Interpol. In this case the National Commissioner was a respected political leader but showed signs of arrogance and a lack of integrity. He was eventually convicted of corruption and sentenced to a 15 year prison sentence. Of importance to this chapter, is the fact that the National Commissioner's followers supported him and issued a declaration in which they confirmed their blind loyalty to him irrespective of the fact that they were senior police officials.

To Schwella (2013, pp. 65–90), this case pointed to various underlying weaknesses in the SAPS including an organizational environment which exhibited weak ethical commitment as well as minimal ethical reasoning. Selebi's followers did not resist his bad leadership and acted in a submissive and suppressed way. Another contributing factor was the serious challenges faced by the SAPS including service delivery, transformation, and the incidence of crime. Increasing pressure in terms of goal setting and realization often leads to the emphasis on goal attainment at the expense of ethical behavior.

These forms of organizational deficiencies such as poor ethical leadership, weak ethical commitment, and minimal ethical reasoning are the focus of this chapter. Complicating these deficiencies even more is the context within which decisions are taken: a public service context within a developmental state.

ETHICAL LEADERSHIP WITHIN A DEVELOPING STATE CONTEXT

Developing states are confronted with unique challenges. The United Nation's Economic Commission for Africa (2011, pp. 6–8) describes a developmental state as a state that has the capacity to deploy its authority, credibility, and legitimacy in a binding manner to design and implement policies to promote transformation and growth. The developmental state should play a positive interventionist role by allocating resources and coordination economic activities. Central themes in the developing state context includes "greater state oversight by citizens," "providing stakeholders with a voice," "the state being assisted by developmentalist coalitions," "pervasive market failures," "promoting transformation and growth," and the "state to play a central role." These attributes provide for a unique context for ethical leadership in developmental states.

According to Lawton et al. (2013, p. 169) research on ethical leadership to date has been inattentive to the nature of the organizational context within which ethical leadership is practiced. The assumption was that a "one size fits all" ethical leadership is adequate for organizations operating in different environments, societies, and cultures. In fact, Loyens and Maesschalk (2010) confirm this observation as they noted that research on ethical decision-making—a key aspect of ethical leadership—is mainly based on the literature in the field of business ethics.

However, according to Lawton et al. (2013, p. 169) ethical leadership is context dependent. For Heres (2014, p. 36) normatively appropriate conduct depends on *inter alia* the institution's own moral norms and values, its primary and secondary values, and the society at large. In the study by Heres and Lasthuizen (2012, pp. 441–466) ethical leadership within public, private, and hybrid organizations, context appears to influence ethical leadership expectations and success. For example, where private sector leaders perceive honesty to be a significant value, public and hybrid sector leaders value an outward and societal focus. In public institutions, leaders may want to emphasize general ethical principles and the value of decisions to the public interest, whereas private sector leaders may relate ethics directly to recognition and rewards. As Lawton et al. (2013, p. 169) notes, the general principles and components of ethical leadership are universally stable, but the implementation of these components varies across contexts.

According to Heres (2014, pp. 61–66) this ethical leadership context is determined by three variables including: public service motivation (PSM), the nature of organizational tasks, and the influence of stakeholders. Public service motivation reflects a person's desire to serve the public interest, one's loyalty to government, and to strive for social equity. Managers in public service institutions may expect subordinates to be intrinsically motivated to serve the greater good and could consider communication on ethics to be unnecessary. Such individuals are often less dependent on monetary and other extrinsic motivations. Secondly, where private institutions are required to maximize profit, public institutions are required to enforce the law and policy, serve the public interest, and provide services that are unavailable in the marketplace. It can be assumed that the nature of dilemmas in the public space would be more pronounced as compared to those in the private sector. Finally, the demand by stakeholders in the public sector could exceed those applied in the private sector. Public institutions are subject to political dynamics, and external oversight that could serve to inhibit the decision-making discretion of public service managers.

Nabatchi in Webb (2015, pp. 98–114) provides a different perspective on public values. In her view, public officials should be responsible to uphold values; especially when they exercise delegated decision-making authority. She recognized the existence of multiple values at play and the complexity of public administration is to find the appropriate balance. Although she acknowledged the common perspective of values as an interplay between bureaucratic ethics—concerned with values such as efficiency, expertise, loyalty, and hierarchy—and the democratic ethos—which is concerned with values such as social equity, justice, citizenship, and constitutionalism—she regarded this conceptual framework of little practical use to public administrators.

Nabatchi identifies four value frames (i.e., political-, legal-, organizational-, and market public values; (cf. De Graaf & Van der Wal, 2010, pp. 623–630). Each value frame has specific content values. For example, the political values frame reflects the values of participation, representation, liberty, equality, and responsiveness. The legal value frame contains the content values of substantive rights, the right to procedural due process, and the equity values of fairness and the protection of the individual's constitutional rights that have been violated by administrative action. The organizational value frame is concerned with administrative efficiency and also specialization and expertise, authority of positions, merit, formalization, and political neutrality. Finally, the market values frame contains the content values of innovation, productivity, customer service, entrepreneurship, and cost savings and efficiency. In her view, the values of accountability, legitimacy, citizenship and possibly integrity could be regarded as floating values that could be interpreted differently depending on the particular values frame through which administrators adjudicate (Webb, 2015, pp. 98–114).

It is not only the public service context and the values found within that create complexity in decision-making. The nature of the developing state is yet another variable which introduces complexity. In Schwella's (2013, pp. 65–90) study on leadership within the SAPS, he describes the public service context as one in which public officials should understand and work with political processes and role players, the need to work with public pressure and protest, and active pursuance of democratic public accountability where openness is encouraged.

It is not only the public–private service contexts that impacts on our understanding of ethical leadership, but also the divide between developed— developing state contexts. In Andrews' (2010, pp. 7–35) publication entitled "Good Government Means Different Things in Different Countries," the author argues that the *one-size-fits-all* model of good and effective government is inappropriate roadmap for developing states to pursue. For example, the Worldwide Governance Indicators suggest that developing states should establish internal audit infrastructure as a means to achieve a "good government." However, in Andrews' (2010) evaluation of 38 governments it is evident that many developed states are less likely to adopt these internal audit practices. In another example, the author cites the scores on legislative oversight as a key reform measure of Australia, Canada, United Kingdom, and the United States; all examples of countries with good governments. In respect of legislative oversight, Australia, Canada, and the United Kingdom scored 1 out of a potential score of 11, whereas the United States scored 10. This variance could be assigned to the presidential governments with higher levels of legislative oversight.

What is evident from the Andrews' (2010) evaluation is the importance of considering the impact of context on our understanding of conceptual models—in this case ethical leadership. As is argued below, the awareness and judgment as components of ethical leadership may be very appropriate in a developed state context but highly undesirable in developing state context. For example, in the context of the South African public service supply chain management practices, the *Treasury Regulations* 16A8.3 issued in terms of the Public Finance Management Act (1999) officials are required to treat all suppliers and potential suppliers equitably. However, in respect of the Preferential Procurement Policy Framework Act (2000), procurement must be guided by goals that promote contracting with persons historically disadvantaged by unfair discrimination by race, gender, or disability. Due to the South African political, historical, and legal context, it seems fair to discriminate in supply chain management decisions.

In the following section, the theories and conceptual models of ethical leadership will be described. The importance of strong leadership and role models impacts directly on the organizational climate and the way people behave within an institution (Kaptein, Huberts, Avelino, & Lasthuizen, 2005, pp. 299–311).

THEORIES OF ETHICAL LEADERSHIP

Perhaps this section should start with a rationale on why the ethics of leadership is so important and consequently the topic of this chapter. According to Lawton & Paez (2014), the decisions by leaders may be far reaching, non-routine, complex, with high stakes, and require the exercise of judgement, and not the application of rules. Whereas subordinates follow policy prescription and emulate the behavior of their leaders, leaders are often confronted with a much greater area of decision-making discretion and consequently have to make a choice between conflicting values. It could also be argued that ethical leaders are more effective too. According to Lawton et al. (2013, p. 166) ethical leaders often inspire employees to be more optimistic and take more initiative which leads them to experience their work as more meaningful.

If it is accepted that ethical leadership is important, then what constitutes such behavior? According to Lawton and Paez (2014) behavioral integrity refers to the alignment between an actor's words and deeds; consistency between a person's beliefs and the way they act. To become an ethical competent leader is not a once off affair; it is a life-long endeavor (Menzel, 2015, p. 317). Ethical leaders should be consistent, coherent, and constant in their decision-making. But also honest, fair, respectful, approachable, loyal, open towards followers (Heres, 2014, p. 45; cf. Lawton & Paez, 2014). Ethical leaders should reflect on the moral implications of their decisions and actions, the end goals they set, and the means they use to achieve these goals (Heres, 2014, p. 45). According to Menzel's (2015, p. 317) ethical leaders should consider the utilitarian trap; calculating the best outcome for most employees. Menzel cites the example of rewarding all employees with the same pay increase: those who work hard as well as those who do not. Although this may make most employees happy it may not be the right thing to do.

As acknowledged above the impact of ethical leaders is wide. Such leaders are not ethical for the sake of earning some form of spiritual recognition. Ethical leadership is the layer between the ethical culture imbedded in its policies and programs on the one hand, and its ethical climate, and employee ethical reasoning, and behavior on the other hand (Lawton et al., 2013, p. 167). Furthermore, ethical leadership requires not only self-motivation, but also the ability to motivate others. In terms of Social Identity Theory followers identify themselves with their leaders when the leaders are fair, just, and caring. Followers emulate the leaders' ethical behaviors (Heres, 2014, p. 45).

Heres (2014, p. 38) defines ethical leadership as the demonstration of normatively appropriate conduct through personal actions and interpersonal relationships, and the promotion of such conduct to followers through two-way communication, reinforcement, and decision-making. Heres (2014), however, is explicit in describing ethical behavior to be context specific. Normatively appropriate conduct depends on inter alia the institution's own moral norms and values, its primary and secondary values, and the society at large (Heres, 2014, p. 36). Expectations of ethical leadership depends on other variables too (e.g., structural characteristics of the work environment, the level of formalization, and work context). The work context may require a leader to demonstrate more task oriented behavior, or more people oriented behavior (Heres, 2014, p. 56).

In shaping our understanding of how ethical leadership works, we could reflect on the attributes of this phenomenon. To Edwards (2010, pp. 93–109), ethical leadership constitutes the following roles: to place institutional interest above personal interest, to create formal mechanisms to enforce ethical conduct, to establish an ethical culture, to act as role models to establish a positive ethical climate. To promote ethical decision-making, to create living conversations about ethics and values among subordinates, to create mechanisms of dissent, and to create a system of shared values within the institution. Edwards provided a to-do list for ethical leadership which includes various dimensions including bringing about *inter alia* ethical alignment, ethical enforcement, and ethical impetus. Ethical alignment is achieved by promoting ethical decision-making in all day-to-day activities, whereas ethical enforcement aligning is brought about by enforcing policies, rules, and codes of conduct. Ethical impetus refers to leading ethical initiatives and rewarding ethical behavior. Her take on servant leadership also seems relevant to the discussion on ethical leadership. Servant leaders—in her view—promote moral reasoning and moral actions, and values institutional interests over self-interest. Although the author clearly articulated the attributes of ethical and servant leadership, she did not distinguish between an ethical climate and an ethical culture.

In the study by Huberts, Kaptein, and Lasthuizen (2007, pp. 587–607), the impact of different ethical leadership styles on integrity violations by police officers were investigated. The authors distinguish between three qualities of ethical leaders *inter alia*: as a role model, strictness of the manager, and openness of the manager. Whereas role modelling and openness are regarded as part of the value based approach, strictness is regarded as a compliance based approach.

The authors developed four separate hypotheses. In the first three hypotheses the authors propose that the display of integrity in managers' behavior (role modeling), more strict enforcement of ethical norms and the punishment of wrongdoers, and greater openness by managers when discussing ethical dilemmas, would lead integrity violations. All three hypotheses were confirmed. While role modelling has the widest impact on the measured integrity violations, the strictness and openness has an impact on 75% of the integrity violations. Role modelling appears to be the most important means to ensure a reduced level of integrity violation. In the final hypothesis, the authors propose that integrity-based leadership styles would contribute more than compliance based leadership styles to reduced levels of integrity violations. The findings of this study refuted the hypothesis and suggested that strictness—as a compliance based approach—is significantly underestimated (Huberts et al., 2007, pp. 587–607).

Different leadership roles may require the application of different virtues. When leaders create vision and purpose the virtues of courage and imagination is important; ethical decision-making require judgement, competence, and prudence, and inspiring others may require the virtues of honesty, transparency, and moral exemplar (Lawton & Paez, 2014). Multidimensional measures of ethical leadership culture enable a more detailed assessment of how such leadership is enacted in practice. Different leadership characteristics and behaviors could curb different types of unethical behaviors (Heres, 2014, p. 41).

Another such multidimensional conceptualization of ethical leadership is provided by Heres and Lasthuizen (2012, pp. 441–466) where they describe the attributes of the moral person versus the moral manager. The authors investigated the differences between ethical leadership in public, hybrid, and private sector organizations. Their literature review pointed to the existence of two main dimensions of ethical leadership: the moral person, and the moral manager. Ethical leadership of the moral person relates to the individual's moral character as well as the moral nature of the individual's own decision-making and behavior. Integrity, trustworthiness, responsibility are the main moral traits of ethical leaders. Ethical leaders make decisions that are consistent, coherent, and constant, and treat followers justly and fairly.

The second dimension of ethical leadership relates to four sub-dimensions. *Role modeling* refers to the extent that the leader's behavior and decision-making is visible and salient, and negative and conflicting signals are not sent out. *Reinforcement* concerns the use of formal and informal measures to reward and punish virtuous or malicious behavior. Communication refers to the extent to which leaders communicate the moral implications of decisions, and promote the open discussion of individual and organizational values. The last dimension of the moral manager refers to the *empowerment* of followers. Ethical leaders empower their followers to participate in decision-making and allow them to voice their own concerns and perspectives. Leadership should be strong in respect of both the moral person and the moral manager dimension (Lawton et al., 2013, p. 167).

The focus of this chapter is on the latter dimension of moral manager. Of course, it could be argued that leaders cannot be moral managers without being moral persons. A focus on the empowerment attribute of Heres and Lasthuizen's (2012) moral manager dimension consequently assumes the existence of leaders who inspire integrity.

ETHICAL LEADERSHIP:
MORAL MANAGER AND EMPOWERMENT

Various authors have noted the positive impact of ethical leadership on employee moral judgment and the prevalence of integrity violations (Huberts, Six, van Tankeren, van Montfort, & Paanakker, 2014, pp. 167–197). As described above, ethical leadership constitute two dimensions: the moral person and the moral manager. Heres (2014, pp. 77–78) noted that empowerment—one of the key variables of the moral manager dimension of ethical leadership—requires ethical leaders to stimulate followers to think for themselves about what is, and what is not, acceptable behavior. Rather than communicate the rules, ethical leaders should emphasize the underlying principles applicable in a specific situation. By emphasizing principles rather than rules, ethical leaders leave space for interpretation and allow different interpretations of appropriate behavior.

This "empowerment" approach to ethical leadership inevitably raises the need to describe discretion and perhaps also those factors that influence discretion. When employees are required to decide what appropriate and inappropriate behavior is, a measure of discretion is required. Loyens & Maesschalk (2010, pp. 67–70) defines discretion as that space—bounded by effective limits—where an employee can make a choice among possible courses of action or inaction. Public officials such as teachers, police officers, and social workers have a high degree of discretion to make choice in a complex and demanding environment. Often this measure of discretion causes these officials to be formulators rather than implementers of public policy. Various factors have an influence on the decision-making discretion of officials including individual decision-makers characteristics such as personal beliefs, gender, and educational background; organizational characteristics such as workload pressure, rules, and organizational culture; and extra-organizational factors such as the media, service providers, and the attributes of clients (Edwards, 2010, pp. 93–109).

Due to a complex and demanding implementation context, public officials are often confronted with ethical dilemmas. Ethical dilemmas do not always require a form of decision-making discretion. For example, reporting a colleague who uses the official vehicle for private purposes does not require official implementation discretion. Similarly, not all decisions involve an ethical dilemma. However, for the purpose of this chapter, the focus is on formal decision-making by officials being confronted by an ethical dilemma (Loyens & Maesschalk, 2010, pp. 81–82).

One could cite various definitions of ethical dilemmas. Heres (2014, p. 36) defines a *moral dilemma*: a situation in which the moral values and norms that are valid in the context that the actor operates conflict with one another and the right decision is not immediately agreed on by various stakeholders. (Heres, 2014, p. 36).

Loyens & Maesschalk (2010, p. 83–84) described three different types of dilemmas. The dilemma of relationships reflects conflicting interests (e.g., interests of employee versus institution; interests of role players within institution; and interests of stakeholders versus institution). A second type is the dilemma of content where the values of justice, upholding self, upholding others, and upholding relationships are significant. A third type is the dilemma of moral intensity: magnitude of consequences, social consensus, probability and proximity of effect, concentration of effect. To the authors this third type of dilemma is most appropriate in identifying dilemmas. Where beneficiaries are harmed, social agreement exist that an act is indeed evil, where there is a high probability that an impact would occur, and the number of people affected is significant, a dilemma is said to exist.

ETHICAL REASONING AND DECISION-MAKING

The study of decision-making models has received most of its attention within the Business Sciences; notably the field of Business Ethics. Most of these models describe either the individual attributes or situational factors that influence decision-making (Ford & Richardson, 1994, pp. 205–221). However, these models often neglect to describe how these actors impact on individual decision-making (Loyens & Maesschalk, 2010, pp. 66–100). In the next section, some of these models are described.

In the first of these models, Cooper (in Lawton et al., 2013, p. 123) describes the responsible administrator as an individual confronted by both objective and subjective responsibilities. Objective responsibilities refer to meeting external expectations such as law, institutional goals, societal values and norms, whereas subjective responsibilities refer to a person's own moral compass; his or her sense of duty when taking ethical decision-making.

We often resolve ethical issues spontaneously based on our emotions and feelings. When moral trade-offs do not work, or evoke tensions, a more systematic reflection of the underlying principles may be necessary to arrive at a decision on the ethical issue. The following ethical decision-making model—which consists of five steps—could be followed for thinking in a more principled fashion:

1. Perception of an ethical problem
2. Describing the problem and the ethical issue
3. Identifying alternatives
4. Projecting probable consequences
5. Selecting one alternative (Lawton et al., 2013, pp. 126–128)

According to Heres (2014, p. 36) the ethical decision-making process consists of the following four stages: ethical sensitivity or awareness of the moral nature of a decision; ethical judgement or reasoning; establishing intent to act in an ethical manner; engagement in ethical behavior (cf. Huberts et al., 2014, pp. 167–197).

According to Loyens & Maesschalk (2010, p. 75), Trevino developed the person-situation interactionist model. In this model both individual and situational factors have an impact on ethical decision-making. Individual factors include moral development and locus of decision-making whereas situational factors include job context, organizational culture, moral content of the organizational culture, and the characteristics of the job itself. Previous models tended to emphasise either the individual or situational factors, but did not capture the interaction of both factors.

To Loyens and Maesschalk (2010, pp. 66–100) most ethical decision-making models are successful in identifying those attributes that impact on decision-making. However, few—if any—models explain how these variables influence decision-making. Due to this weakness, the authors suggest role theory as a social mechanism that could open up the "black box" of decision-making. Role theory attempts to explain how and under which circumstances staff members deal with different and at times conflicting role expectations. In terms of this theory officials often occupy multiple statuses where demands are generated by several sources, for example a mother versus an employee role. This could lead to role strain such as role ambiguity, role conflict, role discrepancy, and role overload. This in turn could impact on the way officials deal with ethical dilemmas.

Whereas the models described above seeks to simplify and perhaps quantify the decision-making processes, the models described below remind us of the complexity and unpredictability of these processes. In Kohlberg's cognitive moral development theory, a person's level of cognitive moral development influences his/ her moral judgement (Lawton et al., 2013,

p. 124). In terms of this theory individuals progress irreversibly from lower to higher levels of moral development to reach moral maturity. Three phases of development exist including the pre-conventional, conventional and post-conventional phase. Kohlberg proposes that all people from all cultures progress to higher stages of moral reasoning. At the pre-conventional phase people tend to be egocentric and are mainly concerned with their own interests. In this phase an individual's moral reasoning is determined by a need to avoid punishment. At the conventional phase, the individual places a greater value on the role of family members and close associates. Moral reasoning is shaped by the majority view and a need to avoid being disliked by others. Individuals tend to conform to authority, doing their duty and maintaining the social order. At the post-conventional phase, individuals attain a sense of moral autonomy in which human life is sacred; therefore the need to avoid violating other's rights (Lynch, Lynch & Cruise, 2002, pp. 347–369; Hinde, 2002, pp. 55–56). However, according to Loyens and Maesschalk (2010, p. 75) this model describes ethical reasoning but does not guarantee ethical behavior.

However, it should be noted that ethical behavior seems not necessarily to follow explicit moral reasoning processes. Individuals with a developed capacity for moral reasoning do not necessarily act ethically, while those who act ethically indicate that they did so without much reflection (Huberts et al., 2014, pp. 167–197).

Deveterre (2002) identifies three main schools of thought forming the basis of ethical behavior: deontology, utilitarianism, and virtue ethics. Immanuel Kant introduced deontology—the study of duty—in which citizens are expected to obey certain maxims or moral precepts. These maxims do not come from God but from ourselves. Through pure practical reason maxims are established that indicates what we ought and ought not to do. Two beliefs formed the basis of Kant's belief: immortality and the belief that in a life after death a god will provide happiness to those worthy of it (Webb, 2010, pp. 76–77)..

John Stuart Mill introduced utilitarianism in 1873 as an alternative school of thought. This approach emphasises that acts should be judged according to its consequences or the greatest happiness for the greatest number of people. Punishment by a god was not the reason why decisions on actions were taken. To Deveterre (2002) virtue ethics presents a third school of thought. Virtue ethics is not about an obligation or duty to pursue moral principles. The motivation for being ethical comes from the deepest human desires. Prudence precedes all moral laws, principles, and rules. To the virtue ethicists, prudence—practical wisdom and reasoning—is the way to make the decisions that will develop a virtuous character. To emphasise the importance of reason Deveterre (2002) quotes Socrates' view that "the unexamined life is not worth living" (Webb, 2010, pp. 76–77; Loyens & Maesschalk, 2010, p. 76; Frederickson, 1997, pp. 157–182).

Hinde (in Webb, 2010, p. 78) also reflects on the sources of morality. Although Hinde acknowledges culture as a source of morality, he is of the view that greater significance should be assigned to human nature as a source of morality. All individuals are born with pan-cultural psychological potentials and characteristics which after birth are influenced by their life experiences. The author argues that babies are born with a measure of pro-social behavior which is interpreted as a desire to co-operate with others in an environment of mutual respect and reciprocity. Critical of the negative views of social scientists of human nature (including public choice theorists) and their selfish and assertive behavior, he argues that is equally important to emphasise the human propensity to pursue pro-social behavior. This to him is a more real view of human behavior. Hinde views the individual not as a passive recipient of cultural influences, but as a driving force behind cultural change. Cultural influences in his view are likely to play a small part in the later moral development of the individual.

When studying ethics and morality in diverse societies it is important to consider the phenomenon of cultural relativity. This simply implies that different cultural communities maintain different ethical codes and what could be regarded as ethical in one society is not necessarily ethical in another. It should further be acknowledged that moral codes are labile and their precepts are in a state of continuous change. A consequence of cultural relativity is the difficulty to arrive at a universal understanding of what conduct is right and wrong; ethical and unethical conduct. In societies with a diversity of cultures determining common values could pose a real dilemma (Webb, 2010, p. 78).

TEACHING ETHICAL DECISION-MAKING

In the first section of this chapter, Schwella identified various forms of organizational deficiencies in the South African public service such as poor ethical leadership, weak ethical commitment, and minimal ethical reasoning. These deficiencies are compounded by the developing state context in which officials are confronted by the complexity of Nabatchi's four identified value frames (i.e., political-, legal-, organizational-, and market public values, the existence (or lack) of public service motivation (PSM), the nature of organizational tasks, and the influence of stakeholders). Furthermore, the moral codes in diverse societies are described as labile and their precepts in a state of continuous change.

Ethics training and education seems to be the only remedy to these deficiencies. These training and education interventions tends to focus solely on the first two stages of the ethical decision-making process: moral awareness and moral judgment (Huberts et al., 2014, pp. 167–197). However, the success of these training interventions appear to be limited. Van Montfort, Beck, and Twijnstra (2013, pp. 117–132) found little empirical evidence supporting the hypothesis that training enhances moral awareness, reasoning, and action. However, in this study it was found that ethical training and education appears to have a positive impact on institutions with a poor ethical climate. The Van Tankeren study also found that training programs could have a sustainable impact if it is more than incidental (Huberts et al., 2014, pp. 167–197).

If South African public officials are subjected to these training and education programs to enhance their moral awareness and moral judgment, it should be a scheduled and long term event. There are four specific moments in a person's career when ethical training is essential: right from the start, shortly after the start, when moving to an ethically vulnerable position, and when moving to a leadership position (Lawton et al., 2013, p. 126).

CONCLUSION

The "one size fits all" model of ethical leadership often neglects the context within which it is applied. The developmental state context is often associated with themes uncommon in developing states including promoting greater public accountability, the need to drive an agenda of transformation and change, and the central role of the state due to the apparent failure of the free market. The complexity of this context is often exacerbated by the multitude of value frames which public officials at the grassroots should consider when taking decisions *id est* political-, legal-, organizational-, and market public values.

Ethical leaders should be strong in respect of both dimensions of ethical leadership: the moral person and the moral manager. However, in this chapter the focus was specifically on the last dimension of the moral manager: empowerment of followers. Ethical leaders empower their followers to participate in decision-making and allow them to voice their own concerns and perspectives. However, in the South African case study by Schwella various ethical deficiencies were identified including poor ethical leadership, weak ethical commitment and minimal ethical reasoning among public officials.

The need for structured ethics training and education for such officials seem evident. Such interventions could bring about greater awareness of moral dilemmas and the ability to make moral judgments. Opponents of ethics training and education often argue that ethical behavior does not necessarily follow on explicit moral reasoning processes. Those individuals who act ethically do so without much reflection. Conversely it could be argued that individuals with a high level of moral development do not always act ethically.

Public officials within developmental state contexts are often confronted by high levels of complexity, uncertainty, and stakeholder pressure. Knowledge and experience of the four stages of the ethical decision-making process including ethical sensitivity or awareness of the moral nature of a decision; ethical judgment or reasoning; establishing intent to act in an ethical manner; engagement in ethical behavior could reduce the moral ambiguity that confronts these officials.

REFERENCES

Andrews, M. (2010). Good government means different things in different countries. *Governance: An International Journal of Policy, Administration, and Institutions, 23*(1), 7–35.

De Graaf, G., & Van der Wal, Z. (2010). Managing conflicting public values: Governing with integrity and effectiveness. *The American Review of Public Administration, 40*(6), 623–630.

Deveterre, R. J. (2002). *Introduction to virtue ethics: Insight of the ancient Greeks.* Washington, DC: Georgetown University Press.

Edwards, T. (2010). A content and contextual comparison of contemporary leadership approaches with specific reference to ethical and servant leadership: An imperative for service delivery and good governance. *Tydskrif vir Christelike Wetenskap.* Eerste en Tweede Kwartaal, 93–109.

Ford, R. C., & Richardson, W. D. (1994). *Ethical decision-making: A review of the empirical literature. Journal of Business Ethics,* 13, 205–221.

Frederickson, G. H. (1997). *The spirit of public administration.* San Francisco, CA: Jossey-Bass.

Heres, L. (2014). *One style fits all? The content, origins, and effect of follower expectations of ethical leadership.* Amsterdam, Germany: Ipskamp Drukkers.

Heres, L., & Lasthuizen, K. (2012). What's the difference? Ethical leadership in public, hybrid, and private sector organizations. *Journal of Change Management, 12*(4), 441–466.

Hinde, R. A. (2002). *Why good is good: The sources of morality.* London, England: Routledge.

Huberts, L. W. J. C, Kaptein, S. P., & Lasthuizen, K. (2007). A study of the impact of three leadership styles on integrity violations committed by police officers. *Policing (Bingley): An international journal of police strategies and management, 30*(4), 587–607. doi:10.1108/13639510710833884

Huberts, L., Six, F., van Tankeren, M., van Montfort, A. & Paanakker, H. (2014). What is Done to Protect Integrity: Policies, Institutions, and Systems. In Huberts, L. (Ed.), *The integrity of governance: What it is, what we know, what is done, and where to go* (pp. 167–197). London, England: Palgrave Macmillan.

Kaptein, M., Huberts, L., Avelino, S., & Lasthuizen, K. (2005). Demonstrating ethical leadership by measuring ethics. *Public Integrity,* 7(4).

Lawton, A., & Paez, I. 2015. Developing a Framework for Ethical Leadership. *Journal of Business Ethics, 130,* 639–649.

Lawton, A., Rayner, J., & Lasthuizen, K. (2013). *Ethics and management in the public sector.* New York, NY: Routledge.

Loyens, K., & Maesschalk, J. (2010). Toward a theoretical framework for ethical decision-making of street-level bureaucracy: Existing models reconsidered. *Administration and Society,* 44(1).

Lynch, T. D., Lynch, C. E., & Cruise, P. L. (2002). Productivity and the moral manager. *Administration and Society,* 34(4), 347–369.

Menzel, D. (2015). Guest editorial: Leadership in public administration: Creative and/or ethical? *Public Integrity,* 17(4), 315–318.

Preferential Procurement Policy Framework Act, (Act 5 of 2000), Section 2 (2000).

Van Montfort, A., Beck, L., & Twijnstra, A. (2013). Can integrity be taught in public organizations: The effectiveness of integrity-training programs for municipal officials. *Public Integrity,* 15(2), 117–132.

Schwella, E. (2013). Bad public leadership in South Africa: The Jackie Selebi case. *Scientia Militaria: South African Journal of Military Studies,* 41(1).

Treasury Regulations for Departments, Trading Entities, Constitutional Institutions, and Public Entities Issued in terms of the Public Finance Management Act, 1999 (Act 1 of 1999), Section 16A.

United Nations Economic Commission for Africa. (2011). *Economic report on Africa: Governing development in Africa: The Role of the state in economic transformation.* Addis Ababa, Ethiopia: United Nations Economic Commission for Africa.

Webb, W. N. (2010). *The public service anti-corruption strategy: A case study of the department of correctional services (*Unpublished Doctoral Dissertation). University of South Africa.

Webb, W. N. (2015). State of the science: A review of international and South African scholarship on public service ethics. *Administratio Publica,* 23(2), 98–114.

CHAPTER 6

ETHICAL LEADERSHIP, VIRTUE THEORY, AND GENERIC STRATEGIES

When the Timeless Becomes Timely

Geoffrey G. Bell
University of Minnesota Duluth

Bruno Dyck
University of Manitoba

Mitchell J. Neubert
Baylor University

ABSTRACT

Rather than see virtue theory as an approach that is constrained and co-opted by the often-unstated materialistic-individualistic assumptions that character-ize mainstream consequential utilitarianism, we offer virtue theory as an al-ternative moral-point-of-view that allows researchers, instructors and leaders to develop theory and practices that challenge the mainstream. We develop a

Radical Thoughts on Ethical Leadership, pages 113–133
Copyright © 2017 by Information Age Publishing
All rights of reproduction in any form reserved.

new model of ethical leadership and its relationship to business strategy that is based on virtue ethics rather than consequentialist-utilitarian assumptions. We use Porter's generic strategy theory as an example, and develop minimizer, transformer, and compounder strategies that reflect virtue theory's concerns with process and well-being in the context of community.

Despite a long history of reminders, scholars seem prone to forget that ethics are not monolithic. In other words, what it means for a leader to be "ethical" within one ethical moral-point-of-view may be very different from what ethical leadership means within an alternative ethical moral-point-of-view. In particular, what constitutes ethical leadership differs between virtue ethics and consequential utilitarianism. This chapter draws attention to how management theory in general is informed by ethics and moral theories (e.g., Bacharach, 1989), and specifically helps to integrate ethical leadership, strategy and virtue theory (Behnam & Rasche, 2009; Hosmer, 1994; Robertson, 2008). It demonstrates that the "preferred" outcomes of a theory depend on the ethical assumptions underlying the theory. We use virtue theory to both *develop* new leadership and strategy theory and to *critique* existing understandings of ethical leadership. This is important because virtue theory may be difficult to operationalize in management theory (e.g., Dyck & Kleysen, 2001), and the application of virtue theory to strategy is rare (notable exceptions include Arjoon, 2000; Bell & Dyck, 2011; Krsto & Ellwood, 2013).

The chapter lies at the intersection of four literatures: ethics, leadership, virtue theory, and strategic management. It contrasts and compares a generic strategy framework associated with consequential utilitarianism (generic strategy 1.0) with one based upon virtue theory (generic strategy 2.0). We pay particular attention to the capacity of virtue-based generic strategy to address socio-ecological challenges facing humankind. We exemplify this by developing a virtue theory-based model of generic strategies. Finally, we discuss the implications for a virtue theory understanding of ethical leadership and strategy.

META-THEORY, ETHICS, AND VIRTUE THEORY

Weber (1958) argued that the formal rationality associated with capitalism was underpinned by the substantive rationality associated with the Protestant ethic, which differed from and replaced society's previously-dominant substantive rationality (Dyck & Schroeder, 2005). Implicit in Weber's analysis is the idea that differing "substantive rationalities" (e.g., moral-points-of-view, such as consequential utilitarianism and virtue theory) would produce differing "formal rationalities" (e.g., alternative conceptions of ethical leadership).

According to Weber (1958), modern corporations are no longer being managed based on a religious Protestant ethic, but rather this ethic has been secularized and replaced by what we today might call "consequential utilitarianism" (Dyck & Neubert, 2010; Dyck & Schroeder, 2005). The historical roots of consequential utilitarianism—developed by the likes of Jeremy Bentham, David Hume, James Mill, and John Stuart Mill—emphasize how desirable (i.e., ethically commendable) *outcomes* of an action are ones that generate the largest net *benefit* (including positive and negative externalities) for *most* people associated with the action (e.g., Gandz & Hayes, 1988; McKay, 2000). Over time, a short-hand version of mainstream consequential utilitarianism in business theory and practice has developed focusing on measuring the *outcomes* of actions in terms of their *financial* costs and benefits (where money serves as a proxy capturing most of the other costs and benefits) at the *firm* level of analysis (consistent with a popularized understanding of "the invisible hand," where what is good for a *business* is good for *society*; Dyck & Neubert, 2010; Gustafson, 2013; Smith, 1986/1776).

Weber was not the first to note that one's moral-point-of-view would give rise to specific associated ways of organizing and understanding of ethical leadership. In particular, already two and a half millennia ago Aristotle and his Greek contemporaries recognized that the "economy is intelligible only as an ethical dilemma" (Booth, 1993 as cited in Leshem, 2016, p. 231), and they debated about organizational strategies and leadership practices that were "formally rational" vis a vis the "substantive rationality" of virtue theory (Arjoon, 2000; Solomon, 1992). Aristotelian virtue theory has at least three hallmarks that differentiate it from mainstream consequential utilitarianism. Virtue theory emphasizes: virtues (versus outcomes), holistic well being (versus maximized financial well-being) and the larger community (versus the firm). We discuss each in turn.

First, virtue theory focuses on processes more than on outcomes. For example, it focuses on the leader's *character,* not *accomplishments.* Virtue theory's emphasis on character and the practice of virtues contrasts with consequential utilitarian ethics. From a consequential utilitarian approach it is unethical for leaders to allow process to impede the maximization of outcomes, which comes perilously close to saying the ends justifies the means. Conversely, from a virtue theory perspective it is unethical for leaders to focus on outcomes at the expense of their everyday practice of virtues. That said, while virtue theory focuses on the internal sphere, it also clearly influences the outer sphere (MacIntyre, 1981). In this way the processes and character of leadership may be observed in organizational practices and outcomes. Thus organizational practices that are developed based on virtue theory can subsequently influence the character of organizational members who work within those structures and systems (Dyck & Wong, 2010).

Second, whereas consequential utilitarianism implies that "more is better" (e.g., firms should grow in size and profits), virtue theory emphasizes knowing when "enough is enough," and moreover asserts that there is enough to sustain everyone (Leshem, 2016, p. 226). Rather than assume that it is inherently good (ethical) to increase economic wealth endlessly, Aristotelian virtue ethics "call[s] into question the pursuit of economic goals as an end in and for themselves" (Leshem, 2016, p. 236) and assert "that a luxurious life (as well as an unending focus on economic life) is a perversion of the good life" (Leshem, 2016, p. 233). In particular, Aristotle distinguished between pursuing economic wealth for its own sake (unnatural *chrematistics*) versus economic activity that enhances the overall good for the larger community (natural *chrematistics*; Aristotle, 2000; Crespo, 2008; Dyck, 2013a; Meikle, 1994). Natural *chrematistics* is evident when someone trades goods for money that is subsequently used to purchase other needed goods. This creates "true wealth" in a community among members who are contributing tangible goods to its well-being. In contrast, unnatural *chrematistics* is evident when someone uses money to purchase goods in order to resell them at a profit—what Aristotle called "spurious wealth"—in a way that does not tangibly improve a community's well-being and which has no satiation (Meikle, 1994). This is consistent with modern economists who realize that there are limits to growth on a finite planet (e.g., Meadows, Randers, & Meadows, 2004).

Finally, the third hallmark that distinguishes virtue theory from consequential utilitarianism is that virtue theory has a distinct focus on the overall well-being of the larger community. In a nutshell, the goal of virtue theory is to optimize *eudemonia* (a deep sense of human flourishing and happiness), which occurs only via enacting the virtues in community (Flynn, 2008; Gavin & Mason, 2004; Koehn, 1998; Sinnicks, 2014). Thus, an ethical leader is someone who exhibits and promotes virtue in community and acts to maximize its collective well-being (*eudemonia*). In an economic context, firms *are* communities (Koehn, 1998; Solomon, 1992), and also *belong to* a larger community of organizations and the broader society. Virtue theory often emphasizes the "common good" (Arjoon, 2000; Pirson, 2011), which transcends both the interests of individuals *per se*, and their material or financial well-being.

In sum, virtue theory has radical implications for the *content* and *meaning* of ethical leadership. From a mainstream consequential utilitarian perspective it is unethical for a leader to incur financial costs that exceed minimum legal requirements in order to reduce her firm's negative social and/or ecological externalities *if doing so compromises the financial outcomes for the firm* (Friedman, 1970). From a virtue perspective, it would be unethical for a leader *not* to reduce her firm's negative social and/or ecological externalities *so long as doing so does not compromise the firm's viability*. The radical nature of our approach is hard to understate. We are not using virtue theory to "tweak" existing mainstream theory about ethical leadership or strategy, for example, by arguing that ethical leaders should exhibit virtuous behavior while maximizing their firm's (and their own) financial well-being. Rather, according to virtue theory, we are suggesting that maximizing financial well-being should not be the primary purpose of business. We are suggesting that nurturing community well-being should become the primary purpose, and that this involves ethical leadership character and practices that nurture organizational structures, systems, and strategies that facilitate *eudemonia*.

In the next section, we examine the implications of ethical leadership through the lens of organizational strategy, contrasting and comparing differences between consequential utilitarianism and virtue theory. In particular, we review the mainstream consequential utilitarian approach to strategy, and then develop a parallel approach based on virtue theory.

VIRTUE THEORY, ETHICAL LEADERSHIP, AND STRATEGY

The influence of organizational leaders is evident in many areas, but perhaps is the most pervasive in the development of firm strategy. Strategy involves the setting of organizational direction (Andrews, 1971), which is inherently an ethical process (Elms, Brammer, Harris, & Phillips, 2010; Hosmer, 1994). Scholars have argued that ethics and strategy have become divorced over time (Hosmer, 1994). We propose an alternate hypothesis— It is not that ethics have become divorced from strategy, but rather that the strategy literature so completely adopts the consequentialist-utilitarian moral framework that the two have become fused together. In this section, we demonstrate this by reviewing Porter's generic strategy theory and then reinterpreting it through a virtue theory lens. Doing so provides the foundation for us to develop a set of generic strategies based on virtue theory paralleling Porter's generic strategies.

Our method of developing alternative theory parallel to mainstream theory is well-established and consistent with those who argue that using paradoxical and competing assumptions provides a helpful framework for developing new theory and a more holistic understanding of management (e.g., Elsbach, Sutton, & Whetten, 1999; Lewis & Grimes, 1999; Poole & Van de Ven, 1989). This parallelism-based approach leverages the strengths associated with long-honored theoretical frameworks and addresses some of their shortcomings. In our case, we develop parallels to Porter's generic strategies. We begin by reviewing Porter's theory.

Generic Strategy 1.0 (Based on Consequential Utilitarianism)

Michael Porter's work on generic strategies, along with his five forces and value chain frameworks, has been highly influential both among practitioners and scholars (Stonehouse & Snowdon, 2007, p. 257). It has robust empirical support delineating a range of direct and moderating effects (e.g., Dess & Davis, 1984; Kotha & Vadlamani, 1995; Miller & Dess, 1993; Wright, 1987). Our intention in describing Porter's generic strategies is not to challenge existing theory and research, but instead to use it as a starting point to develop virtue-based generic strategies, which we call generic strategy 2.0. Because of their ubiquity, we focus on Porter's (1980, 1985) early conceptions of generic strategies. We briefly review the ethical assumptions that underpin them, and highlight their value as "ideal-types" that provide a conceptual foundation for generic strategy 2.0.

The consequentialist utilitarian assumptions underlying Porter's generic strategies are quite evident. First, the strategies primarily focus on maximizing financial outcomes. For Porter (1991, p. 95) the key question in strategy is "why [do] firms succeed or fail" (outcomes, consequences)? Firms succeed when they attain a competitive position that produces "superior and sustainable financial performance" (Porter, 1991, p. 96; Stonehouse & Snowdon, 2007, p. 268). Superior profitability is both "the right goal, and for firms, the only goal" (Stonehouse & Snowdon, 2007, p. 267). Thus, Porter's generic strategy framework reflects consequentialist utilitarian assumptions: generic strategies enable firms to generate competitive advantage (outcomes) characterized by superior financial profitability (a materialistic conception of performance) at the firm-level of analysis (Porter, 1991; Stonehouse & Snowdon, 2007).

In *cost leadership*, firms strive to have a lower financial cost structure than rivals, leading to increased profits and/or enhanced market share (via lower prices). *Differentiation* occurs when a firm offers goods and services with unique features that command a premium price in excess of the extra cost of providing those features. These two strategies occur in the context of competitive scope (broad versus narrow).

A major criticism of the consequential utilitarian paradigm generally, and of generic strategies 1.0 particularly, is that while the theory and practice (formal rationality) associated with this paradigm (substantive rationality) contribute to unprecedented firm-level financial outcomes (which is ethical and good within this paradigm), they have done so at great social and ecological costs. The paradigm's focus on maximizing competitiveness and financial performance diminishes people's well-being and happiness (Kasser, 2003), encourages corporate scandals (Giacolone & Thompson, 2006), and harms the ecology (McCarty & Shrum, 2001).

Hence, there is little wonder that scholars have called for and begun to develop alternative leadership and management theories (Ghoshal, 2005; Mintzberg, Simons, & Basu, 2002; Stahl & De Luque, 2014), particularly those not based on materialist-individualist assumptions (e.g., Ferraro, Pfeffer, & Sutton, 2005; Giacolone & Thompson, 2006). As Hamel (2009) succinctly states, it is time to replace management 1.0 with management 2.0. In light of these concerns, our presentation of generic strategies 2.0 highlights their relative strengths in addressing socio-ecological issues. In other words, rather than focus on how ethical leadership seeks to increase the financial welfare of the firm (consequential utilitarianism), we focus on how ethical leadership improves the socio-ecological well-being of community (virtue theory).

Generic Strategy 2.0 (Based on Virtue Theory)

The generic strategies 2.0 we describe here—minimizer, transformer, and compounder—are grounded in virtue theory, and in important ways parallel the ideal types in Porter's framework. Similar to Porter's original model, in our model the minimizer and transformer strategies draw upon distinct logics, but founded in virtue theory. *Minimizers* <u>reduce</u> multiple costs (e.g., social, financial, ecological), including negative externalities. *Transformers* <u>enhance</u> multiple forms of well-being (e.g., financial, social, ecological), creating positive externalities by redeeming (infusing value into) elements of the environment that were previously undervalued or wasted. Minimizer and transformer strategies emphasize improved socio-ecological well-being (versus having a primary or exclusive focus on financial well-being) for the larger community (recognizing multiple stakeholders; going beyond a primary focus on financial implications at the firm level). This dual emphasis on reducing negative characteristics (minimizer), and enhancing positive characteristics (transformer), reflects ethical leadership (Neubert, Wu, & Roberts, 2013).

Because the business world has so completely adopted the consequentialist-utilitarian worldview, it is hard to look at the business world through "fresh eyes." However, we now try to do so by looking at extant firms that most closely resemble the virtue theory worldview, although we admit that it is sort of like "putting new wine in old skins."

Examples of Minimizer Strategy

Costco exemplifies a firm moving towards a minimizer strategy, though still with a concern for profits. Costco's co-founder James Sinegal recognizes the social costs associated with paying low wages, and Costco has internalized these costs by paying its employees relatively high wages and benefits. Sinegal asserts that doing so "is the right thing" (Holmes & Zellner, 2004, p. 77);

for him this is ethical leadership. Costco also reduces ecological costs, both internally (e.g., using solar energy and reducing packaging materials) and by engaging with suppliers who decrease their ecological footprints. While many of these changes save Costco money, Sinegal is also open to changes where the pay-off is not immediate or guaranteed: "Wall Street is in the business of making money between now and next Tuesday. We're in the business of building an organization, an institution that we hope will be here 50 years from now" (quoted in Nadkarni, Chen, & Chen, 2015).

Another example is AKI Energy, whose leaders draw upon traditional First Nations philosophies and values more akin to virtue theory. AKI Energy provides geothermal heating for First Nations communities in Canada, and thereby reduces the fossil fuels and greenhouse gas emission associated with heating homes, minimizes customers' heating and air conditioning expenses, reduces the money leaving communities, and reduces unemployment rates in Indigenous communities (Wood, Loney, & Taylor, 2015).

Minimizer strategies may also be evident when groups of organizations form communities to reduce their overall costs. For example, a biomass energy plant was developed in Gussing, Austria as a collaboration among multiple organizations to serve the needs of local homeowners and private industry; it reduced both energy costs to the community and greenhouse gas emissions, and reduced unemployment (Turiera & Cros, 2013).

Examples of a Transformer Strategy

Greyston Bakery in Yonkers, New York hires ex-convicts, trains them as bakers, and thereby enables them to "start over again" and become contributing members of society in a way that lowers recidivism (Bertrand, 2015). Its strategy is a reflection of what its founder, Bernie Glassman, considers to be ethical leadership:

> The company's business approach is based on an idea developed from two key Buddhist concepts: mandala (wholeness) and path (transformation). According to these concepts, the company is managed in the belief that everything is interconnected, and that one cannot afford to ignore sections of society. Based on Zen traditions, Greyston places great emphasis on personal empowerment and transformation. Employees are encouraged to develop a sense of responsibility for themselves, their families, and their co-workers. Gainful employment is seen as the first step on an individual's path toward success. Social justice, economic development and personal empowerment are the most important building blocks that support the operations that drive the company. (Zsolnai, 2015, p. 75)

Terracycle, Inc. has some attributes of an ecological transformer strategy. Founder Tom Szaky realized that it is profitable to take waste from institutional kitchens, transform it through a natural process of feeding it to worms, package the worms' excrement into used soda pop bottles, and sell the output as fertilizer (Szaky, 2013). Terracycle now transforms or "upcycles" all sorts of consumer waste into marketable products (Allen & Knight, 2011). It works alongside schools (who get paid to collect waste and send it to Terracycle) and other corporations (who seek to transform their waste into saleable products).

Example of a Compounder Strategy

The compounder strategy is a combination of minimizer and transformer. It represents a departure from Porter's original model, which considered low cost and differentiation strategies to be distinct and mutually exclusive drivers. Thus, Porter thought it very difficult for firms to pursue both simultaneously. Subsequent empirical evidence suggests that firms may successfully execute "mixed" strategies that encompass both cost leader and differentiation (Kotha & Vadlamani, 1995; Miller & Dess, 1993). The same argument that supports the viability of mixed conventional generic strategy (e.g., Dess & Davis, 1984; Rothaermel, 2015) is extended here. We argue that firms may be able to simultaneously pursue *both* minimizer and transformer strategies in what we call a compounder strategy. That is, although the two strategies rely on different logics, some organizations may be able to execute both simultaneously. Firms may find ways to minimize their holistic cost structure *and* transform waste into valuable products and services.

Such a compounder strategy is evident in the ethical leadership approach of First Fruits apple orchard, the largest privately owned contiguous apple orchard in the United States. Consistent with a social transformer strategy, the First Fruits enhances the quality of life its workforce, which includes large numbers of formerly migrant workers. Rather than managing the workforce to maximize firm financial profitability by hiring and laying off (discarding, wasting) workers on an as-needed basis (as commonly occurs in their industry), First Fruits' owners deliberately enlarged the firm to develop year-round jobs for many employees. This emphasis on year-round permanent jobs subsequently prompted the owners to open a day care center to address the child-care needs of their packing plant employees, 80 percent of whom are women. In addition, a social minimizer strategy is evident because the firm minimizes night shifts (especially stressful for employees with children). When the owners became aware of the housing shortage and poor living conditions employees were experiencing, they worked collaboratively with their region's local planning committee to develop nearby affordable housing (Bairstow, 2005; Roberge, 2003; Sparks, 2003). In addition, First Fruits emphasizes elements of an ecological transformer strategy, emphasizing soil-rejuvenating organic practices (Pihl, 2012) and non-GMO apples (Warner, 2014), and its ecological minimizer strategy is evident in reductions of its use of pesticides. The comments from the owners of First

Fruits provide a clear indication that their understanding of ethical leadership is well-aligned with virtue theory:

> When we started our business, we had nothing but a dream and the commitment to work it out. It was with the help of others who gave us every opportunity to learn, to participate, that we learned to fly. We needed an empowering team around us. When we finally became financially successful, it would have been easy to continue stockpiling money (as opposed to true wealth) around us. However, the spiritual values that we are also committed to would not let us. For us, it was impossible to separate business goals from spiritual values which promote the equality and connectedness of all people, using their unique gifts and skills to serve one another while together serving the common good.
>
> Sure, we have to make money or we'd have to shut the doors... But profit isn't our main motive. It becomes the by-product of treating people with dignity, respect, and mutuality, and as equals in every sense of the word. We all have a role to play in creating a community of people who care for a business that then cares for them. We believe that if we ever stopped doing that, we would implode. (cited in Neubert & Dyck, 2014, p. 65)

Finally, it is also possible that firms may come together in community to adopt a region-level compounder strategy. Doing so may allow the firms to access holistic cost reductions and transformations of waste that are unavailable to any of them individually (Asheim, Cooke, & Martin, 2006). One notable example of such an industrial ecological community is Kalundborg, Denmark, where multiple organizations take each other's "waste" and turn it into valuable inputs (Valero, Usón, & Costa, 2012), significantly reducing waste products and converting them into viable uses (cf. Gibbs & Deutz, 2007; Hawken, 1993; Tudor, Adam, & Bates, 2006).

DISCUSSION

In the remaining space we consider the implications of our argument and framework for teaching and practice as well as for theory and future research. In particular, we focus on ethical leadership based on virtue theory as it relates to (a) formulating and implementing strategy and the four functions of management, and (b) new theory and research that contrasts with the three hallmarks of consequential utilitarianism.

Implications for Teaching and Practice

While a conventional understanding of the generic strategies of cost leadership and differentiation still plays a central role among management scholars, educators, and practitioners, there has been a growing volume of what might be called "non-conventional" writing on strategy. Indeed, Michael Porter himself has tweaked his thinking, and challenges practitioners facing contemporary socio-ecological challenges to focus on creating shared value, even if doing so might not enhance short-term profit (Porter & Kramer, 1999, 2011). His work is still within the consequentialist utilitarian paradigm insofar as it is consistent with others who view social and ecological challenges as opportunities for businesses to maximize their long-term profits. Such tweaking may resonate with the ethics of conventional business leaders, but it may be counter-productive to addressing socio-ecological externalities that do not lend themselves to increasing profits (e.g., Gates, 2007; Margolis & Walsh, 2003).

In contrast, generic strategy 2.0 provides a helpful overarching conceptual framework for strategy formulation that assumes businesses care about society as a whole and meeting fundamental human needs, and that socio-ecological well-being is at least as important as financial well-being. It is consistent with calls for the conventional "value capture paradigm" to be supplanted by a "value creation paradigm" (Santos, 2012), with calls for the primary emphasis on self-interested profit maximization to be replaced by an emphasis on balancing multiple forms of well-being for multiple stakeholders (Dyck & Neubert, 2010), and with calls to see a firm's rare and inimitable resources as something to be shared, not hoarded (Bell & Dyck, 2011).

Business schools typically teach an approach to strategy that is steeped in a mainstream consequentialist-utilitarian worldview. Although students who take a course in business ethics may be exposed to multiple worldviews that include both consequentialist-utilitarian and virtue ethics, most of their remaining studies are founded on the consequentialist-utilitarian worldview. As a result, it is difficult for students to appreciate that there are alternative moral points of view that produce different preferred outcomes with regard to everyday organizational practices. This points to the importance for the study of ethical leadership to go beyond courses in ethics, leadership, or leadership ethics. In our view, virtue theory should not be limited to a few select classes; it is a holistic paradigm that encompasses and is very relevant to all of management and business. For an example of what teaching accounting, finance, management and marketing from a virtue theory based understanding of ethical leadership might look like, see Dyck (2013b).

Even though virtue theory can be used to inform alternative theory and practice for all the business functions, the only currently available classroom resources we are aware of that integrate this perspective are textbooks in the areas of Management (Dyck & Neubert, 2010, being revised) and Organizational Behavior (Neubert & Dyck, 2014). Both these textbooks are unique because, in each chapter, they contrast and compare an approach to the topic at hand based on consequential utilitarianism, and an approach based on virtue ethics. In other words, students read about a consequential utilitarian and a virtue theory approach to goal-setting, motivation, organizing, controlling, change, strategy and so on (indeed, some of the ideas in the current chapter are drawn from and build on content from these books). In both texts, the virtue-based alternative to the dominant consequentialist-utilitarian perspective is supported by research and illustrated through the examples of vanguard practitioners. Empirical research shows that students in classes where these books are used tend to improve their critical thinking skills, change their views of ethical leadership (in particular, they come to adopt less materialistic and less individualistic views of management), and believe they have improved their ethical thinking skills (Dyck, Walker, Starke, & Uggerslev, 2011, 2012).

We now draw from these sources to consider how a shift from the consequentialist-utilitarian worldview to a virtue ethics worldview may affect the day-to-day behavior of ethical leaders. As conceptualized by Brown and Trevino (2006), ethical leadership includes behaviors that reflect being a moral *person* as well as a moral *manager*. Here is a brief description of a virtue-based approach to the four functions of management: planning, organizing, leading, and controlling.

Ethical Leadership and Virtuous **Planning**

From a virtue theory perspective, the management function of planning obligates leaders to work alongside others to set organizational goals and to develop strategy (such as the minimizer, transformer, and compounder). Such leaders exercise foresight by taking a long-term holistic perspective on planning. They use measurable goals, however they also use goals that may be difficult to measure, including goals related to human dignity, happiness and environmental sustainability (Neubert & Dyck, 2016). In particular, virtue theory suggests that leaders exercise the virtue of *wisdom* to set, align, and pursue achievement of goals that seek multiple forms of well-being for multiple stakeholders. The virtuous planner includes others in setting goals and making decisions related to their implementation to realize better-informed strategies and greater ownership of their implementation. Practically, this mutual discernment process results in goals throughout the organization that cascade down from and up to the formulation of virtuous strategies.

Ethical Leadership and Virtuous **Organizing**

The process of organizing human and other organizational resources helps to achieve the strategies and goals that are set in the planning function. The virtuous organizer exercises *courage* to challenge current organizational structures and systems which are serving the interest of the powerful but not of the powerless, and to implement organizing fundamentals that empower marginalized stakeholders with opportunity and voice. Virtue theory serves as a basis to develop organizing principles that parallel mainstream organizing fundamentals such centralization, specialization, and standardization (Neubert & Dyck, 2014). Instead of centralizing authority and decision making, ethical leaders promote structures that *dignify* others by distributing authority, information, and respect across the organization, and invite members to exercise their authority to implement participatively-developed strategies. Instead of specialization, ethical leaders promote *sensitization* by expanding the scope of what an organizational member thinks about and does. Interaction with others within and outside of the organization is encouraged to better understand others' needs and the interdependencies among the community of stakeholders. Instead of standardization, ethical leaders welcome *experimentation* that places a premium on learning and innovation that contributes to the sustainability of the strategies.

Ethical Leadership and Virtuous Leading

Rather than an emphasis on positional authority and pressure, a virtue theory approach to leading involves listening and empowering, and welcomes community-wide influence and persuasion. The consequential utilitarian emphasis on techniques that maximize productivity are often extrinsically oriented and short-sighted. In contrast, virtuous leadership exercises *temperance* to resist the temptation to offer merely instrumental enticements to motivate behavior, and seeks to balance short-term and long-term interests (Bell & David, 2015). Instead of focusing on directing and structuring the work environment for primarily instrumental outcomes, the virtuous leader focuses on serving others and nurtures intrinsic motivation through meaningful work and growth. Rather than promoting simple and immediate compliance, this approach yields greater levels of creativity and cooperative behavior among organizational members (Neubert, Kacmar, Carlson, Chonko, & Roberts, 2008). Such leaders are seen as servants who exhibit humility and model temperance in exercising self-control to resist temporal pressures for the sake of the long-term interests of the organization and other stakeholders (Molyneaux, 2003).

Ethical Leadership and Virtuous Controlling

Organizational control exists when organizational members know what they are supposed to do and are held accountable to do it. While this conventionally takes the form of providing specific expectations, monitoring progress, and managing exceptions, a virtuous leader facilitates control by ensuring *justice*. Broadly, justice is a sense of fair treatment (Rawls, 1958). Beyond distributive justice, which is concerned with outcomes distributed according to inputs and thus could be a means of instrumental control, a virtuous perspective would include aspects of fairness associated with respect and inclusive processes (Colquitt et al., 2013). For example, a just approach to working toward fulfillment of a virtuous strategy ensures that everyone connected with an organization is included to some degree in providing input on implementation and that everyone also shares to some degree in success, including those external stakeholders benefited by minimizer and transformer strategies.

Finally, in response to readers who might argue that, because virtue theory is based on ancient ideas it may be esoteric and difficult to operationalize or observe in contemporary organizations, we note that the little empirical evidence that we have on this topic suggests that the opposite may be true. A study by Dyck and Kleysen (2001) asked management students to observe the behaviors of video-taped managers (a sales manager, a financial controller, and a general manager), and to classify their behaviors according to three templates: (a) Mintzberg's (1973) three managerial roles (interpersonal, informational, decisional); (b) three of Fayol's (1949/1919) four functions of management (planning, organizing and controlling); and (c) the four Aristotelian cardinal virtues (wisdom, justice, courage and self-control). Perhaps surprisingly, students were able to classify managers' actions using the Aristotelian framework 89% of the time, more than the 80% and 82% associated with Mintzberg (1973) and Fayol (1949/1919), respectively. In sum, the study:

> provides an oft-called-for empirical basis for further work in virtue theory as an appropriate conceptual framework for the study and practice of management. The results indicate that virtue theory may be used to re-conceive our fundamental *understanding* of management, alongside its capacity to weigh moral judgment upon it. (Dyck & Kleysen, 2001, p. 561)

Implications for Research and Theory

We conclude by reviewing how a virtue theory approach to business contrasts and compares with the three main assumptions of mainstream consequential utilitarianism, and thus helps to develop theory and suggestions for research outside of the conventional (consequential utilitarian) box. First, and perhaps most importantly, virtue theory explicitly questions the mainstream consequence-centric mantra that "more is better." Humankind lives on a finite planet with finite resources (Meadows et al., 2004). There are presently 7 billion of us, compared to 1 billion in 1804, and 2 billion in 1927. Some estimates suggest that we are already living 50% beyond the carrying capacity of the planet (e.g., Moore & Rees, 2013). In short, we cannot have ever-increasing "more"—it is simply unsustainable. Virtue theory provides a moral-point-of-view upon which to develop understandings of ethical leadership in a world where we need to re-learn when "enough is enough," a world where transactions are characterized by natural *chrematistics* rather than unnatural *chrematistics*. The implications extend not only to our understanding and practice of management, or to the functions of business more generally, but also extend to the larger realm of societal institutions, norms and regulations. We invite future research that includes developing theory regarding how actors within industries can collaborate to reduce consumption, and how regulatory and societal institutions can support the development of a less materialistic and less individualistic operating climate for organizations.

Second, a virtue theory understanding of ethical leadership—in direct contrast to the economics-centric nature of mainstream theory and practice—legitimizes the intuitive view that there are more important things in life than money, and that a primary focus on money is dysfunctional (e.g., Kasser, 2003). More than money, people want to feel connected to others and to have a greater purpose; they desire meaningful relationships, reduced social injustice and ecological degradation, and an opportunity to leave the world in a better condition than they found it (Giacolone, 2004). Instead of seeking only to accumulate wealth for themselves, people are motivated to contribute to the well-being of the whole (Aguinis, & Glavas, 2012); people want their actions and those of the organizations they are part of to benefit the broader world in which they live (Neubert & Dyck, 2016). Virtue theory is premised on the understanding that true happiness (*eudemonia*) comes from healthy relationships with others, from working in a community towards larger (non-financial) goals. In particular, it says that ethical leadership is evident when virtues are practiced in community.

Future research can explore the implications of strategy formulation based on virtue theory and test the implicit hypotheses embedded in the suggestions for virtuous strategy implementation. For example, does implementing a strategy consistent based on virtue theory (generic strategy 2.0) enhance socio-ecological well-being (compared to generic strategy 1.0)? What is the effect on followers when leaders enact the four functions of management consistent with implications from a virtue theory perspective? Do followers become more virtuous themselves (as Aristotle predicted), more loyal, more productive, exhibit higher levels of organizational citizenship behavior, perceive their leaders as being more humble and more like servant leaders, and so on?

Third, a virtue theory understanding of ethical leadership draws attention to the dysfunctionality of focusing on the firm-level and thereby downplaying the larger community level (see also Donaldson & Walsh, 2015). Virtue theory is consistent with the intuitive understanding that the so-called "invisible hand" is dysfunctional *unless it is attached to a "virtuous arm."*

Adam Smith (2004/1759, p. 237) himself noted that people should be free to pursue their self-interest *only insofar as their actions are informed by virtues* like justice, self-control, practical wisdom and benevolence. Unabated pursuit of goals to maximize corporate or individual performance encourages excessive risk taking and engaging in unethical behavior (Larrick, Heath, & Wu, 2009; Ordonez, Schweitzer, Galinsky, & Bazerman, 2009). From a virtue theory perspective, it is foolhardy to focus on maximizing one's own financial well-being—whether at the individual or firm level—without regard to the classic virtues, and expect that doing so will create positive outcomes for the larger socio-ecological environment. A narrow strategic focus on individualistic and materialist goals yields a limited set of outcomes organizationally and individually, whereas a virtuous approach prudently and temperately considers a broader range of outcomes for more stakeholders in both the short-term and long-term (Neubert & Dyck, 2016).

Future research could contrast the effects of strategy formulation and implementation based in virtue theory with consequentialist utilitarian theory on the level of negative socio-ecological externalities produced by the firm, on levels of income inequality within the firm, and on the character of relationships with customers. For a more specific example, what might be the implications for executive compensation models, which in most cases are solidly established in the consequentialist-utilitarian worldview? In contrast, as Bell and David (2015) argue, from a virtue theory perspective executive compensation could focus on a range of alternative outcomes that may be related to the minimizer and transformer strategies (e.g., fostering employment of marginalized members of the community, reducing ecological externalities), and to reflect the high level of intrinsic motivation present in the executive function (Moriarty, 2005) that may be impaired by extensive reliance on financial rewards.

In conclusion, ours is a bold vision. We promote virtue theory as a lens and moral foundation that enable and encourage leaders, researchers and educators to develop and promote business theory and practice that challenges dysfunctionalities associated with mainstream consequential utilitarianism. In particular, it is our hope this will enable the development of a more holistic understanding of ethical leadership that places greater emphasis on the *eudemonic* well-being of the whole community, and thus counteracts and subverts the negative socio-ecological externalities associated with the status quo.

REFERENCES

Aguinis, H. & Glavas, A. (2012). What we know and don't know about corporate social responsibility: A review and research agenda. *Journal of Management, 38*(4), 932–968.

Allen, N., & Knight, M. (2011). Recycling the world's trash into cash. Retrieved from http://www.cnn.com/2011/10/10/world/americas/terracycle-recycling-waste-szaky/index.html

Andrews, K. R. (1971). *The concept of corporate strategy*. Homewood, IL: Richard D. Irwin.

Aristotle. (2000). *Politics* (B. Jowett, Trans.). Mineola, NY: Dover.

Arjoon, S. (2000). Virtue theory as a dynamic theory of business. *Journal of Business Ethics, 28,* 159–178.

Asheim, B., Cooke, P., & Martin, R. (2006). The rise of the cluster concept in regional analysis and policy. In B. Asheim, P. Cooke, & R. Martin (Eds.), *Clusters and regional development: Critical reflections and explorations* (pp. 1–29). London, England: Routledge.

Bacharach, S. B. (1989). Organizational theories: Some criteria for evaluation. *Academy of Management Review, 14*(4), 496–515.

Bairstow, R. (2005, July 21). [Site visit and discussions].

Behnam, M., & Rasche, A. (2009). "Are strategists from Mars and ethicists from Venus?"—Strategizing as ethical reflection. *Journal of Business Ethics, 84,* 79–88.

Bell, G. G., & David, J. (2015). What if corporate governance fostered executive dignity? *Journal of Applied Business and Economics, 17*(4), 30–45.

Bell, G. G., & Dyck, B. (2011). Conventional resource-based theory and its radical alternative: A less materialist-individualist approach to strategy. *Journal of Business Ethics, 99,* 121–130.

Bertrand, N. (2015, February 10). The inspiring story behind the brownies in Ben & Jerry's most popular flavors. *Business Insider.* Retrieved from http://www.businessinsider.com/ben-and-jerrys-greyston-bakery-workers-2015-2

Brown, M. E., & Trevino, L. K. (2006). Ethical leadership: A review and future directions. *Leadership Quarterly, 17*(6), 595–616.

Colquitt, J. A., Scott, B. A., Rodell, J. B., Long, D. M., Zapata, C. P., Conlon, D. E., & Wesson, M. J. (2013). Justice at the millennium, a decade later: A meta-analytic test of social exchange and affect-based perspectives. *Journal of Applied Psychology, 98*(2), 199–236.

Crespo, R. F. (2008). *On Aristotle and economics.* IAE Business School, Austral University. Buenos Aries Province, Argentina.

Dess, G. G., & Davis, P. S. (1984). Porter's (1980) generic strategies as determinants of strategic group membership and organizational performance. *Academy of Management Journal, 27*(3), 467–488.

Donaldson, T., & Walsh, J. P. (2015). Toward a theory of business. *Research in Organizational Behavior, 35,* 181–207.

Dyck, B. (2013a). *Management and the Gospel: Luke's radical message for the first and twenty-first centuries.* New York, NY: Palgrave-Macmillan.

Dyck, B. (2013b). A proven way to incorporate Catholic social thought in business school curriculae: Teaching two approaches to management in the classroom. *Journal of Catholic Higher Education, 32*(1), 145–163.

Dyck, B., & Kleysen, R. (2001). Aristotle's virtues and management thought: An empirical exploration of an integrative pedagogy. *Business Ethics Quarterly, 11*(4), 561–574.

Dyck, B., & Neubert, M. (2010). *Management: Current Practices and New Directions.* Boston, MA: Cengage/Houghton Mifflin.

Dyck, B., & Schroeder, D. (2005). Management, theology and moral points of view: Towards an alternative to the conventional materialist-individualistic ideal-type of management. *Journal of Management Studies, 42*(4), 705–735.

Dyck, B., Walker, K., Starke, F., & Uggerslev, K. (2011). Addressing concerns raised by critics of business schools by teaching multiple approaches to management. *Business and Society Review, 116*(1), 1–27.

Dyck, B., Walker, K., Starke, F., & Uggerslev, K. (2012). Enhancing critical thinking by teaching two distinct approaches to management. *Journal of Education for Business, 87*(6), 343–357.

Dyck, B., & Wong, K. (2010). Corporate spiritual disciplines and the quest for organizational virtue. *Journal of Management, Spirituality & Religion, 7*(1), 7–29.

Elms, H., Brammer, S., Harris, J. D., & Phillips, R. A. (2010). New directions in strategic management and business ethics. *Business Ethics Quarterly, 20*(3), 401–425.

Elsbach, K. D., Sutton, R. I., & Whetten, D. A. (1999). Perspectives on developing management theory, circa 1999: Moving from shrill monologues to (relatively) tame dialogues. *Academy of Management Review, 24*(4), 627–633.

Fayol, H. (1949/1919). *General and industrial management.* London, England: Pitman.

Ferraro, F., Pfeffer, J., & Sutton, R. I. (2005). Economics language and assumptions: How theories can become self-fulfilling. *Academy of Management Review, 30*(1), 8–24.

Flynn, G. (2008). The virtuous manager: A vision for leadership in business. *Journal of Business Ethics, 78,* 359–372.

Friedman, M. (1970). The social responsibility of business is to increase its profits. *New York Times Magazine,* 122–126.

Gandz, J., & Hayes, N. (1988). Teaching business ethics. *Journal of Business Ethics, 7*(9), 657–669.

Gates, W. (2007, June 7). Remarks of Bill Gates: Harvard commencement. *Gazettte Online.* Retrieved from http://www.news.harvard.edu/gazette/2007/06.14/99-gates.html

Gavin, J. H., & Mason, R. O. (2004). The virtuous organization: The value of happiness in the workplace. *Organizational Dynamics, 33*(4), 379–392.

Ghoshal, S. (2005). Bad management theories are destroying good management practices. *Academy of Management Learning & Education, 4*(1), 75–91.

Giacolone, R. A. (2004). A transcendent business education for the 21st century. *Academy of Management Learning & Education, 3,* 415–442.

Giacolone, R. A., & Thompson, K. R. (2006). Business ethics and social responsibility education: Shifting the worldview. *Academy of Management Learning & Education, 5*(3), 266–277.

Gibbs, D., & Deutz, P. (2007). Reflections on implementing industrial ecology through eco-industrial park development. *Journal of Cleaner Production, 15*(17), 1683–1695.

Gustafson, A. (2013). In defense of a utilitarian business ethic. *Business and Society Review, 118*(3), 325–360.

Hamel, G. (2009). Moon shots for management. *Harvard Business Review,* 91–98.

Hawken, P. (1993). *The Ecology of commerce: A declaration of sustainability*. New York, NY: HarperBusiness.

Holmes, S., & Zellner, W. (2004). The Costco way. Retrieved from Business Week online https://www.bloomberg.com/news/articles/2004-04-11/commentary-the-costco-way.

Hosmer, L. T. (1994). Strategic planning as if ethics mattered. *Strategic Management Journal, 15*(Summer), 17–34.

Kasser, T. (2003). *The high price of materialism*. Cambridge, MA: Bradford Books, MIT Press.

Koehn, D. (1998). Virtue ethics, the firm, and moral psychology. *Business Ethics Quarterly, 8*(3), 497–513.

Kotha, S., & Vadlamani, B. L. (1995). Assessing generic strategies: An empirical investigation of two competing typologies in discrete manufacturing industries. *Strategic Management Journal, 16*(1), 75–83.

Krsto, P., & Ellwood, P. (2013). Strategic and ethical foundations for responsible innovation. *Research Policy, 42*(5), 1112–1125.

Larrick, R. P., Heath, C., & Wu, G. (2009). Goal-induced risk taking in negotiation and decision making. *Social Cognition, 27*(3), 342–364.

Leshem, D. (2016). Retrospectives: What did the ancient Greeks mean by *oikonomia*? *Journal of Economic Perspectives, 30*(1), 225–238.

Lewis, M. W., & Grimes, A. J. (1999). Metatriangulation: Building theory from multiple paradigms. *Academy of Management Review, 24*(4), 672–690.

MacIntyre, A. (1981). *After virtue: A study in moral theory*. Notre Dame, IN: University of Notre Dame Press.

Margolis, J., & Walsh, J. P. (2003). Misery loves companies: Rethinking social initiatives by business. *Administrative Science Quarterly, 42*, 268–305.

McCarty, J. A., & Shrum, L. J. (2001). The influence of individualism, collectivism, and locus of control on environmental beliefs and behavior. *Journal of Public Policy and Marketing, 20*(1), 93–104.

McKay, R. B. (2000). Consequential uitilitarianism: Addressing ethical deficiencies in the municipal landfill siting process. *Journal of Business Ethics, 26*(4), 289–306.

Meadows, D., Randers, J., & Meadows, D. (2004). *Limits to growth: The 30-year update*. White River Junction, VT: Chelsea Green.

Meikle, S. (1994). Aristotle on money. *Phronesis, 39*(1), 26–44.

Miller, A., & Dess, G. G. (1993). Assessing Porter's (1980) model in terms of generalizability, accuracy, and simplicity. *Journal of Management Studies, 30*(4), 553–585.

Mintzberg, H. (1973). *The nature of organizational work*. Upper Saddle River, NJ: Prentice-Hall.

Mintzberg, H., Simons, R., & Basu, K. (2002). Beyond selfishness. *Sloan Management Review, 44*(1), 67–74.

Molyneaux, D. (2003). "Blessed are the meek, for they shall inherit the earth"—Am aspiration applicable to business? *Journal of Business Ethics, 48*(4), 347–363.

Moore, J., & Rees, W. E. (2013). Getting to one-planet living. *State of the World 2013: Is sustainability still possible?* (pp. 39–50). Washington, DC: Worldwatch Institute.

Moriarty, J. (2005). Do CEOs get paid too much? *Business Ethics Quarterly, 15*(2), 257–281.

Nadkarni, S., Chen, T., & Chen, J. (2016). The clock is ticking! Executive temporal depth, industry velocity, and competitive aggressiveness. *Strategic Management Journal, 37*(6), 1132–1153.

Neubert, M., & Dyck, B. (2014). *Organizational behavior.* New York, NY: John Wiley & Sons.

Neubert, M., & Dyck, B. (2016). Developing sustainable management theory: Goal setting theory based in virtue. *Management Decision, 54*(2), 304–320.

Neubert, M., Kacmar, K. M., Carlson, D. S., Chonko, L. B., & Roberts, J. A. (2008). Regulatory focus as a mediator of the influence of initiating structure and servant leadership on employee behavior. *Journal of Applied Psychology, 93*(6), 1220–1233.

Neubert, M., Wu, J.-C., & Roberts, J. (2013). The influence of ethical leadership and regulatory focus on employee outcomes. *Business Ethics Quarterly, 23*(2), 269–296.

Ordonez, L., Schweitzer, M. E., Galinsky, A., & Bazerman, M. (2009). Goals gone wild: How goals systematically harm individuals and organizations. *Academy of Management Perspectives, 23*(1), 6–16.

Pihl, K. (2012). Acreage down, sales of organic crops up in Washington. *Tri-City Herald.* Retrieved from http://www.tri-cityherald.com/news/local/article32061999.html

Pirson, M. (2011). What is business organizing for? The role of business in society over time. In W. Amann, M. Pirson, C. Dierksmeier, E. von Kimakowitz, & H. Spitzeck (Eds.), *Business schools under fire: Humanistic management education as the way forward* (pp. 41–51). Houndsmills, Basingstoke, Hampshire, England: Palgrave Macmillan.

Poole, M. S., & Van de Ven, A. H. (1989). Using paradox to build management and organization theories. *The Academy Of Management Review, 14*(4), 562–578.

Porter, M. E. (1980). *Competitive Strategy: Techniques for analyzing industries and competitors.* New York, NY: The Free Press.

Porter, M. E. (1985). *Competitive Advantage: Creating and sustaining superior performance.* New York, NY: The Free Press.

Porter, M. E. (1991). Toward a dynamic theory of strategy. *Strategic Management Journal, 12*, 95–117.

Porter, M. E., & Kramer, M. R. (1999). Philanthropy's new agenda: Creating value. *Harvard Business Review,* (November/December), 121–130.

Porter, M. E., & Kramer, M. R. (2011). Creating shared value: How to reinvent capitalism—and unleash a wave of innovation and growth. *Harvard Business Review* (January/February), 2–17.

Rawls, J. (1958). Justice as fairness. *Philosophical Review, 67*(2), 164–194.

Roberge, E. (2003). First fruits—Broetje Orchards. *Washington Business Magazine.* Retrieved from http://www.firstfruits.com/

Robertson, C. J. (2008). An analysis of 10 years of business ethics research in *Strategic Management Journal:* 1996–2005. *Journal of Business Ethics, 80*, 745–753.

Rothaermel, F. T. (2015). *Strategic Management* (2 ed.). New York, NY: McGraw Hill Education.

Santos, F. M. (2012). A positive theory of social entrepreneurship. *Journal of Business Ethics, 111*, 335–351.

Sinnicks, M. (2014). Practices, governance, and politics: Applying MacIntyre's ethics to business. *Business Ethics Quarterly, 24*(2), 229–249.

Smith, A. (1986/1776). *The wealth of nations: Books I–III*. London, England: Penguin Books.

Smith, A. (2004/1759). *The theory of moral sentiments*. New York, NY: Barnes & Noble.

Solomon, R. C. (1992). Corporate roles, personal virtues: An Aristotelian approach to business ethics. *Business Ethics Quarterly, 2*(3), 317–339.

Sparks, B. (2003, August 1). Apple grower of the year is humble, committed, and forward-thinking. Retrieved from http://www.growing-produce.com/fruits/apple-grower-of-the-year/apple-grower-of-the-year-is-humble-committed-and-forward-thinking/.

Stahl, G. K., & De Luque, M. S. (2014). Antecedents of responsible leader behavior: A research synthesis, conceptual framework, and agenda for future research. *Academy of Management Perspectives, 28*(3), 235–254.

Stonehouse, G., & Snowdon, B. (2007). Meet the person: Comparative advantage revisited: Michael Porter on strategy and competitiveness. *Journal of Management Inquiry, 16*(3), 256–273.

Szaky, T. (2013). *Revolution in a bottle: How TerraCycle is redefining green business*. London, England: Penguin.

Tudor, T., Adam, E., & Bates, M. (2006). Drivers and limitations for the successful development and functioning of EIPs (eco-industrial parks): A literature review. *Ecological Economics, 61*(2–3), 199–207.

Turiera, T., & Cros, S. (2013). *Co-business: 50 examples of business collaboration*. Barcelona, Spain: Infonomia.

Valero, A., Uson, S., & Costa, J. (2012). Exergy analysis of the industrial symbiosis model in Kalundborg, Proceedings of ECOS 2012—The 25th international conference on Efficiency, cost, optimization, simulation, and environmental impact of energy systems, June 26–29, 2012, Perugia, Italy.

Warner, G. (2014, April 2). Opal apple verified non-GMO. *GoodFruit Grower*. Retrieved from http://www.goodfruit.com/opal-apple-verified-non-gmo/

Weber, M. (1958). *The Protestant ethic and the spirit of capitalism* (T. Parsons, Trans.). New York, NY: Scribner's.

Wood, D. J., Loney, L., & Taylor, K. (2015). *Social enterprise and the solutions economy: A toolkit for Manitoba First Nations*. Winnipeg, MB: AKI Energy.

Wright, P. (1987). A refinement of Porter's strategies. *Strategic Management Journal, 8*(1), 93–101.

Zsolnai, L. (2015). Post-materialistic business models. *Post-materialistic business: Spiritual value-orientation in renewing management* (pp. 46–77). Houndsmills, London: Palgrave Macmillan.

CHAPTER 7

ETHICAL LEADERSHIP

A Complex and Messy Phenomenon

Leonie Heres, Leo Huberts, and Karin Lasthuizen[1]

"Ethical leadership" conquers the world, in terms of the attention that is paid to it by scholars in research in many countries and contexts as well as by the manifold practitioners involved in policy and organizational development on ethics and integrity. For many, that is a sign of hope and progress on a topic many of us are passionate about: the ethics and integrity of governance. We also cherish that development in comparison with the situation in which the topic was ignored or primarily seen as a corruption problem in poor countries to be countered by more adequate investigation and sanctions.

However, the impressive conquest makes us feel uncomfortable as well. Although we do not wish to "spoil the party" of the many involved researchers and practitioners with their sincere involvement to contribute to good governance and a better world, a bit of radical reflection on the state of the art and the (un)intended consequences seems appropriate.

First we will address the question what ethics and integrity of governance are about, including ethical leadership and integrity management. This leads to some doubts about the tendency to forget that it is about the "moral"

Radical Thoughts on Ethical Leadership, pages 135–150

dimension of the good, amidst other dimensions. This relates to a topic which we will address at the end: we do not seem to cope with the "western" or maybe even "U.S." bias in our rather "monolithical" concepts and theories and the resulting research. In addition we will reflect on the relationship between leadership and different phases in and aspects of "governance."

Second, we focus on our knowledge of the effects of ethical leadership. The overall image—a bit simplified—is that it contributes to about everything that is valued on governance (integrity, effectiveness, satisfaction, altruism et cetera). We doubt that and illustrate that with reference to research results on the effects of leadership on different types of integrity violations (in organizations).

Third, the relationship between leaders and followers and their contradictory interpretations of ethics and ethical leadership is on the agenda. That leads to doubts about the dominance of a "leaders'" perspective in theory and practice.

We conclude with some reflection on a research agenda that might help to address some of the problems and complexities we distinguish.

1. Focus on ethics, on the moral values, norms and rules, is fully justified and seems crucial to understand and explain governance, but more clarity in conceptualization will help and stimulate that.
2. The self-evidence of the positive effects of ethical leadership needs to be countered by more empirical research on the actual intended and unintended effects.
3. Ethical leaders operate in a complex and multidimensional environment and the influence of that context is underestimated in our research. This includes the characteristics of the work, the work environment and the views of followers on ethics and leadership.
4. In addition, there is the limitedness of our research from a "geographical" perspective. As of yet, we seem unable to cope with objections concerning our "Western" or maybe even "U.S." bias in our rather monolithical concepts and theories and the resulting research. More context-oriented research and policy development seems crucial, even though we are the first to acknowledge the complexity of that endeavor.

CONCEPTUAL VAGUENESS ON ETHICS, INTEGRITY, LEADERSHIP, AND GOVERNANCE

The first issue that we want to address is the question of how "ethical" leadership is defined and interpreted in the literature. To investigate the meanings of ethical leadership, Ciulla (2004) proposed that the ethics of leadership be examined along five interlinked dimensions: (a) the ethics of a leader as a person, (b) the ethics of the leader/follower relationship, (c) the ethics of the process of leadership, (d) the ethics of what a leader does or does not do, and (e) the ethics of leadership in the larger context of the community. Most of these dimensions are reflected in the seminal work on the topic by Brown, Treviño and Harrison (2005, p. 120), who define ethical leadership as: "the demonstration of normatively appropriate conduct through personal actions and interpersonal relationships, and promotion of such conduct among followers through two-way communication, reinforcement, and decision-making processes." This definition refers to "ethics," to "normatively appropriate conduct," and therefore to "relevant moral values and norms." But what is the meaning of those concepts? In research on "ethical" leadership it is not very common to be very explicit about the meaning of "ethical," of "normatively appropriate," or "moral values and norms" (Eisenbeiss, 2012).

In addition, a reflection on leadership in different types of decision-making within a broader governance framework seems to be missing as well. In this paragraph we build on research on the integrity and ethics of governance and on leadership in an attempt to make the conceptual framework somewhat clearer (for more extensive discussions, see also Heres, 2014; Huberts, 2014; Lasthuizen, 2008).

First, the terms "ethics" and "integrity" require further conceptual delineation. Ethics and integrity are about moral values and norms (Huberts, 2014). The moral dimension concerns shared ideas about right or wrong, good or bad. They concern values and norms that people feel rather strongly about because fundamental interests are involved and the outcomes affect the community they are part of. Evaluation in terms of right and wrong also implies principles, standards, or criteria by which morality and ethics can be judged. Values and norms are the basis for judgment and decision-making. A "value" is a belief or quality that *contributes to judgments* about what is good, right, beautiful, or admirable. Values thus have weight in the choice of action by individuals and collectives. A norm is more specific. Norms *tell us* whether something is good or bad, right or wrong, beautiful or ugly. For types of behavior, they answer the question "what is the correct thing to do?" (De Graaf, 2003; Fijnaut & Huberts, 2002; Van der Wal, 2008). Yet not all values and norms are relevant for ethical or moral judgments. Ethics are not, for example, concerned with what is beautiful (aesthetics), what is conventional (etiquette), or what works (science and technology; e.g., "ISO norms").

Because moral values and norms are so important—that is, because people feel so strongly about the "good and bad" of issues that matter to the community and involve fundamental community interests—Ethics and integrity are crucial for individuals and organizations. This significance not only makes ethics and integrity important and special, it also makes it crucial that they are related through a clear reference to the moral values and norms (violated), and specific about the *object* being judged. The terms "integritism" and "ethicism" (as also "moralism") refer to analysis and evaluation that does not comply with these criteria (Huberts, 2014). Integritism and ethicism relate to judgments that are inappropriate because the values or norms are non-moral or irrelevant and/or there is misunderstanding about the object being judged. The first aspect concerns the morality (i.e., the right/wrong, good/bad) of the norms and values. When individuals, leaders and organizations behave stupidly, make inefficient and ineffective decisions, or do not listen to their constituencies, it often leads to fierce debates and accusations of errors, wrong judgments, failures, and blunders. In the heat of that debate, the discussants tend to overstretch the integrity and ethics concept, accusing opponents of not being ethical or integritous, while the accusations do not concern fundamental values, or that which is of basic moral significance for the person itself, the profession and/or the organization in which he or she operates.

Concepts as "integritism" and "ethicism" offer food for thought, also for "ethical leadership" as well as its interpretation in terms of the underlying dimensions of "moral person," "moral manager" (Treviño, Hartman, & Brown, 2000) and morality innovator (Kaptein, 2016). What exactly is a moral person, a moral manager, and a morality innovator? Do we interpret that in line with the moral quality of leadership, with the focus on the relevant moral values and norms at stake? Or is our interpretation actually more on the "good" leader in a broader sense (in line with the multiple criteria involved in "good governance"), also taking into account other criteria and values (effectiveness, responsiveness etc.)? And what is the focus of our research on ethical leadership in governance?

In addition, it seems important to us that we be clear about the distinction between (ethical) *leadership* on the one hand and (the ethics and integrity of) *governance* on the other. In general, leadership pertains to "the process of influencing others to understand and agree about what needs to be done and how to do it, and the process of facilitating individual and collective efforts to accomplish shared objectives" (Yukl, 2006, p. 8). Governance, on the other hand, refers to "authoritative policy-making on collective problems and interests and implementation of these policies" (Huberts, 2014, p. 68). The definition refers explicitly to policy-making, as well as to policy implementation. This points at the relationship with bodies of knowledge on the political system and on the policy process. A systems approach focuses on the input, throughput, output, and outcome of the political and administrative system (Easton, 1979). The policy process model explicitly distinguishes between agenda building, policy preparation, decision-making and decision taking, implementation, evaluation, and feedback. In all phases, ethics and integrity play an important but often underestimated role. It is underestimated in dominant governance research, for example, on the legitimacy of political or governance systems, which treats input and output legitimacy as the basics of the legitimacy of political order in democracies (Scharpf, 1999). This focus neglects the legitimacy of the throughput phase, even though there is overwhelming evidence that the quality of governance in the throughput phase is crucial for the problem-solving quality of the output (output legitimacy) as well as the success of policies in terms of the resulting quality of life (Rothstein, 2011), on the importance of impartiality of the governance process.

It seems wise to take into account this distinction between input, throughput and output in our research on the content and consequences of ethical leadership. The different phases might bring along different consequences for the content and effects of types of (ethical) leadership. Ethical leadership in dealing with the environment in the input and output phase might request other qualities and involvement than in the throughout phase (which—contrary to the governance literature—seems to be the central or even the only focus in ethical leadership research).

Two final remarks seem relevant. In our view the limited focus of our research ignores the tension and potential conflict between the plural values that are at stake in ethical leadership and its consequences (Beck Jørgensen & Rutgers, 2015; De Graaf, 2015). A leader with the focus on ethics and integrity might (thus?) undervalue other values of good governance, such as responsiveness or effectiveness and efficiency. At present these tensions and conflicts are discussed more prominently in governance literature than in ethical leadership research. And beyond that and to begin with: what are the valid moral norms and values for leadership and governance, what are good governance or good leadership all about, also and especially when we consider their contextual meaning? We will address that later, putting our specific "Western" interpretation in dominant research at the table.

ETHICAL LEADERSHIP: THE NEGLECT OF FOLLOWERS

A second issue that we want to discuss is the leader-centered focus in both research and practice. In our efforts to find out "what works" we often look at what characterizes an ethical leader and his or her behavior, but neglect the fact that ethical leadership is by its very nature a subjective, dynamic process that involves followers as well. Without followers, there simply can be no ethical leadership. In fact, basic for our theory and research is that it is the followers who provide the terms and conditions for effective (ethical) leadership and that it is followers' perceptions of the leader's behavior, not the leader's actual behavior, that best predict the leader's influence on individual and organizational outcomes (e.g., Lord & Maher, 1991; Brown & Treviño, 2006). And in the words of Lord and Emrich (2000, p. 551): "If leadership, at least partly, resides in the minds of followers, then it is imperative to discover what followers are thinking." Still, followers' role in the constitution and development of ethical leadership is often overlooked and there is a dearth of research on the origins of and mechanisms behind follower perceptions of ethical leadership (Brown & Mitchell, 2010). As such, the leader-centered focus in our research limits our knowledge of how leaders can effectively build a reputation for ethical leadership.

By paying more attention to the role of followers, new and important questions arise that we need to address if we are to gain a full understanding of how ethical leadership works and why. Most notably, most definitions of ethical leadership, including the definition of Brown et al. (2005) that is adopted in most academic research, implicitly suggest that the concept means more or less the same to all parties involved, be they leaders or followers (cf. Kalshoven, Den Hartog, & De Hoogh, 2011; Yukl, Mahsud, Hassan, & Prussia, 2013). A follower-perspective, however, immediately raises doubts about whether such a "one style fits all" conceptualization of ethical leadership is actually tenable. Is there really one best way to be an ethical leader? Is there one meaning of the concept on which followers agree and accept as the "best practice," even though they might be faced with different challenges and dilemmas in their work?

Empirical research on these questions is limited, but the studies that are available point in a clear direction. That is, while followers' assumptions, beliefs and expectations of ethical leadership are consistent with academic definitions on a very general level (e.g., the importance of leader integrity and some form of communication), they differ significantly in the meaning and relative importance attributed to specific leader characteristics and behaviors. Studies for instance found cross-cultural variation in the extent to which people expect ethical leaders to be altruistic or empowering (e.g., Resick, Hanges, Dickson, & Mitchelson, 2006; Resick et al., 2011). And in a more extensive study on follower expectations, Heres' research (2014) uncovered not one but five ideal-typical views on what ethical leadership entails (see Box 7.1).

Follower-centered research thus shows us that ethical leadership is not a simple universal, but rather a *variform* universal phenomenon: While the main components of ethical leadership constitute a strong, generalizable foundation, there is subtle yet important variation in how those components are understood and enacted in practice (cf. Bass, 1997; Heres & Lasthuizen, 2012). This variation is especially important in light of the finding that followers' implicit assumptions, beliefs and expectations serve as a cognitive framework that guides and biases their subsequent perceptions of the behavior a leader demonstrates and determines their acceptance of an

BOX 7.1: FIVE IDEAL-TYPICAL VIEWS
ON ETHICAL LEADERSHIP (HERES, 2014)

The Safe Haven Creator: an ethical leader is a leader who creates an environment in which there is room to make mistakes and followers feel safe to speak up if needed. The leader is open and honest about his or her decisions and actions, but explicit discussions about ethics and values are limited and ethical behavior is expected to be more or less self-evident.

The Practicing Preacher: an ethical leader is a leader who not only role models high ethical standards but also engages in frequent two-way communication about ethics and dilemmas. The leader emphasizes values and principles over rules and procedures.

The Moral Motivator: an ethical leader is a charismatic leader who role models strong moral character, authenticity, self-reflection, and openness to criticism. The leader does not make ethics a priority within the organization and leaves it up to followers to decide for themselves what is and what is not morally appropriate behavior.

The Social Builder: an ethical leader is a leader who emphasizes shared values and norms within the group and creates and maintains a good relationship with followers. The leader always looks at situations from different perspectives, takes account of stakeholder and societal interests in decision-making and shows moral courage, even if that comes at a cost to the organization.

The Boundaries Setter: an ethical leader is a leader who sets clear boundaries and rules to prevent unethical behavior, and maintains these boundaries in strict but just way. The leader is loyal and fair to followers, but does not tolerate unethical behavior.

ethical leader's influence (Heres, 2014). Hence, for leaders to be perceived and accepted as ethical leaders it is important that they are aware of their followers' expectations of ethical leadership and that they align expectations and practices as much as possible (see also Van den Akker, Heres, Lasthuizen, & Six, 2009).

Follower-centered research also provides insights that can help explain why ethical leadership works better in some contexts than in others. For example, differences in follower expectations are related not only to the broader cultural context but also to the moral complexity of the work that followers do. That is, followers whose work evokes more serious and frequent moral dilemmas are also more likely to expect a proactive, principled and explicit approach to ethical leadership (Heres, 2014). Perhaps, then, ethical leadership has no effect in certain contexts (e.g., Detert, Treviño, Burris, & Andiappan, 2007) and may even become counterproductive at some point (e.g., Stouten, Van Dijke, Mayer, De Cremer, & Euwema, 2013) because followers do not experience their work as morally complex and hence do not expect their leaders to be as proactive and explicit about ethics and integrity as the literature prescribes. In such instances, the type of leadership that some scholars would consider to be "ethically neutral" (cf. Treviño, Brown, & Hartman, 2003) or "morally mute" (Bird & Waters, 1989; Menzel, 2007) may suffice in fostering and safeguarding follower ethical behavior.

Lastly, follower-centered research can highlight critical limitations in our research methods (cf. Heres, 2014[2]). Consistent with research on leader categorization and implicit leadership theories (e.g., Epitropaki & Martin, 2005; Lord & Maher, 1991), the follower-based research discussed above points towards an important source of bias in perceptual measures of ethical leadership. Specifically, the results suggest that when filling out questionnaires, respondents may in fact be (partly) regenerating their expectations of ethical leadership rather than critically reviewing their leader's actual behavior and traits (Rush & Russell, 1988). Even more so, processes of pattern-completion may be at play, in which respondents come to associate characteristics and behaviors with their leader that they did not actually observe but which reflect their implicit assumptions, beliefs and expectations of ethical leadership (Lord & Emrich, 2000; Shondrick, Dinh, & Lord, 2010).

Taken together, the above indicates that a broader perspective on both the leaders *and* followers involved in ethical leadership is needed to gain a better perspective on what it means to be an ethical leader and on when and how ethical leadership works. This requires a move away from the "one style fits all" conceptualization currently dominating the literature, towards more nuance and differentiation of ethical leadership.

THE VARYING EFFECTS OF ETHICAL LEADERSHIP

The third issue in ethical leadership research and practice that deserves mentioning here concerns the lack of specificity in how we examine the effects of ethical leadership. In general, research into the effects of ethical leadership shows that counterproductive and unethical behavior are reduced by leadership styles that put ethics in the forefront (e.g., Huberts, Kaptein, & Lasthuizen, 2007; De Hoogh & Den Hartog, 2008; Lasthuizen, 2008; Mayer, Kuenzi, Greenbaum, Bardes, & Salvador, 2009). Moreover, ethical leadership raises followers' moral awareness and judgment and fosters an ethical work climate (e.g., Treviño, Weaver, Gibson, & Toffler, 1999). It is important here to note that the effects of ethical leadership on (un)ethical behaviors go above and beyond the effect of other, more general leadership styles without a specific focus on ethics (Brown et al., 2005; Lasthuizen, 2008). Additionally, ethical leadership appears to be beneficial

beyond ethics and integrity, as it affects more general organizational outcomes as well, such as interpersonal trust, organizational commitment, and
organizational citizenship behaviors (Brown et al., 2005; De Hoogh & Den
Hartog, 2008; Mayer et al., 2009; Toor & Ofori, 2009; Kalshoven, 2010). In
discussion of the effects of ethical leadership, the presumption is thus that
ethical leadership improves the overall organizational performance and
therefore seems to be a good leadership strategy.

However, similar to our critique on the leader-centered focus in ethical leadership research, an important limitation of most ethical leadership
studies is the common assumption that the same approach of ethical leadership is adequate for all kinds of (un)ethical behavior and organizational
climates—under all circumstances. This is further exacerbated in the way
in which ethical leadership tends to be measured in standardized survey
research. For instance, in the previous mentioned work of Brown, Treviño,
and colleagues, a concept of ethical leadership is used containing dimensions of the moral person and the moral manager (Treviño et. al., 2000,
Brown et al., 2005). Yet the authors' parsimonious 10-item ethical leadership scale for standardized surveys combines both dimensions assumed to
be important for the ethical leader and is therefore little sensitive to its
contingencies. Such lack of specificity in ethical leadership measurement
raises the question whether the prevention of a specific type of unethical
behavior such as corruption and fraud, for example, demands a different
ethical leadership approach than the prevention of other types of unethical
behavior such as conflicts of interest, discrimination, or misuse of information. We think it does.

Huberts et al. (2007) discussed three aspects of leadership—role modeling, strictness, and openness—and examined them in relation to a typology
of integrity violations as developed by Huberts, Pijl, and Steen (1999; see
also Lasthuizen, Huberts, & Heres, 2011), by means of a survey amongst
police officers. In a latter study of Lasthuizen (2008) two empirically distinct types of ethical leadership are found: role modeling leadership and
integrity-focused leadership. Both studies indicate that ethical role modeling of public sector leaders is especially effective in minimizing integrity
violations that relate to interpersonal relationships within the organization,
including bullying, sexual harassment, or gossiping about colleagues. But
when it comes to integrity violations that concern organizational resources
(e.g., misuse of working hours for private purposes, falsely calling in sick
or carelessness in the use of organizational resources), it is essential that a
leader is strict and reinforces behavior through rewards and punishments.
And, finally, clarifying ethical values and norms and being open to discuss
ethical dilemmas seem most effective in reducing favoritism within the organization and discrimination of the public outside the organization. In
addition, as Lasthuizen's (2008) study shows, it appears that role-modeling

leadership works primarily via the ethical culture dimension of clarity (cf. Kaptein, 2008), while integrity-focused leadership works primarily via the ethical culture dimensions of discussability, sanctionability and supportability on the incidence and prevalence of integrity violations. These findings are outlined in Figure 7.1 (cf. Lsthuizen, 2008, p. 156).

Another study of Kalshoven et al. (2011) confirm this basic argument that ethical leadership is in fact a multi-dimensional construct with different consequences for the "ethics" of the organization, including the occurrence of integrity violations. Ethical leadership involves different behaviors that each have different antecedents and outcomes. Kalshoven et al. (2011) provide an Ethical Leadership at Work (ELW) questionnaire in which seven dimensions of ethical leadership are developed and tested. In line with our studies, she found different relationships between the various behaviors of ethical leadership and outcomes (cf. Lawton & Paez, 2015).

In sum, these findings lead us to the conclusion that the various aspects and components of ethical leadership differ in their respective effect on follower unethical behaviors and the ethical organization (cf. Jurkiewicz & Giacalone, 2016). Many authors in leadership studies—either ethical leadership or the broader organizational leadership—stress that dimensions or styles are interdependent and should be combined. However, as important as this work may be, a too narrow focus on the concept or its measurement prohibits specific knowledge on which leadership styles work under what conditions and with what results. Fortunately, differentiation in (ethical) leadership is gaining territory in scholarly work,[3] giving new impetus for approaches known as situational or contingency leadership (Hersey & Blanchard, 1993). Although this latter theory has been criticized (cf. Fernandez & Vecchio, 1997; Graeff, 1997), its underlying rationale that leadership effectiveness depends on the specific situation and followers remains appealing.

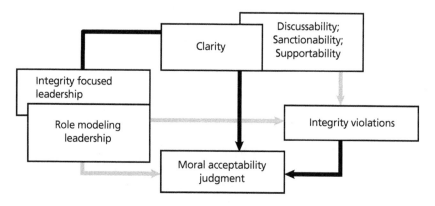

Figure 7.1   Working of ethical leadership styles on integrity violations.

DISCUSSION AND CONCLUSION

In this chapter, we addressed three key issues in ethical leadership research and theory. Each of these issues provides food for thought for future research, theory development, and possible implications for governance practice—some of which may indeed be considered quite "radical," messy, and complex when compared to the clean and clear message that dominates ethical leadership research and practice. As a research community, we are able to make valuable and interesting progress, but we nevertheless seem to be a bit "stuck" within our own boundaries and limitations... Our reflection on these limitations concerned doubts about the conceptual clarity on basic concepts as "ethics" and "integrity," as well as on the content and interpretation of "ethical leadership" in different contexts. More differentiation and nuance seems necessary, taking into account different phases of governance, different interpretations, and experiences within organizations (including followers' perspectives). In addition, we need to distinguish more between types of ethical leadership with differing consequences for the organization and its outcomes. This offers a complex but also challenging agenda for future research and theory development. More international comparative research should be put on that agenda, with more clarity about the validity of the insights on the types of ethical leadership and their consequences in varying circumstances. In addition more clarity about the basic concepts and their context might help to make more explicit what ethical leadership is all about, with more specificity on the consequences of types of leadership. This of course also is crucial for our contribution to the practice of governance and leadership.

An additional point for serious reflection (cf. Huberts & Lasthuizen, in press) stems from scholars who question the Western or cultural bias in dominant perceptions of ethics, integrity and corruption (De Graaf, Wagenaar, & Hoenderboom, 2010; Mungiu-Pippidi, 2006). Sissener (2001), for example, claimed that Western approaches to corruption are often peculiarly Western, influenced as they are by Weber's famous ideal type of bureaucracy and not easily applied to non-Western societies. In many countries, the public official who issues favors towards an established network is not corrupt; his or her actions can simply be conceived as the social obligation to help; and deals within the network are considered as a normal practice (Sissener, 2001). The definition issue thus raises questions of cultural bias. Accordingly, Chadda (2004, p. 122) was particularly outspoken on the use of TI's definition in developing countries: "To judge transactions originating in the traditional sphere as corrupt because they clash with the requirements of the legal rational order can be seen as simply an ideological argument for the rapid destruction of the traditional sphere."

In the same vein, Andersson and Heywood (2009) argued that the concept of corruption is politically misused, claiming that the very concept has been increasingly instrumentalized for political ends since the end of the Cold War—most especially in those countries where corruption is perceived as a major issue.

This issue seems to be more prominent in the mentioned literature on corruption and integrity of governance then in our research and theory development on the content and consequences of "ethical leadership." Nevertheless, more reflection on cultural subjectivity issues, and the limitations of our "western perspective," seem important to progress in our field of study.

This of course relates to our previous topics, on what ethics and leadership are about, on the perceptions of followers and leaders and on the effects of ethical leadership styles. In addition to research implications and theory-oriented conclusions, our "journey of doubt" also suggests consequences for the practice of ethical leadership and integrity management. More nuance and differentiation seem inevitable, on the styles of (ethical) leadership, on the types of consequences or effects of those styles and on the importance of taking into account the context.

NOTES

1. The authors are listed alphabetically and contributed equally to this chapter. In this chapter we build on previous works of the authors, most notably Huberts (2014), Heres (2014) and Lasthuizen (2008), referencing the aforementioned works only when referring to specific research results. We thank Carlo de Cocq for his assistance on adequate referencing.
2. Other methodological implications of follower-based research and recommendations on how to deal with bias in perceptual measures of ethical leadership include: the inclusion of more detailed behaviors in measurement instruments; the use of multidimensional measures that allow for in-depth examination of measurement models, and; the employment of a wider range of measurement instruments. See Heres (2014) for a more extensive discussion.
3. See for instance studies from Bedi, Alpaslan, & Green (2016); Huang & Paterson (2017); Kottke & Pelletier, 2013; Lamboo, Lasthuizen, & Huberts, 2008; Lawton, Rayner, & Lasthuizen, 2013; Lu, 2014; Neubert, Wu, & Roberts, 2013; Ruiz, Ruiz, & Martinez, 2011; Stouten et al., 2010; Taylor & Pattie, 2014.

REFERENCES

Andersson, S., & Heywood, P. M. (2009). The politics of perception: Use and abuse of Transparency International's approach to measuring corruption. *Political Studies, 57*(4), 746–767.

Bass, B. M. (1997). Does the transactional-transformational leadership paradigm transcend organizational and national boundaries? *American Psychologist,* *52*(2), 130–139.

Beck Jørgensen, T., & Rutgers M. R. (2015). Public values: Core or confusion? Introduction to the centrality and puzzlement of public values research. *The American Review of Public Administration, 45*(1), 3–12.

Bedi, A., Alpaslan, C. M., & Green, S. (2016). A meta-analytic review of ethical leadership outcomes and moderators. *Journal of Business Ethics, 139*(3), 517.

Bird, F. B., & Waters, J. A. (1989). The moral muteness of managers. *California Management Review, 32*(1), 73–88.

Brown, M. E., & Treviño, L. K. (2006). Ethical leadership: A review and future directions. *The Leadership Quarterly, 17*(6), 595–616.

Brown, M. E., & Mitchell, M. S. (2010). Ethical and unethical leadership: Exploring new avenues for future research. *Business Ethics Quarterly, 20*(4), 583–616.

Brown, M. E., Treviño, L. K., & Harrison, D. A. (2005). Ethical leadership: A social learning perspective for construct development and testing. *Organizational Behavior and Human Decision Processes, 97*(2), 117–134.

Chadda, M. (2004). India: Between majesty and modernity. In R. A. Johnson (Ed.), *The struggle against corruption* (pp. 109–143). New York, NY: Palgrave Macmillan.

Ciulla, J. B. (2004). The relationship of ethics to effectiveness in leadership. In R. J. Sternberg, J. Antonakis & A. T. Cianciolo (Eds.), *The Nature of Leadership.* Thousand Oaks, London and New Delhi: SAGE.

De Graaf, G. (2003). *Tractable morality. Customer discourses of bankers, veterinarians and charity workers.* Rotterdam, Holland: ERIM.

De Graaf, G., Wagenaar, P., & Hoenderboom, M. (2010). Constructing corruption. In G. De Graaf, P. von Maravic, & P. Wagenaar, (Eds.), *The good cause. Theoretical perspectives on corruption causes* (pp. 98–114). Opladen & Farmington Hills, MI: Barbara Budrich.

De Graaf, G. (2015). The bright future of value pluralism in public administration. *Administration and Society, 47*(9), 1094–1102.

De Hoogh, A. H. B., & Den Hartog, D. N. (2008). Ethical and despotic leadership, relationships with leader's social responsibility, top management team effectiveness and subordinates' optimism: A multi-method study, *The Leadership Quarterly, 19*(3), 297–311.

Detert, J. R., Treviño, L. K., Burris, E. R., & Andiappan, M. (2007). Managerial modes of influence and counterproductivity in organizations: A longitudinal business-unit-level investigation. *Journal of Applied Psychology, 92*(4), 993–1005.

Easton, D. (1979). *A systems analysis of political life.* Chicago, IL: University of Chicago Press.

Eisenbeiss, S. A. (2012). Re-thinking ethical leadership: An interdisciplinary integrative approach. *The Leadership Quarterly, 23*(5), 791–808.

Epitropaki, O., & Martin, R. (2005). From ideal to real: A longitudinal study of the role of implicit leadership theories on leader-member exchanges and employee outcomes. *Journal of Applied Psychology, 90*(4), 659–676.

Fernandez, C. F., & Vecchio, R. P. (1997). Situational leadership theory revisited. A test of an across-jobs perspective. *The Leadership Quarterly, 8*(1), 67–84.

Fijnaut, C., & Huberts, L. W. J. C. (Eds.). (2002). *Corruption, Integrity and Law Enforcement*. Dordrecht, The Netherlands: Kluwer Law International.

Graeff, C. L. (1997). Evolution of situational leadership theory: A critical review. *The Leadership Quarterly, 8*(2), 153–170.

Heres, L. (2014). *One style fits all? The content, origins, and effect of follower expectations of ethical leadership*. Amsterdam, the Netherlands: VU University Amsterdam. Free download available via www.leonieheres.com.

Heres, L., & Lasthuizen, K. (2012). What's the difference? Ethical leadership in public, hybrid, and private organizations. Special issue of the *Journal of Change Management, 12*(4), 441–466.

Hersey, P., & Blanchard, K. (1993). *Management of organizational behavior. Utilizing human resources* (6th ed). Englewood Cliffs, NJ: Prentice Hall.

Huang, L., & Paterson, T. A. (2017). Group ethical voice: Influence of ethical leadership and impact on ethical performance. *Journal of Management, 43*(4), 1157–1184.

Huberts, L. W. J. C. (2014). *The integrity of governance. What it is, what we know, what is done, and where to go*. Basingstoke, England: Palgrave Macmillan.

Huberts, L. W. J. C., Pijl, D., & Steen, A. (1999). Integriteit en corruptie. [Integrity and corruption]. In C. Fijnaut, E. Muller, & U. Rosenthal, (Eds.), *Politie. Studies over haar werking en organisatie*. [Police studies on work and organization] (pp. 433–472). Alphen aan den Rijn, The Netherlands: Samsom.

Huberts, L. W. J. C., Kaptein, M., & Lasthuizen, K. (2007). A study of the impact of three leadership styles on integrity violations committed by police officers. *Policing. An International Journal for Police Strategies and Management, 30*(4), 586–607.

Huberts, L. W. J. C., & Lasthuizen, K. (in press). Corruption in context: What goes wrong in governance. In M. Powell, D. Wafa, & T. A. Mau (Eds.), *Corruption in a global context. Restoring public trust, integrity, and accountability among public leaders and governing institutions*. Brussels, Belgium: Bruylant.

Jurkiewicz, C. J., & Giacalone, R. A. (2016). How will we know it when we see it? Conceptualizing the ethical organization. *Public Organization Review, 16*(3), 409–420.

Kalshoven, K. (2010). *Ethical leadership through the eyes of employees*. Amsterdam, The Netherlands: University of Amsterdam.

Kalshoven, K., Den Hartog, D. N., & De Hoogh, A. H. B. (2011). Ethical leadership at work questionnaire (ELW): Development and validation of a multidimensional measure. *The Leadership Quarterly, 22*(1), 51–69.

Kaptein, M. (2008). Developing and testing a measure for the ethical culture of organizations: The corporate ethical virtues model. *Journal of Organizational Behavior, 29*(7), 923–947.

Kaptein, M. (2016). *Leadership in ethics: The morality innovator as third component of ethical leadership*. Retrieved from: https://www.researchgate.net/publication/297556029

Kottke, J. L. & Pelletier, K. L. (2013). Measuring and differentiating perceptions of supervisor and top leader ethics. *Journal of Business Ethics, 113*(3), 415–428.

Lamboo, M. E. D, Lasthuizen, K., & Huberts, L. W. J. C. (2008). How to encourage ethical behavior. The impact of police leadership on police officers taking gratuities. In L. W. J. C. Huberts, C. L. Jurkiewicz and J. Maesschalck (Eds.), *Ethics and integrity of governance: perspectives across frontiers* (pp. 159–177). Cheltenham, England: Edward Elgar.

Lasthuizen, K. (2008). *Leading to integrity. Empirical research into the effects of leadership on ethics and integrity.* Enschede, The Netherlands: Printpartners Ipskamp.

Lasthuizen, K., Huberts, L. W. J. C., & Heres, L. (2011). How to measure integrity violations, towards a validated typology. *Public Management Review, 13*(3), 383–408.

Lawton, A., & Paez, I. (2015). Developing a framework for ethical leadership. *Journal of Business Ethics, 130*(3), 639–649.

Lawton, A., Rayner, J., & Lasthuizen, K. (2013). *Ethics and management in the public sector.* London, England: Routledge.

Lord, R.G., & Emrich, C. G. (2000). Thinking outside the box by looking inside the box: Extending the cognitive revolution in leadership research. *The Leadership Quarterly, 11*(4), 551–579.

Lord, R. G., & Maher, K. J. (1991). *Leadership and information processing.* London, England: Routledge.

Lu, X. (2014). Ethical leadership and organizational citizenship behavior: The mediating roles of cognitive and affective trust. *Social Behavior and Personality: An International Journal, 42*(3), 379–389.

Mayer, D. M., Kuenzi, M., Greenbaum, R., Bardes, M., & Salvador, R. (2009). How low does ethical leadership flow? Test of a trickle-down model. *Organizational Behavior and Human Decision Processes, 108*(1), 1–13.

Menzel, D. C. (2007). *Ethics management for public administrators. Building organizations of integrity.* Armonk, NY: M. E. Sharpe.

Mungiu-Pippidi, A. (2006). Corruption: Diagnosis and treatment. *Journal of Democracy, 17*(3), 86–99.

Neubert, M. J., Wu, C., & Roberts, J. A. (2013). The influence of ethical leadership and regulatory focus on employee outcomes. *Business Ethics Quarterly, 23*(2), 269–296.

Resick, C. J., Hanges, P. J., Dickson, M. W., & Mitchelson, J. K. (2006). A cross-cultural examination of the endorsement of ethical leadership. *Journal of Business Ethics, 63*(4), 345–359.

Resick, C. J., Martin, G. S., Keating, M. A., Dickson, M. W., Kwan, H. K., & Peng, C. (2011). What ethical leadership means to me: Asian, American, and European perspectives. *Journal of Business Ethics, 101*(3), 435–457.

Rothstein, B. (2011). *The quality of government. Corruption, social trust, and inequality in international perspective.* Chicago, IL: University of Chicago Press.

Rush, M. C., & Russell, J. E. (1988). Leader prototypes and prototype-contingent consensus in leader behavior descriptions. *Journal of Experimental Social Psychology, 24*(1), 88–104.

Ruiz, P., Ruiz, C., & Martínez, R. (2011). The cascading effect of top management's ethical leadership: Supervisors or other lower-hierarchical level individuals? *African Journal of Business Management, 5*(12), 4755–4764.

Scharpf, F. W. (1999). *Governing in Europe: Effective and democratic?* Oxford, England: Oxford University Press.

Shondrick, S. J., Dinh, J. E. & Lord, R. G. (2010). Developments in implicit leadership theory and cognitive science: Applications to improving measurement and understanding alternatives to hierarchical leadership. *The Leadership Quarterly, 21*(6), 959–978.

Sissener, T. (2001). *Anthropological perspectives on corruption, working paper/development studies and human rights.* Bergen, Norway: Chr. Michelsen Institute (CMI).

Stouten, J., Baillien, E., Broeck, A., Camps, J., Witte, H., & Euwema, M. (2010). Discouraging bullying: The role of ethical leadership and its effects on the work environment. *Journal of Business Ethics, 95*(1), 17–27.

Stouten, J., Van Dijke, M., Mayer, D. M., De Cremer, D., & Euwema, M. C. (2013). Can a leader be seen as too ethical? The curvilinear effects of ethical leadership. *The Leadership Quarterly, 24*(5), 680–695.

Taylor, S. G., & Pattie, M. W. (2014). When does ethical leadership affect workplace incivility? The moderating role of follower personality. *Business Ethics Quarterly, 24*(4), 595–616.

Toor, S. U. R., & Ofori, G. (2009). Ethical leadership: Examining the relationships with full range leadership model, employee outcomes, and organizational culture. *Journal of Business Ethics, 90*(4), 533–547.

Treviño, L. K., Weaver, G. R., Gibson, D. G., & Toffler, B. L. (1999). Managing ethics and legal compliance: What works and what hurts. *California Management Review, 41*(2), 131–151.

Treviño, L. K., Hartman, L. P., & Brown, M. E. (2000). Moral person and moral manager: How

executives develop a reputation for ethical leadership. *California Management Review, 42*(4), 128–142.

Treviño, L. K., Brown, M. E., & Hartman, L. P. (2003). A qualitative investigation of perceived executive ethical leadership: Perceptions from inside and outside the executive suite. *Human Relations, 56*(1), 5–37.

Van den Akker, L., Heres, L., Lasthuizen, K., & Six, F. E. (2009). Ethical leadership and trust: It's all about meeting expectations. *International Journal of Leadership Studies, 5*(2), 102–122.

Van der Wal, Z. (2008). *Value solidity. Differences, similarities and conflicts between the organizational values of government and business.* Amsterdam, The Netherlands: VU University.

Yukl, G.A. (2006). *Leadership in organizations* (6th ed). Upper Saddle River, NJ: Prentice Hall.

Yukl, G., Mahsud, R., Hassan, S., & Prussia, G. E. (2013). An improved measure of ethical leadership. *Journal of Leadership and Organizational Studies, 20*(1), 38–48.

CHAPTER 8

RADICAL HEROIC LEADERSHIP

Implications for Transformative Growth in the Workplace

Scott T. Allison
University of Richmond

Allison Toner
University of Richmond

Carl Sagan (1949) once wrote, "Extraordinary claims require extraordinary evidence." A corollary of this claim might read, "Radical times require radical leadership." Our observation of current world conditions suggests that we live in such radical times. As we write this chapter, the United States is averaging more than one mass-fatality shooting per day (Ingraham, 2015). Terrorism sponsored by the Islamic state and other extremist groups threaten world peace and stability (Hoffman, 2013). Rising sea levels due to global warming are projected to submerge the world's coastal cities within a few decades (Fagan, 2014). Our planet's oceans are dying from humans

Radical Thoughts on Ethical Leadership, pages 151–168

disposing over a dozen metric tons of plastic and other rubbish into it over several millennia (Roberts, 2013). If radical times such as these require radical leadership, then it is incumbent on us to define the exact nature of such leadership and to take immediate steps toward encouraging, developing, and implementing it before the world's problems become irreversible. To avoid cultivating radical leadership is to invite collective disaster.

The purpose of this chapter is to describe an approach to leadership that is grounded in the ideal of encouraging and developing heroes and heroism in the workplace. Specifically, our radical approach recognizes the heroic potential of all organizational members and focuses on its cultivation, especially in those individuals already occupying leadership positions or who are on leadership tracks within organizations. Our approach is founded on the two assumptions that all leaders are capable of heroic transformative development, and that the key to such development is found in the classic hero's journey as described by Joseph Campbell in his iconic 1949 book, *The Hero with a Thousand Faces*. This chapter outlines a conceptual framework, based on the hero's journey, for developing leadership that can meet the radical needs of our desperate times. In doing so, we draw from theory and research in numerous sub-disciplines of psychology, most notably from the areas of developmental, social, personality, organizational, and positive psychology.

THE CLASSIC HERO'S JOURNEY

Our radical approach to promoting heroic development in organizations begins with Campbell (1949), a comparative mythologist who noticed a distinct pattern within hero myths from around the world. In virtually all mythological stories from all time periods in human history, a hero embarks on a journey that begins when she is cast into a dangerous, unfamiliar world. The hero is charged with accomplishing a daunting task and receives assistance from unlikely sources. There are formidable obstacles along the way and villainous characters to overcome. After many trials and much suffering, the hero learns an important truth about herself and about the world. Succeeding on her journey, the hero is forever changed and returns to her original world. There she bestows some type of gift to that society, a gift that is only made possible by her own personal journey of growth and change. In short, heroes undergo personal transformations that include the development of a motive to improve the lives of others.

From the perspective of advancing radical leadership, what is the source of this motive to make others better? An examination of the hero's journey suggests that people must complete all the stages of the journey to acquire this pro-social motive. Campbell (1949) proposed that this prototypical heroic path, which he called the hero *monomyth*, consists of three parts: *departure*, *initiation*, and *return*. The initial *departure* phase refers to the forces that set the hero's journey in motion. Heroes embark on their journeys to achieve a goal that requires the acquisition of an important quality that the hero lacks. All heroes start out "incomplete" in some sense. They are missing some essential inner strength or quality that they must develop to succeed. This quality can be self-confidence, humility, courage, compassion, faith, resilience, a moral compass, or some fundamental insight about themselves and the world. The second phase, *initiation*, refers to the challenges, obstacles, and foes that must be overcome for the hero to prevail. Heroes cannot triumph over these obstacles without help from others. Campbell (1949) calls these helpers *mentors*, who bear a resemblance to the Jungian archetype of the "wise old man." These mentors can be friends, teachers, love interests, sidekicks, or father figures. The role of the mentor is to help the hero discover, or recover, the missing quality that is needed to overcome challenges and obstacles on the journey. Good mentors are leaders in the classic sense; they help others discover their strengths and raise them to new levels of competence and morality. Campbell (1949) believed that the most satisfying heroes we encounter in mythic storytelling are heroes who are transformed by the mentoring they have received. Transforming mentorship is a pivotal component of the hero's journey.

Of central importance in the hero monomyth is the phase involving the hero's *return* to his or her original world. Upon returning, the hero brings a great boon, or benefit, to the world. Having been personally transformed, the hero is drawn to a higher calling of giving back to his or her group, organization, or society. This transition from self-transformation to a desire for a wider, social transformation is similar to Maslow's (1943) distinction between the need for self-actualization and the need for self-transcendence. It also bears a resemblance to the progression from Erik Erikson's (1975) stage of identity formation to the later stages of generativity and integrity. The hero's journey is the human journey, replete with struggle, growth, learning, transformation, and an ascendency from followership to leadership. In this sense it is similar to the dramatic story form that Howard Gardner (1995) suggests that leaders use to influence followers' identities. The hero evolves from one who is incomplete and in need of mentoring to one who later becomes a mentoring figure for others. The process is remarkably similar to James MacGregor Burns' (1978) vision of followers being transformed and elevated by mentors and leaders to create a "new cadre of leaders" within an organization.

Burns (1978) proposed that "leaders and followers raise one another to higher levels of motivation and morality." How might this raising occur? Research on heroic leadership suggests that heroes lead by example, demonstrating high degrees of competence and morality to followers (Allison

& Goethals, 2011, 2013). Our analysis suggests that a heroic leader's demonstration of exemplary morality exerts a profound emotional effect on followers. Recent work suggests that moral exemplars evoke a unique emotional response which Jonathan Haidt and his colleagues have called *elevation* (Algoe & Haidt, 2009). Haidt borrowed the term "elevation" from Thomas Jefferson, who used the phrase *moral elevation* to describe the euphoric feeling one gets when reading great literature. When people experience elevation, they feel a mix of awe, reverence, and admiration for a morally beautiful act. The emotion is described as similar to calmness, warmth, and love. Haidt (2003) argues that elevation is "elicited by acts of virtue or moral beauty; it causes warm, open feelings in the chest." Most importantly, the feeling of elevation has a concomitant behavioral component: A desire to become a better person. Elevation motivates people to behave more virtuously themselves. A form of moral self-efficacy, elevation transforms people into believing they are capable of engaging in significant prosocial action. Abundant research evidence supports this idea (Allison, Goethals, & Kramer, 2017; Csikszentmihalyi, Condren, & Lebuda, 2017).

BENEFITS OF EXPOSURE TO HERO NARRATIVES

Both Gardner (1995) and Sternberg (2011) have argued that effective leaders promote a narrative of heroism in their communications with followers and during their efforts to recruit prospective followers. Evidence that humans have always been drawn to hero stories can be found in the earliest known human narratives that describe stirring accounts of the exploits of heroes and heroic leaders (Kerenyi, 1978). These ancient hero tales from around the globe included the tales of Hesiod, Vishnu, Gilgamesh, Etana, Sundiata, Beowulf, Samson, Thor, Leonidas, Guan Yu, among others (Durant, 2002; Hamilton, 1999). In all of these stories, including ones used by contemporary leaders, the hero's journey describes a voyage of self-realization and transformation (Allison & Smith, 2015). The hero's message to others contained within the narrative is one of growth, redemption, resilience, selflessness, and courage.

Recent research has shown that heroes and hero stories nourish the minds and hearts of people who read them or listen to them (Allison & Goethals, 2014, 2016). Hero narratives fulfill important cognitive and emotional needs, such as our need for wisdom, meaning, hope, inspiration, and development (Allison & Goethals, 2017). A central underlying theme in this research is the idea that our most basic human needs underlie our thirst for heroes, and these needs explain why we are drawn to heroes, how we benefit from them, why we stick with flawed ones, and why we repudiate heroes only after they have outlived their psychological usefulness (Goethals & Allison, 2017).

Research on the psychological benefits of hero narratives draws from the abundance of work underscoring the significance of narrative storytelling for both individuals and collectives (Cajete, Eder, & Holyan, 2010; McAdams, 1997; Sternberg, 2011). Stories crystalize abstract concepts and endow them with contextual meaning (Boje, 1995). Stories are more than tools for influencing others; they also promote self-change. McAdams (1997, 2014) has argued that personal self-narratives shape life trajectories and the maintenance of subjective well-being. Stories are rich, emotionally laden capsule summaries of wisdom for which the human mind was designed (Green & Brock, 2005; Haidt, 2012; Wyer, 1995). According to Price (1978), "a need to tell and hear stories is essential to the species—Homo sapiens—second in necessity apparently after nourishment and before love and shelter" (p. 3).

Hero stories fulfill two principal human functions: an *epistemic* function and an *energizing* function (Allison & Goethals, 2014). The epistemic function refers to the knowledge and wisdom that hero stories impart to us. The energizing function refers to the ways that hero stories inspire us and promote personal growth. In our model of radical leadership, we argue that such leadership must tap into both of these functions if followers within organizations are to reach their full heroic potential. We now examine these two functions in more detail below.

Epistemic Function of Hero Stories

Stories of heroic action impart wisdom by supplying mental models, or scripts, for how one could, or should, lead one's life. For example, Martin Luther King, Jr., based his strategy of nonviolent resistance on stories of similar tactics used successfully by Mahatma Gandhi (Bennett, 2003). Heroic narratives also teach us how we should behave in crisis situations (Allison & Goethals, 2011; Goethals & Allison, 2012). The heroic actions of Wesley Autrey offer a compelling example of the wisdom imparted by hero stories. Autrey was a construction worker who received international acclaim when he rescued a complete stranger from an oncoming New York subway train in 2007 (The Hero in the Subway, 2007). Autrey provided a script for heroic action to millions of New York citizens hungry for such a script. Heroes such as Autrey are role models who perform behaviors that affirm our most cherished worldviews (Kinsella, Ritchie, & Igou, 2015a; Solomon, Cohen, Greenberg, & Pyszczynski, 2008).

Hero narratives are more than simple scripts prescribing prosocial action. According to Rohr (2011), hero stories contain instances of *transrational* phenomena, which he defines as human experiences that resist or defy rational analysis. Transrational phenomena in hero stories reveal truths and life patterns that our limited minds have difficulty understanding using our best logic or rational thought. Examples of transrational experiences that commonly appear in hero stories include *suffering, sacrifice, meaning, love, paradox, mystery, God,* and *eternity.* The ultimate transrational phenomenon may be the eternal battle between good and evil, a theme that pervades all of human literature and is a universal characteristic of the human condition (Miller, 2005; Zimbardo, 2008). Transrational events beg to be understood but cannot be fully known using conventional tools of human reason. We believe that radical leaders can use hero stories to unlock the secrets of transrational phenomena, from which their followers can benefit.

Hero narratives promote wisdom in several ways. First, the classic hero narrative reveals *deep truths* about human life. Truths are considered deep when their insights about human nature and motivation are not only profound and fundamental but also hidden and nonobvious. Campbell (1949) believed that most readers of mythic hero stories remain oblivious to their deep truths, their meaning, and their wisdom. Deep truths contained in hero myths are difficult to discern and appreciate because they are disguised within symbols and metaphors. One type of deep truth is called *deep time,* which refers to the timelessness that connects us with the past, the present, and the future. Deep time is evident when stories contain phrases such as, "Once upon a time," "A long time ago in a galaxy far, far away," and "they lived happily ever after." Hero stories also emphasize *deep roles* in our human social fabric. Moxnes (2012) has argued that the deepest roles are archetypal family roles such as mother, child, maiden, and wise old man or grandparent. Family role archetypes abound in classic hero tales and myths, as when stories feature kings and queens, parents, stepparents, princesses, children, and stepchildren. The family unit is an ancient device, still useful today, for understanding our social world (Moxnes, 1999). Another deep truth centers on the essential role of sacrifice in the hero's journey and in human growth and development. Franco, Blau, and Zimbardo (2011) have argued that self-sacrifice may be the principal defining feature of the hero's journey.

Another epistemic function of hero stories resides in their ability to shed light on meaningful life paradoxes. We propose that most people have trouble unpacking the value of paradoxical truths unless the contradictions contained within the paradoxes are illustrated inside a good story. Campbell (1949) believed that a paradoxical truth about the hero's journey is that heroes must leave home to find home. All mythic hero stories involve a necessary departure into a new, dangerous world that, paradoxically, requires a descent into hell before an ascent into enlightenment. For the hero, "the way down is the way up" (Rohr, 2011, p. 18). This counterintuitive journey is not just reserved for mythic heroes; all human beings face painful challenges that are a necessary path toward personal growth. "Where you stumble," wrote Campbell (1949), "there lies your treasure" (p. 75). Campbell (1949) often used dragon-slaying as a metaphor for describing how the confrontation of our fears is necessary for later redemption. When heroes summon the courage to face their challenges, they enter the dragon's lair, and only when they defeat these demons is their personal transformation complete. According to Campbell (1949), when we slay our dragons, we are slaying our false, egocentric selves thereby allowing our true heroic selves to emerge.

A final epistemic benefit of the hero narrative focuses on the development of emotional intelligence. This type of intelligence refers to people's ability to identify, understand, use, and manage emotions (Caruso, Fleming, & Spector, 2014; Mayer, Salovey, Caruso, & Sitarenios, 2001). Psychoanalyst Bruno Bettelheim believed that children's fairy tales are useful in helping people, especially children, understand emotional experience (Bettelheim, 1976). The heroes of these fairy tales are usually subjected to dark, foreboding experiences, such as encounters with witches, evil spells, abandonment, neglect, abuse, and death. Listeners to these tales vicariously experience these dark stimuli, allowing them to develop strategies for resolving their fears and distress. Bettelheim (1976) believed that even the most distressing fairy tales, such as those by the Brothers Grimm, add clarity to confusing emotions and give people a greater sense of life's meaning and purpose. The darkness of fairy tales allows children to grow emotionally, thus developing their emotional intelligence and preparing them for the challenges of adulthood.

Energizing Function of Hero Stories

In addition to enriching their followers with the wisdom of hero stories, radical heroic leaders can use hero narratives to energize and inspire others. As we have noted, the recently identified emotion of elevation refers to a form of moral self-efficacy, transforming people into believing they are capable of significant prosocial action (Britton, 2008). Consistent with research on elevation, Kinsella et al. (2015b) propose that heroes serve important life-enhancing functions. Heroes who "behave in ways that benefit others, sometimes at great personal risk, are likely to increase positive feelings towards the hero and others, reminding people of the good in the world" (p. 7). Heroes take risks that inspire us. Franco et al. (2011) argue that in addition to sacrifice, risk-taking differentiates heroism from altruism, with heroes taking risks and making self-sacrificing decisions in ways that altruists do not. This risk-taking aspect of heroism is what makes heroism especially desirable and emotionally inspiring.

We propose that hero stories energize us by healing our psychic wounds, promoting our personal growth, inspiring us to action, and demonstrating the power of charisma in leadership. One way that hero narratives promote healing is through social bonding that results from group storytelling. Ancient humans gathered around campfires for storytelling as a means of establishing social connections. This sense of family, group, or community was, and remains, central to human emotional well-being (Aberson, Healy, & Romero, 2000; Leary & Baumeister, 2000). The content of hero stories also promotes a strong sense of social identity. Effective heroes perform actions that exemplify and affirm the community's most cherished values. The validation of a shared worldview, expressed in storytelling, serves important healing and self-esteem-building functions (Leary & Baumeister, 2000; Solomon et al., 2008).

Group storytelling, we argue, is a quasi-group therapy setting that involves bringing people together to share stories about how an individual (the hero) has overcome challenging, traumatic situations. We believe that hero stories share many of the benefits of group therapy as identified by Yalom and Leszcz (2005). These benefits include the instillation of hope; the relief of knowing that others' share one's emotional experiences; the sharing of information; the development of socialization skills; the acquisition of modeling behavior; the fostering of self-awareness; the building of group cohesiveness; the relief of stress; and the development of a sense of existential meaning about life. The anxiety-buffering role of heroic action is consistent with the tenets of terror management theory (Solomon et al., 2008). Moreover, many 12-step recovery groups, such as Alcoholics Anonymous, also promote healing through the open sharing of members' stories. Some clinical psychologists even use hero stories in their practice to help their clients develop the heroic traits of strength, resilience, and courage (Garloch, 2013).

Psychiatrist Karl Stern (1966) once observed that "the evolution of human growth is an evolution from an absolute need to be loved towards a full readiness to give love" (as cited in Fernandez, 2007, p. 114). Stern's observation is consistent with Erich Fromm's (1956) claim that the ability to love others first requires self-respect and self-love. We believe that Stern (1966) and Fromm (1956) have aptly summarized the transformation that the mythic hero undergoes during the hero journey. Campbell (1949) believed that the hero journey parallels human developmental stages. All young adults, according to Campbell (1949), are driven out of their safe, familiar worlds and into the fearful real world, and "the big question is whether you are going to be able to say a hearty yes to your adventure" (p. 43). Eric Erikson's (1975) stages of development suggest a hero trajectory during the human lifespan, with young adults driven to establish competencies and carve out an identity for themselves. Older adults reach a stage of generativity, which Erikson (1975) defines as people's desire to create things that will outlast them and to give back to the society that has given them so much.

Campbell's (1949) stages of the hero's journey culminate with the gift, boon, or elixir that the hero bestows upon the society from which he originated. Both Campbell (1949) and Erikson (1975) believed that personal transformation is the key to reaching the generativity stage of development and, finally, the apex of integrity. In all good hero stories, the key to achieving transformation is the discovery of an important missing inner quality that has heretofore hindered personal growth. Good heroes use the power of transformation not only to change themselves for the better, but also to transform the world. Campbell (1988) describes the power of mythic transformation in this way: "If you realize what the real problem is—losing yourself, giving yourself to some higher end, or to another—you realize that this itself is the ultimate trial. When we quit thinking primarily about ourselves and our own self-preservation, we undergo a truly heroic transformation of consciousness. And what all the myths have to deal with is transformations of consciousness of one kind or another" (p. 112)

HEROIC LEADERS FOSTER TRANSFORMATIVE GROWTH

The importance of leaders and leadership in fostering a heroic motive in followers is highlighted by Gardner (1995). Gardner (1995) proposed that leaders influence significant numbers of their fellow human beings through their words and example and that they do so through stories that they both relate and embody. Furthermore, the most powerful stories are stories about identity, about the leader's identity and followers' personal identities and the identity of their group. The story concept underlines the fact that leaders frequently offer a dynamic perspective, about where a group has come from, where it is going, and what obstacles it has faced and is facing. Leaders and followers are central and heroic figures in these dramatic narratives. Gardner's (1995) examples include Robert Oppenheimer who successfully led the Manhattan Project to completion by relating, through what he said and what he did, a story of dedicated scientists pushing back the frontiers of knowledge to build a weapon that would win the war against despotism but also, perhaps, make future wars unthinkable. That story was important in mobilizing thousands of young scientists toward the common goal of creating the atomic bomb. Another example is Pope John XXIII, who reached back to the early teachings of Jesus to relate a story about a caring, nonhierarchical, inclusive church that concerned itself with uplifting the human condition.

Gardner (1995) argues, in a way that resonates with Burns' (1978) emphasis on leaders mobilizing followers "in competition or conflict with others," that there are counter-stories to most leaders' narratives. Followers are often presented with competing stories about who they are and what goals and challenges lay ahead. Which stories prevail depends on complex interactions between the nature of the identity story that leaders relate, and the mindset with which followers process competing stories. Gardner (1995) first makes an important distinction between stories that are inclusive versus exclusive. Most of the leaders Gardner (1995) considers in detail told an inclusionary story. The identity they related to their followers embraced the similarity and common humanity of different kinds of people, and their shared challenges. Pope John's simple warmth and humanity recognized the value of non-Catholics and even non-Christians. Working with Soviet and American leaders, including Khrushchev and Kennedy, in the early 1960s, Pope John once said to a Russian diplomat, "I know you are an atheist, but won't you accept an old man's blessing." George Marshall, as Secretary of State in the 1940s, told an inclusionary story about how Americans needed to help Europeans, both former allies and former enemies, after World War II to take the lead in rebuilding the world economy. On the other hand, Hitler told an exclusionary story about a "master race" that was destined to rule the world in part by ridding it of lesser races and groups.

Whether inclusionary or exclusionary stories prevail depends in large measure on the level of sophistication with which potential followers understand the story. Gardner (1995) describes the "unschooled" or five year old mind that tends to see the world in rigid good and evil categories, through what he refers to as a Star Wars mentality. Exclusionary "us versus them" stories appeal to this simple way of thinking. While adults may achieve higher levels of cognitive sophistication, they can be pulled back to a simpler more primitive way of thinking by powerful exclusionary stories. Cognitive development as described by Piaget, where once an individual reaches a more sophisticated level of thinking there is no backsliding, does not quite capture the way people process leaders' stories. A more Freudian perspective incorporates the fact that people can regress to more primitive modes of thinking and feeling, making them open to simple, exclusionary stories. During the 2016 U.S. Presidential election, Donald Trump is said to have appealed to this same simplistic, exclusionary type of thinking (Pahari, 2015).

Gardner's discussion of "minds" that differ in their level of sophistication, and that leaders can pull people back or attempt to pull them forward is entirely consistent with Burns considerations of cognitive, emotional and moral stages of development, and their relevance to transforming leadership. Transforming leaders can be seen to not only raise levels of motivation and morality, but also levels of cognitive processing. In this regard, as Burns

(1978) notes, the theories of Erikson (1975) and Kohlberg (1969) about adult development are highly relevant to our understanding of transforming leadership. In Erikson's (1975) formulation, each stage of adult development offers leaders and followers the possibility of attaining ever higher levels of motivation and morality, that can move people toward Maslow's state of self-transcendence.

According to Kohlberg (1969), the capacity to see the world from multiple perspectives enables post-conventional morality where ethical judgments are not based on conventional wisdom or values but rather one's own carefully deliberated morality based on fundamental ethical principles and values such as justice and equality. The fact that post-conventional morality is based on perspective taking, an orientation that psychological research shows degrades with power, highlights the potential for altruistic, generative behavior among mature adults. People who have reached these higher levels of emotional, cognitive, and moral development described by Erikson (1975), Gardner (1995), and Kohlberg (1969) are likely to have the "resource and motive," in Burns' (1978) terms, to be transforming leaders, raising others as well as themselves to higher levels of motivation and morality. They will have discovered that their powerful need for value and significance propels them to lead and transform others in the direction of values that produce significant, lasting, and positive change.

Mentors and leaders can also use their charisma to exert a transformative effect on their followers. Goethals and Allison (2014) reviewed the transforming leadership of three heroic leaders from the 20th century whom they dubbed "the three kings": Muhammad Ali, Elvis Presley, and Martin Luther King, Jr. These kings radiated powerful charisma that transformed their followers. All three kings had exceptional personas. All three made an emotional connection with their audiences. All three related and embodied compelling stories. All three enacted theatrical leadership that gave people what they wanted and needed. Two of them, King and Ali, used words, delivered in riveting styles, often touching on religious precepts, to influence their followers' thoughts, feelings, and behavior. The three kings used their charisma to transform others, through both their words and their example.

IMPLICATIONS FOR CULTIVATING ETHICAL LEADERSHIP

We believe that our heroic leadership framework has important implications for leadership research and for the development of ethical leadership in organizations. In our view, the most promising attempt to investigate these issues empirically has been undertaken by Kramer (2017). Kramer's (2017) work is based on the idea that the cultivation of heroic leadership begins with the development of *existential courage*. His working definition of existential courage is "the courage associated with the pursuit of longed-for or yearned for identities—even if the pursuit of those identities might be daunting, arduous, audacious, difficult, or challenging." For leaders on the heroic path, existential courage represents their willingness to choose a brand of leadership that accepts, even embraces, the prospect of psychological risks and social dangers in order to grow, thrive, and pursue morally correct action. Existential courage is related to Biswas-Diener's (2012) definition of courage as "the willingness to act toward a moral or worthwhile goal despite the presence of risk, uncertainty, and fear" (p. 10). It also incorporates elements of Staub (2015) definition of moral courage as "the courage to express important values in words and actions, even in the face of opposition, potential disapproval, and ostracism or a violent response" (p. 47).

The goal of Kramer's (2017) work is to help potential leaders develop a conception of their *identity strivings* or *identity work*. Identity work is aimed at cultivating people's intentional pursuit of imagined, valued, and desired future identities (Kramer, 2004). One of the central assumptions of Kramer's (2017) methodology is the idea that nearly everyone possesses the potential for heroic leadership, and for heroism more generally. Consistent with research on heroism, Kramer's (2017) work assumes also that people are largely aware that they are on the hero's journey, and as a result they can benefit from exercises and practices designed to bring elements of the journey into conscious attention (see also Allison & Goethals, 2016).

Using a new method of cultivating existential courage, Kramer (2017) has established an "identity lab" as a setting in which people work individually and collaboratively on their respective identity strivings. The lab is designed as a reflective and experiential resource where individuals can (a) identify their desired future identities, (b) develop an inventory of identity-relevant attributes that support the cultivation of those desired future identities, (c) design behavioral exercises to explore and further develop those self-selected identity attributes, and (d) consolidate their discoveries from these practices through reflection and assessment.

To stimulate his participants' ability to think holistically about their desired future identities, Kramer (2017) asked a recent group to write their own obituaries and eulogies. From these writings, participants gleaned their *personal identities* (e.g., parent, spouse) and *professional identities* (e.g., founder and chief executive office [CEO] of a major tech company). Participants were then instructed to select "one important but challenging or difficult *identity attribute* you perceive as vitally linked to the successful realization of one of these future identities and on which you would like to work now in the context of the identity lab." Participants were then subjected to three phases of heroic leadership training. In Phase 1, they "designed a behavioral experiment intended to stimulate them to strive to be or to become the *opposite* of that *current* characteristic or attribute for some identified time period." They were encouraged to think "outside the box" and to develop "stretch goals" in pursuit of their chosen attribute. Participants were encouraged to research the attribute on which they had chosen to work. If a student wanted to work on developing more empathy, for example, they were told to research what is known about the causes and consequences of empathy.

In Phase 2, participants executed their experiments over the given time period. They were instructed to systematically "audit" the results of their behavioral experiments, thereby keeping track of what they attempted and how well it worked, as well as noting any behavioral, psychological, and social consequences. In Phase 3, participants were asked to reflect back on their overall experiences and to attempt to consolidate their findings from their experiment. They could perform this consolidation privately or with trusted friends and colleagues.

The results were promising in terms of enabling participants to identify and develop several key aspects of effective and heroic leadership. One notable result was that Kramer's (2017) participants experienced enhanced self-perceptions of their creativity and competence at self-change. The behavioral experimental approach was also perceived as powerful, transformative, impactful, and effective at helping participants pursue their identity aspirations. These participants enjoyed a sense of enlarged self-capacity for change, persistence, enormously energized and "re-charged" by their successful experiments. Several participants reported feeling more resilient regarding their prospects for successfully facing future challenges. They expressed exuberance and exhilaration at the perceived success of their work. One participant described the "intense joy," feeling "tremendous zest, especially for the future." The results of this study in existential courage suggests that strategically chosen and carefully constructed behavioral experiments can stimulate individuals to take significant psychological and social risks in order to challenge their current sense of self in the pursuit of a desired future sense of self. Participants reported that the identity laboratory experience significantly increased their leadership skills by making them more cooperative, collaborative, kinder, empathic, generous, compassionate, meaningful, consequential, authentic, ethical, moral, courageous, philosophical, wiser, spiritual, faithful, and transcendent.

Overall, Kramer's (2017) methodology represents a promising new way of helping people develop their most heroic qualities, thereby assisting in producing the personal transformation that is the centerpiece of the classic hero's journey. We believe that organizations can easily adopt this methodology in their training practices for both current and prospective leaders. Such training programs can unleash the heroic potential in organizational members, permitting them to identify their most desired heroic qualities and providing them with the tools and resources to cultivate and apply those qualities.

CONCLUDING THOUGHTS

We began this chapter by emphasizing the dire need for a new type of leadership that is based on heroic transformative development of leaders and followers in organizations. Our chapter has highlighted the many ways that radical heroic leadership can take advantage of the wisdom and insights inherent in hero mythology. The hero narrative, according to Campbell (1949), is designed to teach us that society is not a "perfectly static organization" but represents a "movement of the species forward" (p. 48). During the process of experiencing personal transformation, the hero obtains the "elixir" that empowers and enables her to help guide others on their personal transformative journeys. Having once been mentored, the hero ultimately becomes a mentor to others. As a mentor, the hero's goal is to transform others. This idea is consistent with contemporary theories of leadership that focus on the role of enlightened leaders to transform their followers, elevating them toward greater levels of motivation and morality (e.g., Burns, 1978).

All of the world's most revered leaders have traveled the hero's journey of personal transformation and, in turn, have used their gifts to transform others. Martin Luther King, Jr., came from humble origins to organize the American civil rights movement. He transformed himself and then heroically transformed others, as evinced in his famous quote: "Life's most persistent and urgent question is: what are you doing for others?" (King, 2001, p. 3). The hero's journey also characterizes the lives of indirect leaders such as Helen Keller. Born with illness that left her without sight or hearing, Keller overcame her severe disability to achieve a life of extraordinary philanthropy and humanitarianism. She said, "I long to accomplish a great and noble task, but it is my chief duty to accomplish humble tasks as though they were great and noble" (Wallis, 1983, p. 240). Keller's personal transformation played a role in transforming the world.

A cynic might decry the necessity of assigning the label of "radical" onto a form of leadership that is based on loving others and nurturing their full potential. The current heroism activism movement is based on the idea that every person is capable of heroism, not just great leaders or comic book superheroes (Efthimiou, 2017). Because every person is capable of the kind of self-transformation that this chapter has addressed, it follows that every person is also capable of assisting in the positive transformation of others. Giacalone (2015) expresses this ideal nicely: "Joy and meaning can be achieved only through a process by which we align our behavior toward remembering, understanding and living our gifts, toward sharing them with others for the common good" (p. 81). Giacalone also observes that "We are beings of love, gifted in ways that are truly unique, and yet connected to all that is" (p. 92). We hope that our chapter has illuminated the myriad ways that leaders can dare to be radical in loving and connecting to their followers to a transformative degree.

REFERENCES

Aberson, C. L., Healy, M. R., & Romero, V. L. (2000). Ingroup bias and self-esteem: A meta-analysis. *Personality and Social Psychology Review, 4*, 157–173. doi: 10.1207/S15327957PSPR0402_04

Algoe, S. B., & Haidt, J. (2009). Witnessing excellence in action: The "other-praising" emotions of elevation, gratitude, and admiration. *Journal of Positive Psychology, 4*, 105–127. doi: 10.1080/17439760802650519

Allison, S. T., & Goethals, G. R. (2011). *Heroes: What they do and why we need them.* New York, NY: Oxford University Press.

Allison, S. T., & Goethals, G. R. (2013). *Heroic leadership: An influence taxonomy of 100 exceptional individuals.* New York, NY: Routledge.

Allison, S. T., & Goethals, G. R. (2014). "Now he belongs to the ages": The heroic leadership dynamic and deep narratives of greatness. In G. Goethals, S. Allison, R. Kramer, & D. Messick (Eds.), *Conceptions of leadership: Enduring ideas and emerging insights.* New York, NY: Palgrave Macmillan.

Allison, S. T., & Goethals, G. R. (2016). Hero worship: The elevation of the human spirit. *Journal for the Theory of Social Behaviour, 46*, 187–210.

Allison, S. T., & Goethals, G. R. (2017). The hero's transformation. In S. Allison, G. Goethals, & R. Kramer (Eds.), *Handbook of heroism and heroic leadership.* New York, NY: Routledge.

Allison, S. T., & Smith, G. (2015). *Reel heroes & villains.* Richmond, VA: Agile Writer Press.

Allison, S. T., Goethals, G. R., & Kramer, R. M. (Eds.). (2017). *Handbook of heroism and heroic leadership.* New York, NY: Routledge.

Bennett, S. H. (2003). *Radical pacifism: The war resisters league and Gandhian nonviolence in America, 1915–1963.* Syracuse, NY: Syracuse University Press.

Bettelheim, B. (1976). *The uses of enchantment: The meaning and importance of fairy tales.* New York, NY: Knopf. doi: 10.1037/e309842005-008

Biswas-Diener, R. (2012). *The courage quotient: How science can make you braver.* San Francisco, CA: Jossey-Bass.

Boje, D. M. (1995). Stories of the storytelling organization: A postmodern analysis of Disney as Tamara-land. *Academy of Management Journal, 38*, 997–1035. doi: 10.2307/256618

Britton, K. (2008, May 7). Awe and elevation. *Positive Psychology News Daily.* Retrieved from http://positivepsychologynews.com/news/kathryn-britton/20080507738

Burns, J. M. (1978). *Leadership.* New York, NY: Harper & Row.

Cajete, G., Eder, D., & Holyan, R. (2010). *Life lessons through storytelling: Children's exploration of ethics*. Bloomington, IN: Indiana UP.

Campbell, J. (1949). *The hero with a thousand faces*. New York, NY: New World Library.

Campbell, J. (1988). *The power of myth, with Bill Moyers*. New York, NY: Doubleday.

Caruso, D. R., Fleming, K., & Spector, E. D. (2014). Emotional intelligence and leadership. In G. R. Goethals, S. T. Allison, R. Kramer, & D. Messick (Eds.), *Conceptions of leadership: Emerging ideas and enduring insights*. New York, NY: Palgrave Macmillan. doi: 10.1057/9781137472038.0010

Csikszentmihalyi, M., Condren, M., & Lebuda, I. (2017). Deviant heroes and social heroism in everyday life: Activists and artists. In S. Allison, G. Goethals, & R. Kramer (Eds.), *Handbook of heroism and heroic leadership*. New York, NY: Routledge.

Durant, W. (2002). *Heroes of history: A brief history of civilization from ancient times to the dawn of the modern age*. New York, NY: Simon and Schuster.

Efthimiou, O. (2017). The hero organism: Advancing the embodiment of heroism thesis in the 21st century. In S. T. Allison, G. R. Goethals, & R. M. Kramer (Eds.), *Handbook of heroism and heroic leadership*. New York, NY: Routledge.

Erikson, E. H. (1975). *Life history and the historical moment*. New York, NY: Norton.

Fagan, B. (2014). *Rising oceans: The past, present, and future of rising sea levels*. London, England: Bloomsbury Press.

Fernandez, I. (2007). *Through the eye of a needle: Transforming relationships*. New York, NY: New Dawn Press.

Franco, Z. E., Blau, K., & Zimbardo, P. G. (2011). Heroism: A conceptual analysis and differentiation between heroic action and altruism. *Review of General Psychology*. 1–15. doi: 10.1037/a0022672

Fromm, E. (1956). *The art of loving*. New York, NY: Harper & Row.

Gardner, H. E. (1995). *Leading minds: An anatomy of leadership*. New York, NY: Basic Books.

Garloch, K. (2013). *Charlotte psychologists use movie and comic book superheroes to help clients find strength and resiliency*. Retrieved from http://www.charlotteobserver.com/2013/09/02/4276377/charlotte-psychologists-use-movie.html#.UpksHY1RYT7

Giacalone, R. A. (2015). *The essence of living: Three stories on the path to a meaningful life*. Richmond, VA: Thinkable Press.

Goethals, G. R. & Allison, S. T. (2012). Making heroes: The construction of courage, competence and virtue. *Advances in Experimental Social Psychology, 46*, 183–235. doi: 10.1016/B978-0-12-394281-4.00004-0

Goethals, G. R., & Allison, S. T. (2014). Kings and charisma, Lincoln and leadership: An evolutionary perspective. In G. R. Goethals, S. T. Allison, R. Kramer, & D. Messick (Eds.), *Conceptions of leadership: Enduring ideas and emerging insights*. New York, NY: Palgrave Macmillan. doi: 10.1057/9781137472038.0011

Goethals, G. R., & Allison, S. T. (2017). Transforming motives and mentors: The heroic leadership of James MacGregor Burns. In G. R. Goethals (Ed.), *Politics, ethics and change: The legacy of James MacGregor Burns*. Northampton, MA: Edward Elgar.

Green, M. C., & Brock, T. C. (2005). Persuasiveness of narratives. In M. C. Green & T. C. Brock (Eds.), *Persuasion: Psychological insights and perspectives* (pp. 117–142). Thousand Oaks, CA: SAGE.

Haidt, J. (2003). Elevation and the positive psychology of morality. In C. L. M. Keyes & J. Haidt (Eds.), *Flourishing: Positive psychology and the life well-lived* (pp. 275–289). Washington DC: American Psychological Association.

Haidt, J. (2012). *The righteous mind: Why good people are divided by politics and religion.* New York, NY: Pantheon.

Hamilton, E. (1999). *Mythology: Timeless tales of gods and heroes.* New York, NY: Grand Central.

Hoffman, B. (2013). *Inside terrorism.* New York, NY: Columbia University Press.

Ingraham, C. (2015, August 26). We're now averaging more than one mass shooting per day in 2015. *The Washington Post*, pp. 37–39.

Kerenyi, K. (1959, Reissue edition 1978). *The heroes of the Greeks.* New YorK, NY: Thames & Hudson.

King, C. S. (2001). *The words of Martin Luther King, Jr.* New York, NY: William Morrow.

Kinsella, E. L., Ritchie, T. D., & Igou, E. R. (2015a). Zeroing in on heroes: A prototype analysis of hero features. *Journal of Personality and Social Psychology, 108,* 114–127. doi: 10.1037/a0038463

Kinsella, E. L., Ritchie, T. D., & Igou, E. R. (2015b). Lay perspectives on the social and psychological functions of heroes. *Frontiers in Psychology, 6,* 130. doi: 10.3389/fpsyg.2015.00130

Kohlberg, L. (1969). Stage and sequence: The cognitive-developmental approach to socialization. In D. A. Goslin (Ed.), *Handbook of socialization: Theory and research.* Boston, MA: Houghton Mifflin.

Kramer, R. M. (2004). The imperatives of identity: The role of identity in leader judgment and decision making. In D. van Knippenberg & M. A. Hogg (Eds.), *Leadership and power: Identity processes in groups and organizations,* (pp. 184–197). London, England: SAGE.

Kramer, R. M. (2017). To be or not to be? Existential courage and the quest for identity. In S. T. Allison, G. R. Goethals, & R. M. Kramer (Eds.), *Handbook of heroism and heroic leadership.* New York, NY: Routledge.

Leary, M. R., & Baumeister, R. F. (2000). The nature and function of self-esteem: Sociometer theory. In M. Zanna (Ed.), *Advances in Experimental Social Psychology,* Vol. 32 (pp. 1–62). San Diego, CA: Academic Press.

Maslow, A. (1943). A theory of human motivation. *Psychological Review, 50,* 370–396.

McAdams, D. P. (1997). *The stories we live by: Personal myths and the making of the self.* New York, NY: Guilford Press.

McAdams, D. P. (2014). Leaders and their life stories: Obama, Bush, and narratives of redemption. In G. R. Goethals, S. T. Allison, R. Kramer, & D. Messick (Eds.), *Conceptions of leadership: Enduring ideas and emerging insights.* New York, NY: Palgrave Macmillan. doi: 10.1057/9781137472038.0014

Mayer, J. D., Salovey, P., Caruso, D. L., & Sitarenios, G. (2001). Emotional intelligence as a standard intelligence. *Emotion, 1,* 232–242. doi: 10.1037/1528-3542.1.3.232

Miller, A. G. (Ed.). (2005). *The social psychology of good and evil.* New York, NY: The Guilford Press.

Moxnes, P. (1999). Deep roles: Twelve primordial roles of mind and organization. *Human Relations, 52,* 1427–1444. doi: 10.1177/001872679905201104

Moxnes, P, (2012). Deep roles: Are they real? A model of positive and negative interpersonal fantasies. *International Journal of Psychology,* Special Issue: SI Supplement, 1(47), 724–725.

Pahari, A. (2015, December 23). "Make America exclusionary again": The threat of Donald Trump. Retrieved from http://theodysseyonline.com/mount-holyoke/america-exclusionary-threat-donald-trump/255038

Price, R. (1978). *A palpable God.* New York, NY: Atheneum, p. 3.

Roberts, C. (2013). *The ocean of life: The fate of man and the sea.* New York, NY: Penguin Books.

Rohr, R. (2011). *Falling upward.* New York, NY: Jossey-Bass.

Sagan, C. (1980). *Cosmos: A personal voyage* [Television series]. In G. Andorfer & R. McCain (Producers). Arlington, VA: PBS.

Solomon, S., Cohen, F., Greenberg, J., & Pyszczynski, T. (2008). Knocking on heaven's door: The social psychological dynamics of charismatic leadership. In C. L. Hoyt, G. R. Goethals, & D. R. Forsyth (Eds.), *Leadership at the crossroads, (Vol. 1). Leadership and psychology* (pp. 45–61). Westport, CT: Praeger.

Staub, E. (2015). *The roots of goodness and resistance to evil.* New York, NY: Oxford University Press.

Stern, K. (1966, November 18). *Institute of man symposium on neurosis and personal growth.* Duquesne University, Pittsburgh, PA.

Sternberg, R. J. (2011). Leadership and education: Leadership stories. In M. Harvey & R. Riggio (Eds.), *Leadership studies: The dialogue of disciplines* (pp. 88–1-1). New York, NY: Edward Elgar. doi: 10.4337/9780857936486.00019

The Hero in the Subway. (2007, January 5). *The New York Times.* Retrieved from http://www.nytimes.com/2007/01/05/opinion/l05hero.html?_r=0

Wallis, C. L. (1983). *The treasure chest.* New York, NY: HarperCollins.

Yalom, I., & Leszcz, M. (2005). *Theory and practice of group psychotherapy.* New York, NY: Basic Books.

Wyer, R. S. (1995). *Knowledge and memory: The real story.* New York, NY: Erlbaum.

Zimbardo, P. (2008). *The Lucifer effect: Understanding how good people turn evil.* New York, NY: Random House.

CHAPTER 9

RETHINKING ETHICAL LEADERSHIP USING PROCESS METAPHYSICS[1]

Mark Dibben
University of Tasmania

Martin Wood
RMIT University

Rob Macklin
University of Tasmania

Ronald E. Riggio
Claremont McKenna College

ABSTRACT

Ideas and knowledge of ethical leadership as something accomplished between the leader and the led, are becoming increasingly valuable. We propose a view from process philosophy in which relations determine individual leaders and followers, not the reverse. Each individual is a locus, in which a plurality of relational determinations interacts; the ethics of leadership is situated within this. The process perspective views leadership as an occasion

Radical Thoughts on Ethical Leadership, pages 169–198
Copyright © 2017 by Information Age Publishing
All rights of reproduction in any form reserved.

we experience subjectively within ourselves, instead of simply looking at it objectively from the outside. Such a process perspective, grasping leadership as an internally complex occasion of experience, has implications for our understanding of what it means to be an ethical leader.

Leaders and leadership are cornerstones of the human endeavor. Much that has been achieved by humanity can be traced to our capacity to lead and be led. Arguably, much of the good done has been founded on sound leadership ethics. Yet the world we now live in is deeply constrained by the effects of business that has focused on a rationalism that gives priority to economic over ecological concerns. We live at the end of an age and within an ecological crisis (Cobb, 2014) that, at least in part, was caused by established understandings of "who" leaders are, what leaders do, and how they might be genuinely ethical. New ways of understanding leadership are required to navigate a new age.

We argue in this chapter that one of these new ways may be found in a process-relational worldview that takes as its basis the philosophical work of the Cambridge Mathematician and Harvard Philosopher Alfred North Whitehead. Using a process-relational approach we begin to develop an understanding of ethical leadership that is not only intimately connected to what it means to be a human being but also what it means for leaders to positively influence our humane becoming. First, we provide a brief introduction to process thought. Second, we consider some of the traditional and indeed entrenched conceptualizations of leadership and look to unpack the problems therein. Third, we explore how leadership might be understood from within a process perspective. Fourth, we re-frame relational leadership, and thus ethical leadership, from this process perspective. In doing so, we consider a number of contemporary ethical leadership issues such as the moral aspect of leadership and the ever-present question of power.

PROCESS PHILOSOPHY

Process thought traces its origins as far back as Heraclitus' "you never step into the same waters twice"; reality is perpetual change. This is important for our understanding of leadership and ethics, because it emphasizes the fact that organizations constantly evolve and adapt as a result of the thinking of, and the relations between, their key strategic actors. Processual ideas have found emphasis in the work of a number of philosophers, including Spinoza, Leibniz, Heidegger, Bergson, Mead, James, Pierce, Deleuze and Whitehead (see e.g., Cobb, 2008b; Griffin, 1988; also Helin, Hernes, Hjorth, & Holt, 2014). Of all these, it is the work of Alfred North Whitehead (1929/1978), particularly as envisioned in his magnum opus "Process and Reality: An Essay in Cosmology" (1929/1978) that is arguably the most comprehensive rendering of processual thought.

To provide a brief exposition, we shall first consider process thought in the context of the most obvious connection we standardly make to process and change, namely the question of time (see Dawson and Sykes, 2016). Everyday understandings of time are often confused by the question of space; relational time is intimately connected to our appreciation of the changefulness of collections of things (Capek, 1976). For example, the vast collection of cells we recognize as people, change over time. An extension of this is to think of time as the coordinate along which events are spread, such that from our experience of yesterday, today and tomorrow, it is irreversible (Griffin, 1986; Prigogine, 1980).

The connection to space is made more immediate with the notion of relativity (ie., rather than time being absolute, it alters in relation to the speed travelled between two given points of the one observing it; Bohm, 1980; Angel, 1980); on this view it is not possible to draw a clear-cut distinction between space and time. What is rather more clear-cut is that, despite the time equations of Newton, Maxwell and quantum physics conceptually allowing for time to run backwards (ie., $-t$ as well as t), in practical application a region or boundary condition always needs to be selected to allow the calculation of the equations, by setting the values of the other variables in the equations (Jungerman, 2000). As soon as these values are set, the equations have inherent within them the assumption that time begins; there is an inherent causality in natural processes (Bohm, 1957). Whether or not one subscribes to the view that time is a primary condition (ie., it is real in and of itself) or a secondary or relative condition of other real things (see also e.g., Fraser, 1982), real systems are irreversible. This means that, while the past changes insofar as it is perpetually added to moment by moment, what is already in the past cannot in reality (as opposed to theory) be changed.

From the Whiteheadian process view, therefore, whatever is in the past now was at one moment in the present, and this accords with the irreversible view of time outlined above. The key feature is that at the moment it was in the present, that present is not characterised as a substantive object but rather as an experiencing subject and its experience is in large part that of its relation to the past-as-object. As Whitehead (1929/1978, p. 88) explains, his process "philosophy of organism"

> is the inversion of Kant's philosophy. *The Critique of Pure Reason* describes the process by which subjective data pass into the appearance of an objective world. The philosophy of organism seeks to describe how objective data pass into subjective satisfaction, and how order in the objective data provides intensity in the subjective satisfaction. For Kant, the world emerges from

the subject; for the philosophy of organism, the subject emerges from the world—a superject rather than a "subject."

For Whitehead (1929/1978), the universe consists in the now, and is a myriad of subjects. It follows, in Whitehead's "concept of the material world, space is not absolute, matter is not ultimate... Instead, relations between nonmaterial geometrical entities are at the base of a relational theory of space" (Desmet & Eastman, 2008, p. 238). The closest Whitehead comes to "space-time," what he calls "the extensive continuum," is construed as potential rather than actual (Cobb, 2008b). This is because his thinking was based on geometry, in which he was expert (Lowe, 1990) and from which he sought to "build a bridge between the apparent space of immediate perception and the physical space of mathematical abstraction" (Desmet & Eastman, 2008, p. 238; see also Bracken, 2014).

Since Whitehead (1929/1978) was clear that he "fully accepts Descartes discovery that subjective experiencing is the primary metaphysical situation that is presented... for analysis," objectification is a "derivative abstraction [that is] delusive as a metaphysical starting point (p. 160; also Lango, 2008). The subjective experience of relations is rather less delusionary, and Whitehead (1929/1978) steps us towards this by arguing the principle of relativity is best stated as "it belongs to the nature of a 'being' that it is a potential for every 'becoming'" (p. 22). Much current work using aspects of his thought in management tends to hold to Robert Cooper's (1976) original notion of the "open field" as "the space between." That is, and although Cooper's (1976) process form coincides with novelty and denies existing structures, at best, there is a focus on the minutiae of process in terms of the relations between things (also 1993 and 2005).

This approach to appreciating the nature of reality entails an understanding that experience is always active, not passive (Griffin, 2008). This is immediately counter-intuitive but, put simply, it is not what happens to us that counts (what in process thought is termed the "external relation"), but rather what we make of what happens to us for ourselves and others (the internal relation; Wood & Dibben, 2015; Cobb, 2007a; 2008a). In this view, our common understandings of past, present, and future are not aspects of Whitehead's extensive continuum, but rather are better understood in a relational sense as extensively connected. This relational connectedness is made real as "serially ordered societies of occasions of experience" (Whitehead, 1929/1978), such that two occasions occurring at the same moment cannot be directly causally related. In this, Whitehead is perhaps the ultimate sociologist of the individual (Wood & Dibben, 2015; Halewood, 2014).

For Whitehead, "duration" just precisely is that facet of reality in which contiguous occasions are contemporaneous (Cobb, 2008b). The present occasion always takes past occasions into account and, in its becoming, turns them to its own use. In this sense, the present is "perpetually per-ishing" but is "immortal in the past," such that "the many become one, and are increased by one," *ad infinitum* (McDaniel, 2015; Sherburne, 1966; Whitehead, 1929/1978). Thus the past is all around us, but it is not quite the past because there is a novel aspect to it, which just precisely makes it the present—which then in the next moment is past. For Whitehead, the future is undecided since creativity is the ultimate feature of reality; even God has a "primordial" (passively ever-the-same) and a "consequent (actively changing-in-response) nature (Cobb, 2007b; Hartshorne, 1984; Whitehead, 1929/1978). Crucially, for social science in general and man-agement in particular, this means all occasions are inherently active sub-jects in their experience of becoming; they are only passive objects once they have perished to the past, for subsequent occasions to appreciate (see above; Whitehead, 1929/1978, p. 88, Dibben, 2015; Neesham & Dibben, 2012). Almost without exception, the world is a world of fleetingly present experiential subjects, not of permanently present material objects; process philosophy closes the quality–quantity, man–nature and mind–matter bi-furcation gaps of classical science that still largely dominate the intellectual tradition that underpins management as a social science.

The full complexities of Whitehead's (1929/1978; also 1927, 1933, 1956, 1967A and 1967b) panexperientialist process metaphysics are beyond this chapter but in some respects it bears comparison with that of Henri Berg-son (1991). Aspects of it have formed the basis of a great deal of work, notably by Deleuze (1994) and a range of management writers in recent times relying largely on him, such as the work of Hari Tsoukas and Robert Chia (e.g., 2002; see also Langley and Tsouas, 2017), and more recently Tor Hernes (2014; also 2007). In this regard, much current work using aspects of his thought in management tends to hold to Robert Cooper's (1976) original notion of the "open field" as "the space between." That is, and although Cooper's (1976) process form coincides with novelty and denies existing structures, at best there is a focus on the minutiae of process in terms of the relations between things. It will already be apparent, however, that this view—which forms the basis of recent work in management stud-ies—is insufficient for a complete appreciation of the potential of process thought in management and, from this, ethical leadership. This is because it has led to process thinking in management theory being reliant on the work of management writers who use certain aspects of Whitehead, Berg-son, and Deleuze's work (e.g., Carlsen, 2006), rather than being directly reliant on the work of the philosophers themselves and, just as importantly, on the secondary literature in philosophy that has grown up around them.

The problem with this is that, quite understandably, people are lured back to the predominant metaphysics of our time, that which holds to the idea that there are, and only are, thoroughly passive objects that are largely unrelated to each other. While this does not stand up to serious-minded common sense scrutiny (see Griffin, 2008), it nonetheless is the dominant worldview not so much of the sciences—which thanks to work in theoretical physics and epigenetics that has uncovered the processual nature of phenomena—but rather of the social sciences.

Process thought, by contrast to the Descartian predilection, is founded in the principle of actively experiencing subjects; this moves us far beyond that which appears presentationally immediate to us. In process thought, to be conscious of something one must first have experienced it. "Consciousness presupposes experience, and not experience consciousness" (Whitehead, 1929/1978, p. 83). This is not quite as counter-intuitive as it at first seems. After all, we know that we do not need to be conscious of gravity, to experience its effects. Otherwise, we would be floating around all the time, until the moment we thought "gravity!"—at which point we would come crashing to earth. There we would presumably be so preoccupied nursing sore limbs we would forget gravity whereupon we would soar into the air. Another obvious example concerns the way the skin around our jowls sags as we grow older, the effect of gravity on the cells. The facelift industry would not exist if our bodies only experienced the effect of gravity when we thought about it.

For process thought, there is an interesting connection between time and consciousness. Work in physics has long since understood that the light from stars takes light-years to reach us since they are often billions of miles away, and thus what we see is the star as it was when the light left the star, rather than the star as it is at the moment we see it; we are looking into the past. This principle holds even for the smallest gap: The light that bounces from the computer screen into the iris, is then converted by the brain into an image that we first appreciate as a shape that we then consciously recognize as a computer, left the computer long before we are conscious of it. The past is all around us, then, but in the immediacy of the *now* an aspect of novelty is brought to bear. That aspect of novelty consists in what we make of what happens to us for ourselves and others. For Whitehead (1929/1978, p. 21) such novelty, or creativity, extends far beyond us. It is the ultimate category of metaphysics; creativity, inherent novelty, is the very essence of the universe.

This is quite different to more commonly viewed understandings of process (i.e., "change"), which are happy to maintain that things first are, then they change, then they are stable again as something else. Process thought argues in contrast that individual occasions are, in and of themselves, dynamic acts of experience—what Whitehead (1929/1978. p. 7) termed actual occasions in *concrescence* (i.e., their momentary coming into existence). This means that the sorts of things that seem to endure through time—what we ordinarily call individuals—are better thought of as (what are generally termed in process metaphysics) "serially ordered societies of occasions of experience" (e.g., Cobb & Griffin, 1976). As Neesham and Dibben (2012, pp. 72–73) have noted, an actual occasion in concrescence

> is the "self-enjoyment of being one among many, and of being one arising out of the composition of many" (Whitehead, 1929/1978: 220). In this sense, enjoyment is not necessarily anything conscious or anything intrinsically and exclusively the preserve of higher grade animal bodies. For Whiteheadian process thought, an experience of subjective unity is an occasion's subjective enjoyment of its very existence, in that "the experience enjoyed by an actual entity [is] what the actual entity is, for itself" (Whitehead, 1929/1978: 81). Which is to say that the experience each occasion has is of the intrinsic value inherent in its actualisation, its capacity to be part of a wider community that informs the concrescence of future occasions. Once its process is completed (is in the past), that unit of process then becomes an object for new process subsequent to it to take into account as part of its enjoyment of an inner reality in and for itself.

While the foregoing is inevitably an incomplete account, it is nonetheless sufficient to appreciate that for process philosophers, when fully worked-through, Whitehead's contribution is to reveal an inherently active, intra-connected, fully relational, and ever evolving, open (ie., not externally predetermined) universe (Phipps, 2009; Jungerman, 2000). Using this understanding, "organization" can be rendered in process terms not just as verb or adverb, but as noun (Dibben, 2009). In sum, for Whitehead, reality is founded on momentary events (cf. Weik, 2004, p. 306) although unlike Deleuze, Whitehead never used the term "event" in any technical sense. A wedding is an event for Whitehead just as it is for us. That is, technically speaking, what we tend to understand as an event would for Whitehead consist of a multiplicity of "durations," which we retrospectively or prospectively artificially delineate into a unit of analysis for descriptive, explanatory, or analytical purposes; we will pick this point up and deal with it in more detail later in the chapter. Before that, and having now provided a very basic overview of process philosophy as the basis for our radical approach to ethical leadership, we will next ground the idea in the established leadership literature in terms of what sparked our new approach and what informs it; and finally provide some insight into the utility of our approach for other researchers, managers/administrators, and organizations at large.

TRADITIONAL CONCEPTUALIZATIONS OF LEADERSHIP

It is extremely hard to critique or displace powerful and very rational theories underlying leadership research. Nevertheless, a problem is that past studies (see, e.g., Bass, 1985, 1990; Burns, 1978; Conger & Kanungo, 1998; Meindl, Ehrlich, & Dukerich, 1985) focused almost exclusively on the insights psychology provides into leadership, both as a field of study and an area of practice. Psychological research and theorizing posit an elementary unit—an individual leader—upon which leadership is accomplished and to which organizational work is reducible (but see Meindl et al., 1985). However, by conceptualizing leadership as a property of individual leaders and their behaviors, a psychological interpretation sets leaders apart, grading them as different, affirming a leader in his or her position. Too often, researchers highlight what is interesting and important in theory and practice without fully appreciating leadership as something beyond the "heroic" or "great man" views of "the leader."

Earlier studies by Blake and Mouton (1964), Fiedler (1967), and Hersey and Blanchard (1977) did challenge conventional theories and practices and offered critical insights into the potential pitfalls of examining personal and behavioral characteristics alone. Because of their original work, most contemporary research has an explicit focus on the relation between leaders and followers. The more visible approaches pay attention to the beliefs and values followers ascribe to leaders (Hogg, 2001; Lord & Smith, 1983; Meindl et al., 1985), and the relationship between transformational vision and the charismatic (Bass, 1985; Bass & Avolio, 1993; Conger, 1989; Klein & House, 1995). Subsequent studies place importance on followership (Collinson, 2006), and shared or group leadership processes (Gronn, 2002; Pearce & Conger, 2002; also Bolden, 2006 and Bolden & Gosling, 2011). A substantial body of empirical work has also drawn on organizational role (Dansereau, Graen, & Haga, 1975; Dienesch & Liden, 1986; Liden & Graen, 1980) and social exchange theory (Graen & Uhl-Bien, 1995; Keller and Dansereau, 1995; Scandura & Graen, 1984; Sparrowe & Liden, 1997) to understand how exchange relationships develop between the leader and the led.

An examination of the literature, thus, quickly reveals an underlying assumption that leaders and followers jointly affect leadership (Brewer & Gardner, 1996; Graen & Uhl-Bien, 1995; Hogg, 2001; Klein & House, 1995). However, most of the research in this area limits its attention to the idea of interactions extending across the leader/follower interface. Very little, if any, attention is given to how a relation determines its terms, and not the reverse (cf. Drath, McCauley, Palus, & Van Velsor, 2008; Hosking, Dachler, & Gergen, 1995; Uhl-Bien, 2006).

While they do permit a connection of the leader and the led, inter-subjective "relationship-based" (Graen & Uhl-Bien, 1995) approaches perceive ideas of leadership in terms of "clear cut" individuals (Whitehead, 1929/1978), or groups, each capable of existing separately in their own right and each determining their own relations. In fact, inter-subjective relationship-based theories seem to commit a tautology, or else a logical fallacy, which holds well only because leadership is read into the content of the process which actually conditions it. In such a context, research does nothing but establish a series of relations between individuals or groups but neglects to show how such relations determine these terms. Researchers (Hosking, 1988; Hosking et al., 1995; Uhl-Bien, 2006; Uhl-Bien & Ospina, 2012; for a recent literature review see Denis, Langley, & Sergi, 2012) wanting to focus on relations more directly believe in processes of social construction and their implications for understanding the course of leadership. It is to this that we now turn.

LEADERSHIP RELATIONSHIPS

As process thinkers, we note that it is common enough for contemporary mainstream research to articulate leadership as the product of relationships between leaders and followers (Cunliffe & Eriksen, 2011; Hosking, 1988; Hosking et al., 1995; Uhl-Bien, 2006; Uhl-Bien & Ospina, 2012). The original elaboration of relationship-based approaches to leadership lies in early research (Blake & Mouton, 1964; Fiedler, 1967; Hersey & Blanchard, 1977) suggesting that leadership effectiveness is contingent upon both an internal organizational context and the external environment. The contingency perspective of leadership had wide currency up to the 1980s and most streams of work coming later have drawn on it to underline the importance of the relationship between leaders, followers and organizational outcomes (see e.g., Bennis, 2007).

One of the most familiar recent approaches to "relational leadership" is leader-member exchange (LMX) theory (Dienesch & Liden, 1986; Graen & Uhl-Bien, 1995; Sparrowe & Liden, 1997; for meta analyses see also Dulebohn et al., 2012; Gerstner & Day, 1997). An important feature of LMX theory is its emphasis on manager-subordinate relationships rather than on individual behavior. Drawing from role theory (Dansereau et al., 1975; Dienesch & Liden, 1986; Liden & Graen, 1980) and social exchange theory (Graen & Uhl-Bien, 1995; Scandura & Graen, 1984; Sparrowe & Liden, 1997), LMX research shows that leaders and managers develop different quality relationships with members of their teams (Dansereau et al., 1975; Graen & Uhl-Bien, 1995; Dansereau, 1995). Managers and team members use a dyadic process to evaluate one another through a series of role taking and role making stages (Graen & Scandura, 1987). Essentially, effective leadership develops when the quality of these relationships is high (Dulebohn, Bommer, Liden, Brouer, & Ferris, 2012; Gerstner & Day, 1997).

Considering how managers and subordinates gauge interpersonal exchanges opens up ways of seeing leadership as a result of everyday talk and interaction (Korsgaard, Roberson, & Rymph, 1998). How leaders and followers employ language effectively so they can define and shape the meaning of formal and informal situations (Smircich & Morgan, 1982) is a key issue of research on "framing" (Fairhurst 2005, 2010; Fairhurst

& Uhl-Bien, 2012; Shotter & Cunliffe, 2003). Seeing leadership in terms of framing, avoids casting leaders and followers in specific positions and roles that exist independently from the interactional behavior that bring their framing of personal visions and priorities and formal policies and procedures to life by means of everyday talk and interaction. Because roles are typically not held in advance of the interactional behavior, subordinates can meet a leader's attempt to frame the situation with acceptance or rejection: "Each turn at talk is coded as to whether it asserts control, acquiesces or requests control, or neutralizes the control move of the previous utterance" (Fairhurst, 2004, p. 339).

PROBLEMS WITH RELATIONAL LEADERSHIP RESEARCH

The ability to frame reality provides insight into the relationship between leaders and followers in here-and-now situations. However, scholars also need to be aware that discursively based social constructions, as exemplified by Fairhurst's (2007) approach (see also Fairhurst & Uhl-Bien, 2012), tend to conceive leadership in terms of external relations between distinct and self-contained leaders and followers. Too often, and with few exceptions, discursive accounts take leadership to be an inter-subjective performance, constructed through talk and text. Our point is that, while discursively constructed understandings might help us create leadership through language and discourse, the construction has not come from direct contact with experience itself but from analysis. In a sense, framing the meaning of a situation imposes a sort of intellectual "strait jacket" for the mind that stifles the perception of affective experience.

Mistaking the framing of leadership for leadership itself introduces a great deal of confusion. Framing expresses leadership in general communication concepts but leadership is not reducible to sentences and propositions (Tourish, 2014). Leadership is more than leaders, managers, and subordinates performing and enacting discourses. As Whitehead (1956) writes:

> Some of us struggle to find words to express our ideas. If the words and their order together constitute the ideas, how does the struggle arise? We should then be struggling to obtain ideas, whereas we are conscious of ideas verbally unexpressed. (p. 49)

In short, language and discourse are expressions of leadership, not its essence (cf. Whitehead, 1956). For Whitehead (1929/1978), language remains only a technical "approximation to the general truths" of experience (p. 13). Thus, extending from Whitehead (1929/1978), the only possible start for knowledge of leadership must be with experience.

Some scholars (Bradbury & Lichtenstein, 2000; Dibben, 2009; Drath et al., 2008; Hosking, 1988; Hosking et al., 1995; Koivunen, 2007; Uhl-Bien, 2006; Wood, 2005, Wood & Ladkin, 2008; for a recent review see Denis et al., 2012) see leadership as a center of affective and cognitive experience rather than a position or role taken by people possessing their own thoughts, emotions, and purposes. These commentators describe relationships as encounters or passages of intensity that produce leaders and followers as factors of activity and not as "clear-cut" connections produced by the efforts put into them by clear-cut individuals already given to or lying in the way of experience. Seeing leadership as a direct encounter with experience poses questions about the adequacy of research that speaks of relations in exchange-based terms and demands an investigation of leadership as an intra-subjective (rather than merely inter-subjective) process in the midst of things and (immanent) relations.

Further, because the event field (Bracken, 1989) individuates leadership in many ways, we cannot give a specific position or role directly to a distinct and self-contained figure in advance. Leaders have no essence or substances beyond exhibiting those characteristics that cause us to see, feel, and think about them in a particular "occasion of experience" (Whitehead, 1967a, p. 176). The lived experience of leadership is difficult to perceive because classic and conventional approaches persist in the quasi-objective study of some sort of dialectical interaction between distinct and self-contained leaders and followers, rather than the process constituting their becoming. In the following section we offer an alternative, affective process.

LEADERSHIP AS PROCESS

Relationship-based thinkers have shown us how cozy images of functional relationships between leaders and followers falsely acquire an air of authority and objectivity. These images make individual leaders seem "natural," a causal law, and part of the necessary structures of reality. Instead, they point out how values and roles are often social and personal constructs. Unfortunately, in doing so, some thinkers seem at times to deny that we have any real connection to the world "out there"; that the "real" world is only that world we construct. As process thinkers, how might we respond?

Set against process ontology, which is replete with explanations of the fallacies of presentational immediacy, objectification, and simple location (Whitehead, 1929/1978), etc., studies examining leadership as a shared property between extrinsically related terms find it difficult to comprehensively understand the fundamental nature of internal relations. According to Fairhurst (2004), following Hosking (1988) and colleagues (Hosking et al., 1995), analyses of external relations traditionally take an entity or substance view of reality. This views leadership as an apparent unfolding of real qualities inhering in individually distinct and self-contained leaders and followers.

Entity-based views have the advantage of giving us an objective means of examining the role played by leaders and the expectations of employees at work. Even so, as we have argued, it gives a false sense of intellectual security that only ends up stifling the life out of leadership (Bergson, 1983). Here, the emphasis is on processes of leadership always underway as "moment[s] of interaction frozen in time" (Fairhurst, 2004, p. 341). This simple "fixing" of process—"reality caught in flight" (Pettigrew, 1997, p. 338)—involves reaching beneath the surface appearance of processes to extract supposedly underlying mechanisms driving leadership. Yet, as Whitehead (1929/1978) reminds us, it is a fallacy to imagine abstract conceptions concretely instantiating in the actual process of leadership, removed from the wider context of its occurrence.

We might not be able to think without postulating an arrangement of leaders and followers as the objects of ordinary perception—leaders seem to act toward followers and followers seem to respond to leaders—but we ought not to be deceived into treating these impressions as fundamental things: "they are tendencies, and not things" (Bergson, 1983, p. 135). By contrast, we take the position that the terms "leader" and "follower" are simply an intellectual shorthand for a more fundamental type of internal relation at work behind the scenes. A process view removes leadership entirely from belonging to a person or group of persons—now its "substance" is "relational" (Whitehead, 1929/1978, p. 57)—and invites us to see and to feel leadership as a genuine occasion (Whitehead, 1929/1978, pp. 208–211). Following Bergson (1983), we should talk of the process of qualitative movement through which leaders and followers continually segue into each other rather than plotting clean-cut connections between clearly defined individuals. Intrinsically, the internal coherence of leadership is no longer an abstract relationship between variables but rather a fleeting moment in an on-going process of fleeting moments of affective "matterings" (Seigworth & Gregg, 2010).

Whitehead (1929/1978) argues that our immediate perception of a portion of the world in front of us does not automatically sit there in the atomic isolation of which Bergson (1983, p. 29) speaks—this only gives half the truth. There is, rather, a unity when immediate physical feelings meet their conceptual counterpart; our fundamental perceptions blend together perfectly with the big picture, so that a wonderful sense of meaning and value emerges. On such fleeting occasions the two modes do not merely intersect, they are "fused into one" (Whitehead, 1929/1978, p. 18).

THE "INTERNALITY" OF LEADERSHIP

In order to expand the possibilities for relational leadership research we must shift toward the idea of internal relations. This enables us to break from claims made by leadership researchers that relations remain external to their terms. Leadership is a novel moment, a continuously renewed relational experience, rather than something we can essentialize (e.g., by suggesting that he or she is a leader). Pre- or non-personal relational determinations constitute themselves by grasping some aspect or part of the surrounding generality and appropriating them in the event or concrete act of their becoming (Whitehead, 1967a). We however view leadership as novel events that cause us to see, feel, and think in terms of movement rather than of something that we should define with desired concreteness.

Coordinating the insights of process philosophy with the work of leadership researchers, our premise is that relations are not only as real as everything else is, they are experienced, and directly so, as things in their own right. We consider leadership as a felt occasion bringing to the fore new relational innovations, experiential novelties grasped as purposive affect. What do we mean by experience, here? Psychologists confine experience to processes of mental representation. In a sense, thought and emotion are cognitive processes we use to construct intelligible stories in our minds. From the point of view of process philosophy, experience has a more expansive meaning. Now, our task is not only to understand our environment in a cognitive and analytic sense but also to grasp the "intensity" of experience that arises out of the physical world through our immersive—bodily, affective, and cognitive—encounters. As humans, we move to meet experience; we are sensitive to something, feel a contact with it, appreciate it in mind and body.

This is not to say necessarily that the foregoing describes a conscious "moving," "sensitivity," or "appreciation," and so we must ask how leadership arises out of experience? Our answer is that both the cognitive-analytic representations that we bring to leadership (e.g., the physiological responses that make possible judgements about good or bad leadership) and the physical feelings and emotions that we receive from moments of leadership in return (e.g., what makes leadership come alive for us as a living occasion here and now) are two parts of experience. Thus, set against the tendency in extant relational leadership research to look at/for extrinsic connections between separate leaders and followers, all we find are dynamic, changing bundles of affective and cognitive experiences, each with its own subjective immediacy, communicated via thoughts and feelings.

RETHINKING THE LEADERSHIP OCCASION

We commonly recognize that which we call "an event" as either an "effect" or "situation" that simply occurs, such as an organized social occasion, or as something that simply reveals familiar definitions or objects in the world (Williams, 2003). Nonetheless, an event does not mean that "a man has been run over," or "a storm is coming," or "a friend is arriving" (Deleuze, 1993, p. 76). According to process thought, we always miss an event if we understand it in terms of essential characteristics (Williams, 2003). Instead, events are about affect, they become affect, running through and re-arranging the relations between familiar histories and the situations at hand along the way (Deleuze, 1994).

In this understanding, events often exceed our apprehension but nonetheless are always going on within sensations and affects. The coming event arises in the middle of experience at a point realizing the potentialities of the past in the production of the future. If we might put this yet another way, events absorb us. However, we cannot think of the middling moment of activity without a change in the relation among familiar subjects and objects within experience. Leaders and followers, as familiar coordinates, do not constitute a "personal" experience relative to a subject but, on the contrary, become synonymous with a certain feeling that arises in an occurring event (Whitehead, 1929/1978). The qualitative dimension of the event's occurring arises "as the bringing together into one real context of diverse perceptions, diverse feelings, diverse purposes, and other diverse activities" (Whitehead, 1985, p. 9) into an "organic unity" (Whitehead, 1929/1978). Thus, a characteristic of each unique occasion is how it grasps (prehends) those entities in its event field and renders them as a new subjective form.

At this point it is worthwhile repeating a point made earlier, namely that while "an event" has a technical meaning for Deleuze (1984), for Whitehead (1929/1978) this is not the case. In Whiteheadian process thought, an event can only be subjectively prehended—in the case of higher occasions of experience such as in human beings, recognized as such—retrospectively as perhaps enduring objectively. It is important to note that an event observed in the past as one comprising leadership, therefore, is made up of a multitude of occasions (Cobb, 2008a, pp. 23–30). As an object, an event relies on subjects for its recognition by the subject, its remembering by the subject, in its own immediacy-of-the-*now*. Yet, this recognition, the remembering is a matter purely for the subject. In this sense, most events are better understood as nexus of occasions having an objective existence for the observer (e.g., the follower). As such, there is much that is lost to the observer; the richness of leadership is lost to the follower, however much she responds to the affect. On this view, leadership is not the thing; it is the bringing about and the playing out of leadership as a unique content of experience that is the thing. Each occasion of experience involves immediate sensations and our on-going needs, which together "carve out" (Whitehead, 1929/1978; see also James, 1996) portions of sensible reality in a process that is creative of the leadership subject.

The conditions of possibility and dynamic substance of leadership inherent in the subjective experience of it both in the follower(s) and the leader(s) arise from the distinctiveness inherent in perceiving the relation between the leadership figure and the background. In process terms, this is an act of conscious discrimination of effective contrasts through an experience of intensive integration of the subject in the context of the wider environment. We become aware of leadership by the intensity of our experience of it in contrast to other experiences. It becomes "more fully situated and influential in the world that emerges subsequent to and inclusive [of itself]" (Jones, 2008, p. 283). Leadership intensity is beyond the mere triviality of making an event in the world sensible to a reflecting subject. Rather it is a coherent integration of affective experience, "much as a narrow beam of light focuses a wide array of light trajectories as one" (Jones, 2008, p. 284), separating out the trivial from the important, the vague from the definite in the contrast of what is illuminated to us in consciousness. Together these two affective movements, sensation and reception in a specific context, determine the stance taken on a leadership event and subsequently our active response to it.

SOME IMPLICATIONS FOR ETHICAL LEADERSHIP

Throughout the current discussion, we have been concerned with showing that leadership neither lends itself to any clarity of definition nor depends on the leader-follower dyad (Drath et al., 2008). Under a process view, there is no essence or substance to leadership events other than the novelty of their occurring (Massumi, 2011). Importantly, subjectivity is thus inherent in transition between positions objectively perceived after the fact. Further, a processual understanding of leadership orients around the idea of something continually emergent or "unfolding" (Bohm, 1980) rather than specified from the outset. We can replace the idea of leaders and followers entering into relations with the awareness that leaders and followers are relations. Leadership does not exist in the external relation between the leader and the follower but rather as a felt experience in which each grasps some aspect or part of the other and appropriates them in the formation of a new and unique assemblage. The thing that has a substance, therefore, is the internal relation within the follower—that is, in their own response to their own perception of the actions of the leader—and vice-versa also within the leader, in their own response to their own perception of the follower's actions. What matters is not so much the relationship between the parties, as what each makes of that relationship for themselves, and for others (Cobb, 2007a).

For a process-relational view leadership is not "a way of being-in-relation-to-others" (Cunliffe and Eriksen, 2011, p. 1430; Shotter, 2005; also Uhl-Bien, 2006), but rather more quite genuinely a way of becoming-in-relation-to-others, as a relational ontology. Process-relational leadership is a way of becoming-in-the-world (contra being-in-the-world), in which the moral responsibility of leadership rests just precisely in our own responses as followers—and subsequently too as leaders. The relational integrity brought to the fore in "post-heroic" approaches to leadership is now a function not so much of our response to others but rather more our response in ourselves. The moral impact lies in our subsequent characterization of the present intensive experience, which determines its relevance and influence in future events. In process terms, "morality is now a question of the intensive significance of present becoming in the future that will be derived from that present and which impinges on the felt contours of becoming" (Jones, 2008, p. 288). In other words, the moral responsibility of leadership now lies in our own responsiveness—what we choose to make of the actions of others as a part of our experiences, and how we choose to respond ethically as leaders as a consequence of our experiences. This perspective is consistent with a recent re-emphasis on the role of character in determining ethical leadership (Riggio, Zhu, Reina, & Maroosis, 2010; Thompson & Riggio, 2010). Through developing strong character, leaders (and followers) are better able to respond in a morally responsible way to ethical challenges.

Clearly, our intra-subjective processual perspective on leadership is quite different from an inter-subjective one. So too, our rendering/image of power is quite different from the explicitly bi-lateralist approach. If leadership is relational, as we argue, then the power that surrounds it as manifest in the responses of others must also be inherently relational. Furthermore, with the argument (Murray, 2009) that there is both a receptive side to experience in receiving data from the past, and an active side in making something of that data for oneself in terms of actualizing the possibilities manifest in the present moment, power resides in the decisive capacity for reception, prehension, and actualization. Taken together, power concerns not only "the power to affect, to carry out a purpose, but also the capacity to undergo an effect, to be acted upon" (Murray, 2009, p. 242–243).

In appreciating power as the capacity to be acted upon as well as to affect, we also gain a new approach to describe "struggles for power." Rather than an inter-subjective rendering of power struggles between parties, our intra-subjective view suggests a direct experience of the wishes of others which each appropriates in the formation of its own nature. Each party, as a center of experiencing, contributes to the process of the becoming of another to the extent to which it responds and acts toward the other. Being able to achieve one's wishes is thus more a function of the responses and actions of the other because the desire to achieve the affect is an aspect or part of the capacity to undergo an effect.

From a process perspective, the synthesis of relations conveys a mode of inclusion by which "the differences initially experienced in our encounter with a diverse world" are "reconciled" and "worked up into a unified whole" (Allan, 1998, p. 91). If taken seriously, as theorists of power have done (see e.g., Foucault, 1980), the "unity of self-experience" (Whitehead, 1929/1978, p. 57) makes it impossible to think about ethical leadership in terms of individual agents as detached substances imposing their will *upon* others. It is a function of the personal felt experiences of the individual intentions of the parties; they are each quite literally *in-tension.*

How might we now extend our understanding of an ethical leadership focused on the question of power, to a more holistic appreciation of the way in which leaders might treat employees? An article published recently in *Process Studies* (Macklin, Matheson, & Dibben, 2014) has suggested that, as complex societies of occasions of experience, humans are perhaps sufficiently (if perhaps not uniquely) complex that we must understand our actions in terms of moral responsibility. As Whiteheadian societies, we are sufficiently complex that the idea of moral responsibility is explicable as a result of our capacity to engage in acts of conceptual reflection (see also Henning, 2005, p. 73). This emphasis on ethical and fair treatment of employees as critical to organizational performance is becoming quite clear (Cropanzano, Bowen, & Gilliland, 2007; Qin, Ren, Zhang, & Johnson, 2015).

This being the case, each act of conceptual reflection represents an experience having intrinsic value. Since value is intrinsic to experience, and choice is inherent in experience, then uniqueness comes to the fore. If beauty is a combination of value and uniqueness, for example, in our capacity to elicit harmony through and in the contrasts we find at work, then it is the responsibility of the manager to preserve the beauty manifest in the nature of human beings as moral agents (Henning, 2005, p. 143).

In this sense, the creativity inherent in our capacity to unify experience of contrasts sets aside the question of moral laws as such, and concerns a more immediate and real set of ethical obligations. For Henning (2005, pp. 145–146) these are interrelated and represent a challenge to enable as far as is possible in any situation: beauty, value, and importance; an intensity and harmony of self-respect, an intensity and harmony of respect for others; peaceful avoidance of destruction, and; an educative imperative to expand the depth and breadth of one's own understanding and that of others.

Leaders are now moral agents in organizations charged with helping others, in essence, be the best they can be—for themselves (and then by extension for the organization)—in terms of these five overlapping obligations of beauty, self-respect, respect for others, peaceful co-existence, and learning. From the organizational level of analysis, we suggest any endurance of its common form occurs through instances of power, technology and culture that act to constrain the extent of creative novelty. Leaders act to mitigate or even enhance the influence of each on the organization as it inevitably changes through the personal conceptualizations and actions of individuals and groups. The moral relations between individuals in the organization must be enhanced by the decision-making actions of leaders in terms of the way they treat employees. This may include, for example, the leader's role in shaping an ethical context or climate in a group or organization that helps underscore the value of respectful treatment of employees (Johnson, 2007).

This focus on leaders as moral agents requires leaders to first appreciate what beauty there is in individuals, and the effect of their actions relationally on individuals; does it limit or enhance the beauty they find before them? This means ensuring that as far as possible the individual's needs are met without fundamentally compromising the organization as a whole. What is important here is the emphasis: Leaders should not focus, in a static modern way, on the needs of the organization as primary but rather on the needs of the individual employee. It is not enough to say that leaders meet the needs of the organization and do only what they can get away with to barely sustain the needs of the individuals. The emphasis is now on not destroying the experience of individuals but on enhancing it, by maintaining a sound creative balance between maintaining the status quo and offering opportunity for development. Too much change in organizations is self-defeating because it is fatiguing. The introduction of new contrasts into an individual worker's experience in the organization is about achieving a harmony between variety and intensity of enjoyment (Henning, 2005, p. 155).

This sort of leaderful process ethics requires leaders to take the time to thoroughly understand and appreciate the beauty, as we have just defined it, of the people they are responsible for and orient themselves in their own work practices and leadership strategies primarily towards its sustenance. With a clear intention to develop and maintain harmony, they should strive to strike a balance between freedom of action and rigid order. This means actually stopping the sort of incentivization schemes that fail to take into account the different capabilities, idiosyncrasies, and talents of the people they are responsible for in the pursuit of deliverable objective and identical outcomes. Such identical outcomes do not foster human well-being; they foster at best a resigned acquiescence.

Instead, a process ethics focuses very much on the relational context of an individual's work life in the setting of their wider lived experience. It places the individual at the heart of the considerations in regard to the work that individual is being asked to undertake, in and for herself and then in terms of its contribution to the organization. As such, we see the humanity of people resides in their inherent quality-relatedness. The Cartesian approach to leadership sees employees in fundamentally means-ends terms, understood almost entirely in light of their contributions to the core objectives of a business. A process ethics is clear, as a process leadership is clear, that if leaders genuinely look after the people they are responsible for, the people will look after everything else. If on the other hand, they put in place systems and ways of managing and assessing people that do not pay sufficient respect to those peoples' essential relatedness—their humanity— the result will be a disaffection that is detrimental to not simply the organization, but more importantly, to the health and well-being of the people themselves. Enrichment of the life of the employee is therefore central to the leader's role in the organization, recognizing the well-being of the individual has a value in itself and for herself to which the employer must positively enable at least, and preferably enrich. Indeed, certain leadership theories, such as servant and transformational leadership (Bass, 1985; Bass & Riggio, 2006), to some extent, place attention to followers' needs at the forefront.

Clearly, to achieve this, truth is important—unlike the approach taken in many organizations. A leaderful process ethics cannot be one based on falsehood, or even be ill-informed. A process approach relies on honesty in feedback since it is always cognizant of the fact that all people are genuinely responsive human beings. More than this, though, a process view suggests that ethical leadership does not congeal into human subjects but is always an achievement that it is momentary within an ever-evolving field of relations. Thus, subjectivities dissolve if we consider they are themselves created along with the ever-changing event field that runs through them. To that extent, ethical leadership relationships are not given or give-able but are always in the process of becoming, on the way in or out.

IMPLICATIONS FOR RESEARCH

A process approach to leadership and organizational dynamics is relatively new, and runs counter to the history of leadership and organizational studies, which has focused on leader and follower roles and traditional relationships among these individuals. There has been, however, some discussion in the management literature on viewing leadership and organizations as complex and dynamic systems (e.g., Marion & Uhl-Bien, 2001; Uhl-Bien & Marion, 2009). More recently, Lord and colleagues (Lord, Dinh, & Hoffman, 2015), suggest a "quantum" approach to organizational change— based on quantum mechanics and probability—that views organizational change (and leading change) from a dynamic, process approach. Lord et al. (2015) argue that future research must avoid the traps of both seeing leadership (and followership) as residing in the individuals playing those roles, and suspend the traditional simplistic understandings of time. Future research, according to Lord and colleagues (2015), must incorporate the situational context and time into understanding organizational (and leadership) phenomena.

In terms of measurement, the study of leadership has relied primarily on retrospective survey reports of past phenomena (e.g., "My leader behaves like this... "), and they are framed traditionally in such a way as to view leaders as the agents of leadership and followers' reactions and behavior as the outcomes. Until recently, little attention has been given to the context, to time, and to the idea that leaders, followers, context, and other elements come together to create leadership and organizational processes. The complexity of a process approach to leadership in general, and ethical leadership, in particular, requires more complex measurement of variables than has been previously done in leadership research. Currently, in most leadership research, measurement takes place at a single point in time and variables are analyzed for their interrelationships. Moving forward, it is important to assess processes longitudinally, over time in order to gain a true understanding of the leadership process.

IMPLICATIONS FOR PRACTICE

A process philosophy of leadership argues for a more holistic approach to the practice of leadership, with both a broader view of what the leadership process entails, and an expansion of focus on the outcomes of leadership and organizational processes. Leaders and organizations need to broaden their conceptualizations of outcomes—moving beyond just a focus on profit and shareholder value, and considering the impact on employees, the environment, customers, and the community.

Leaders must be better equipped to deal with the complexity that is modern leadership. Critically important are the roles that flexibility, interpersonal skills, and character play in leadership, and these need to be considered in leader selection and development. Importantly, all organizational members need to be included in the leadership process. The days of focusing only on the development of those in identified positions of power and authority are over, as everyone in the organization contributes to the leadership process and outcomes. Finally, greater attention needs to be given to the wellbeing of organizational members, and of the community at large. Modern organizations need to be full participants in the larger world, concerned about the impact that they have on people and the planet.

CONCLUSION

The radical approach to ethical leadership we have outlined in this chapter contributes to the literature in three ways. We have endeavored to state explicitly the shortcomings in existing literature concerned with exploring the concept of relational leadership. While this work highlights some important insights for research practice, we note it does not tackle inadequacies in current theory, in which, ontologically, studies assume a conventional person-to-person exchange. Second, we have turned to a more technical terminology to account for leadership as an intra-subjective experience, which we grasp in terms of affective engagement. Set against the tendency in studies to consider leadership functions in the guise of an external contact between leaders and followers, we argue internal relations provide insights into the actual nature of leadership. Finally, we have considered how an understanding of the internal constitution of leadership can supplement existing analyses and expand the possibilities for more thoroughgoing process relational ethical leadership research.

We are suggesting in this chapter that leaderfulness is something that is momentary, hard to essentialize, in other words hard to objectify. The point is we might be losing the essence of leadership when we try to focus objectively; the experience of it is entirely in and of the subject. This is not to deny the reality of human beings as "leaders" and moral agents, be this through action or through identification by others as experiencing subjects. Rather, a Whiteheadian reading of experience affirms the immediacy of the present as experiential reality, and that is predominantly subjective; objectivity is reduced to the past. Thus, process philosophy allows us to bring the momentary reality of (morally?) leaderful events that leaders co-create, enable and inform to the fore, in ways that offer new insight into what ethical leadership might mean.

Our contribution therefore situates ethical leadership firmly within "applied process thought" (Dibben, 2008; Dibben & Kelly, 2008; Dibben & Newton, 2009). We anticipate this helps to build toward a shift in perspective from external relations, typically conceived to act as direct one-to-one correspondences between two substantial individuals, to one more fitted to recognize the complexity of processes constituting leadership as an occurrence or event. Our contention is that ethical leadership is neither a personal quality nor an attribute, nor an instrumental interaction extending between a pair of related terms.

We see leaders and followers arising in what, extending from Deleuze (1990), we might call the most "contracted points" or "concentrated moments of leadership's event field. These precise points or moments (relational determinations), which involve the interplay of many elements, are not the same as the general field of events but rather the individuations in-context that give it its defining essence. While we cannot reduce leadership to a person or persons, if we are to give sense to it in a particular experience, it must insist or inhere in both the individuation and at the same time the relationality inherent in "persons-in-community" (Cobb, 2007a). Thus, a process of mutual relating gives rise to leaderful occasions replete with leadership as affect, which, in their cooperative unfolding, enable a sense of leadership to emerge, objectively perceivable retrospectively as an event in which leadership could be seen to have had an effect.

In sum, a leaderful process ethics genuinely invites and enables others to become positively and intra-relationally involved in the organization. The result will be a culture soundly based on trust and selfless giving precisely because it is properly underpinned by a thoroughly balanced (i.e., genuinely aware of the internal relation) relational understanding of people in terms of how they change and can adjust to changes in the workplace. In this way, and in contrast to many modern organizations, the process-informed organization takes a process ethical approach as the appropriate way for the business to operate. As Moore (2009) notes, "value, experience, and subjectivity are always in the process of becoming, whereas intellectually complex events like human consciousness are particularly complex instances of the subjective experience of value" (p. 274). In short, an ethical leadership practice rejects the undermining modern fragmentation of life, work, and culture. It moves beyond the economistic focus on profit and thereby takes a far more integrated view of corporate values being the sum of personal values.

Leadership ethics cannot be understood as constant, nor can it be constant. This is because the context for leadership ethics, the organization, is itself not constant but is, instead, perpetually evolving; ethical leadership as managerial acts is a contribution to that evolution. Organizations are made up of increasingly diverse workforces. A process perspective on ethical leadership speaks directly in recognizing the value of human beings as individuals who are "internally related" to those around them (i.e., it is not what happens to you that counts [the external relation] but what you make of what happens to you [the internal relation] for yourself and others). The sort of process thinking that underpins this simple but profound insight can be worked into leaderful behavior if managers appreciate the notion of inherent freedom implicit within it. This brings with it a holistic view of experience as it is individually felt in the context of life in community as lived. A process view of ethical leadership thus rejects traditional distinctions often rendered in the business literature between corporate and personal values, and business and ethics.

For people to "work towards a living whole in which each person plays a part" (Gare, 2008, p. 375), leaders must therefore actively and genuinely enable rather than passively and dismissively allow; an organization that embodies a principle of benign neglect is not particularly virtuous. Instead, there should be a freely derived orientation toward the common good (see Daly & Cobb, 1994), in which employees can adopt a holistic approach to work in which culture, life, and work are rendered inseparable rather than fragmented. The normative modern science that forces the individual to inhabit the "great cleft" between their lives as part of nature and their work as separate from it, has without doubt been a major factor in late 20th century business. Our argument in this chapter has been that the sort of quasi-ethical leadership it has produced will be insufficient for a world forced to come to terms with the environmental consequences of such business. In response our radical solution is to reconnect our understanding and our practice of leadership with a more complete understanding of what it means to be *in-community*. Ethical leaderful behavior is fully cognizant of the interconnected, fully relational, ever-evolving character of natural systems and the place of human beings *within* them.

Finally, we have placed stress on the fact that it makes sense to speak of relations themselves—and more than this, how we respond to our experiences of these relations—before enquiring about the substance and hence fixity associated with simply located things. As such, we have outlined a distinctive way of conceptualizing ethical leadership as an event *in the making*. Considering ethical leadership in this manner overcomes some humanist beliefs and replaces the familiar bifurcation of distinct and self-contained leaders and followers with a more diverse, novel, and coherent appreciation. This is important for mankind's capacity, for example, to navigate the difficult ecological crisis that appears to lie before us.

NOTES

1. An earlier version of the leadership components of this paper were originally published in Wood, M. & Dibben, M. (2015). "Leadership as relational process," Process Studies, 44(1), 24–47. The authors are grateful for the copyright permission contained therein.

REFERENCES

Allan, G. (1998). Harmony and holism in process philosophy of education. *Interchange, 29*, 87–99.

Angel, R. (1980). *Relativity: The theory and its philosophy.* Oxford, England: Pergamon Press.

Bass, B. M. (1985). *Leadership and performance beyond expectations.* New York, NY: Free Press.

Bass, B. M. (1990). *Bass & Stogdill's handbook of leadership* (3rd ed.). New York, NY: Free Press.

Bass, B. M., & Avolio, B. J. (Eds.). (1993). *Improving organizational effectiveness through transformational leadership.* Thousand Oaks, CA: SAGE.

Bass, B. M., & Riggio, R. E. (2006). *Transformational leadership* (2nd ed.). New York, NY: Routledge.

Bennis, W. (2007). The challenges of leadership in the modern world: An introduction to the special issue. *American Psychologist, 62,* 2–5.

Bergson, H. (1983). *Creative evolution* (A. Mitchell, Trans.). New York, NY: Henry Holt.

Bergson, H. (1991). *Matter and memory* (N. Paul & W. S. Palmer, Trans). New York, NY: Zone.

Blake, R. R., & Mouton, J. S. (1964). *The managerial grid.* Houston, TX: Gulf.

Bohm, D. (1957). *Causality and chance in modern physics.* Philadelphia, PA: University of Pennsylvania Press.

Bohm, D. (1980). *Wholeness and the implicate order.* London, England: Routledge.

Bolden, R. (2011). Distributed leadership in organizations: A review of theory and research. *International Journal of Management Reviews, 13,* 251–269.

Bolden, R., & Gosling, J. (2006). Leadership competencies: Time to change the tune. *Leadership, 2,* 147–163.

Bracken, J. A. (1989). Energy events and fields. *Process Studies, 18,* 153–165.

Bracken, J. A. (2014). Whiteheadian metaphysics, general relativity, and string theory. *Process Studies, 43,* 129–143.

Bradbury, H., & Lichtenstein, B. M. B. (2000). Relationality in organizational research: Exploring the space between. *Organization Science, 11,* 551–564.

Brewer, M., & Gardner, W. (1996). "Who is this we"? Levels of collective identity and self-representations. *Journal of Personality and Social Psychology, 71,* 83–93.

Burns, J. M. (1978). *Leadership.* New York, NY: Harper & Row.

Carlsen, A. (2006). Organizational becoming as dialogic imagination of practice: The case of the indominatible Gauls. *Organization Science, 17,* 132–149.

Capek, M. (1976). *The concepts of space and time: Their structure and their development.* Boston, MA: D. Reidel.

Cobb, J. B. (2007a). Persons-in-community: Whiteheadian insights into community and institution. *Organization Studies, 28,* 567–588.

Cobb, J. B. (2007b). *A Christian natural theology* (2nd ed.). London, England: Westminster John Knox Press.

Cobb, J. B. (2008a). *Whitehead word book: A glossary with alphabetical index to technical terms in process and reality.* Claremont, CA: Process and Faith Press.

Cobb, J. B. (Ed.). (2008b). *Back to Darwin: A richer account of evolution.* Cambridge, England: Eerdmans.

Cobb, J. B. (2014). Series preface: Toward ecological civilization. In R. B. Edwards (Ed.), *An axiological process ethics.* Claremont, CA: Process Century Press.

Cobb, J. B., & Griffin, D. R. (1976). *Process theology: An introduction.* Philadelphia, PA: Westminster Press.

Collinson, D. (2006). Rethinking followership: A post-structuralist analysis of follower identities. *The Leadership Quarterly, 17,* 179–189.

Conger, J. A. (1989). *The charismatic leader: Behind the mystique of exceptional leadership.* San Francisco, CA: Jossey-Bass.

Conger, J. A., & Kanungo, R. N. (1998). *Charismatic leadership in organizations.* Thousand Oaks, CA: SAGE.

Cooper, R. (1976). The open field. *Human Relations, 29,* 999–1017.

Cooper, R. (1993). Heidegger and Whitehead on lived-time and causality. *The Journal of Speculative Philosophy, 7*(4), 298–312.

Cooper, R. (2005). Relationality. *Organization Studies, 26,* 1689–1710.

Cropanzano, R., Bowen, D. E., & Gilliland, S. W. (2007). The management of organizational justice. *Academy of Management Perspectives, 21,* 34–48.

Cunliffe, A. L., & Eriksen, M. (2011). Relational leadership. *Human Relations, 64,* 1425–1449.

Daly, H., & Cobb, J. B. (1994). *For the common good: Redirecting the economy toward community, the environment, and a sustainable future* (2nd ed.). Boston, MA: Beacon Press.

Dansereau, F. (1995). A dyadic approach to leadership: Creating and nurturing this approach under fire. *The Leadership Quarterly, 6,* 479–490.

Dansereau, F., Graen, G., & Haga, W. J. (1975). A vertical dyad linkage approach to leadership within formal organizations: A longitudinal investigation of the role making process. *Organizational Behavior and Human Performance, 13,* 46–78.

Dawson, P., & Sykes, C. (2016). *Organizational change and temporality: Bending the arrow of time.* London, England: Routledge.

Deleuze, G. (1990). *The logic of sense* (M. Lester & C. Stivale, Trans.). New York, NY: Columbia University Press.

Deleuze, G. (1993). *The fold: Leibniz and the Baroque* (T. Conley, Trans.). Minneapolis, MN: University of Minnesota Press.

Deleuze, G. (1994). *Difference and repetition* (P. Patton, Trans.). London, England: Athlone Press.

Denis, J., Langley, A., & Sergi, V. (2012). Leadership in the plural. *Academy of Management Annals, 6,* 211–283.

Desmet, R. & Eastman, T. (2008). Whitehead, Physics, and Relativity. In M. Weber & W. Desmond (Eds.), *Handbook of Whiteheadian Process Thought* (pp. 235–258). Frankfurt, Germany: Ontos Verlag.

Dibben, M. (2008). Organizations and organizing: Understanding and applying Whitehead's processual account. *Philosophy of Management, 7,* 97–108.

Dibben, M. (2009). Exploring Whitehead's understanding of organizations: Moving beyond the organising experience of individual managers. *Philosophy of Management, 7*(2), 13–24.

Dibben, M. (2015). Management and the care of our common home. In J. B. Cobb & I. Catuera (Eds.), *For our common home: Process-relational responses to Laudato Si'* (pp. 274–285). Claremont, CA: Process Century Press.

Dibben, M., & Kelly, T. (2008). *Applied process thought (Vol. 1): Initial exploration in theory and research.* Frankfurt, Germany: Ontos Verlag.

Dibben, M., & Newton, R. (Eds.). (2009). *Applied process thought (Vol. 2): Following a trail ablaze.* Frankfurt, Germany: Ontos Verlag.

Dienesch, R. M., & Liden, R. C. (1986). Leader-member exchange model of leadership: A critique and further development. *Academy of Management Review, 11*, 618–634.

Drath, W. H., McCauley, C. D., Palus, C. J., & Van Velsor, E. (2008). Direction, alignment, commitment: Toward a more integrative ontology of leadership. *The Leadership Quarterly, 19*, 635–653.

Dulebohn, J. H., Bommer, W. H., Liden, R. C., Brouer, R. L., & Ferris, G. R. (2012). A meta-analysis of antecedents and consequences of leader-member exchange: Integrating the past with an eye toward the future. *Journal of Management, 38*, 1715–1759.

Fairhurst, G. T. (2004). Textuality and agency in interaction analysis. *Organization, 11*, 335–353.

Fairhurst, G. T. (2005). Reframing the art of framing: Problems and prospects for leadership. *Leadership, 1*, 165–185.

Fairhurst, G. T. (2007). *Discursive leadership: In conversation with leadership psychology.* Thousand Oaks, CA: SAGE.

Fairhurst, G.T. (2010). *The power of framing: Creating the language of leadership.* San Francisco, CA: Jossey-Bass.

Fairhurst, G. T., & Uhl-Bien, M. (2012). Organizational discourse analysis (ODA): Examining leadership as a relational process. *The Leadership Quarterly, 23*, 1043–1062.

Fiedler, F. E. (1967). *A theory of leadership effectiveness.* New York, NY: McGraw Hill.

Foucault, M. (1980). *Power/knowledge: Selected interviews and other writings, 1972–1977.* London, England: Vintage Books.

Fraser, J. T. (1982). *The genesis and evolution of time.* Amherst, MA: University of Massachusetts Press.

Gare, A. (2008). Process philosophy and ecological ethics. In M. Dibben and T. Kelly (Eds.), *Applied process thought I: Initial explorations in theory and research* (pp. 363–382). Frankfurt, Germany: Ontos Verlag.

Gerstner, C. R., & Day, D. V. (1997). Meta-analytic review of leader-member exchange theory: Correlates and construct issues. *Journal of Applied Psychology, 82*, 827–844.

Graen, G. B., & Scandura, T. A. (1987). Toward a psychology of dyadic organizing. *Research in Organizational Behavior, 9, 175–208.*

Graen, G. B., & Uhl-Bien, M. (1995). Development of leader-member exchange (LMX) theory of leadership over 25 years: Applying a multi-level multi-domain perspective. *The Leadership Quarterly, 6*, 219–247.

Gronn, P. (2002). Distributed leadership as a unit of analysis. *The Leadership Quarterly, 13*, 423–451.

Griffin, D. R. (Ed.). (1986). *Physics and the ultimate significance of time.* Albany, NY: State University of New York Press.

Griffin, D. R. (Ed.). (1988). *The reenchantment of science.* Albany, NY: State University of New York Press.

Griffin, D. R. (2008). *Unsnarling the world-knot: Consciousness, freedom, and the mind-body problem.* Berkeley, CA: University of California Press.

Halewood, M. (2014). Rethinking the social through Durkheim, Marx, Weber and Whitehead. London, England: *Anthem Press.*

Hartshorne, C. (1984). *Omnipotence and other theological mistakes.* Albany, NY: State University of New York Press.

Helin, J., Hernes, T., Hjorth, D., & Holt, R. (Eds.). (2014). *The Oxford handbook of process philosophy and organization studies.* Oxford, England: Oxford University Press.

Henning, B. G. (2005*). The ethics of creativity: Beauty, morality, and nature in a processive cosmos.* Pittsburgh, PA: University of Pittsburgh Press.

Hernes, T. (2007). *Understanding organization as process: Theory for a tangled world.* New York, NY: Routledge.

Hernes, T. (2014). *A process theory of organization.* Oxford, England: Oxford University Press.

Hersey, P., & Blanchard, K. (1977). *Management of organization behavior* (4th ed.). Englewood Cliffs, NJ: Prentice-Hall.

Hogg, M. (2001). A social identity theory of leadership. *Personality and Social Psychology Review, 5,* 184–200.

Hosking, D. (1988). Organising, leadership, and skillful process. *Journal of Management Studies, 25,* 147–166.

Hosking, D., Dachler, P. H., & Gergen, K. J. (Eds.). (1995). *Management and organization: Relational alternatives to individualism.* Aldershot, England: Avebury.

James, W. (1996). *Essays in radical empiricism.* Lincoln, NE: University of Nebraska Press.

Johnson, C. E. (2007). Best practices in ethical leadership. In J. A. Conger & R. E. Riggio (Eds.), *The practice of leadership* (pp. 150–171). San Francisco, CA: Jossey-Bass.

Jones, J. (2008). Intensity and subjectivity. In M. Weber (Ed.), *Handbook of Whiteheadian process thought* (pp. 279–290). Berlin, Germany: De Gruyter.

Jungerman, J. A. (2000). *World in process: Creativity and interconnection in the new physics.* Albany, NY: State University of New York Press.

Keller, T., & Dansereau, F. (1995). Leadership and empowerment: A social exchange perspective. *Human Relations, 48,* 127–146.

Klein, K. J., & House, R. J. (1995). On fire: Charismatic leadership and levels of analysis. *The Leadership Quarterly, 6,* 183–198.

Koivunen, N. (2007). The processual nature of leadership discourses. *Scandinavian Journal of Management, 23,* 285–305.

Korsgaard, M. A., Roberson, L., & Rymph, R. D. (1998). What motivates fairness? The role of subordinate assertive behaviour on manager's interactional fairness. *Journal of Applied Psychology, 83,* 731–744.

Lango, J. W. (2008). Time and Experience. In M. Weber & W. Desmond (Eds.), *Whiteheadian Handbook of Porcess Thought* (pp. 653–663). Frankfurt, Germany: Ontos Verlag.

Langley, A., & Tsoukas, H. (Eds.) (2017). *The SAGE Handbook of Process Organization Studies.* London, England: SAGE Reference.

Liden, R. C., & Graen, G. (1980). Generalizability of the vertical dyad linkage model of leadership. *Academy of Management Journal, 23,* 451–465.

Lord, R. G., Dinh, J. E., & Hoffman, E. L. (2015). A quantum approach to time and organizational change. *Academy of Management Review, 40,* 263–290.

Lord, R. G., & Smith, J. E. (1983). Theoretical, information processing, and situational factors affecting attribution theory models of organizational behavior. *Academy of Management Review, 8*, 50–60.

Lowe, V. (1990). *Alfred North Whitehead: The man and his work, 1910–1947, (Vol. 2)*. Baltimore, MD: Johns Hopkins University Press.

Macklin, R., Matheson, K., & Dibben, M. (2014). Process ethics and business: Applying process thought to enact critiques of mind-body dualism in organizations. *Process Studies, 43*, 61–86.

Marion, R., & Uhl-Bien, M. (2001). Leadership in complex organizations. *The Leadership Quarterly, 12*, 389–418.

Massumi, B. (2011). *Semblance and event: Activist philosophy and the occurrent arts*. Cambridge, MA: MIT Press.

Meindl, J. R., Ehrlich, S. B., & Dukerich, J. M. (1985). The romance of leadership. *Administrative Science Quarterly, 30*, 78–102.

McDaniel, J. (2015). The many become one and are increased by one: Whitehead's understanding of process. In J. McDaniel and P. A. Farmer (Eds.), *Replanting ourselves in beauty: Towards an ecological civilization* (pp.41–47). Anoka, MN: Process Century Press.

Moore, D. (2009). Propositions in corporations. In M. Dibben & R. Newton (Eds.), *Applied process thought II: Following a trail ablaze* (pp. 263–277). Frankfurt, Germany: Ontos Verlag.

Moses, G. J. (2003). Big things from little things? The problem of the compound individual. *Concrescence: The Australasian Journal of Process Thought, 4*, 1–7.

Murray, L. (2009). Empire, relational power and a multi-polar world. In M. Dibben & R. Newton (Eds.), *Applied process thought II* (pp. 239–246). Frankfurt, Germany: Ontos-Verlag.

Neesham, C., & Dibben, M. (2012). The social value of business: Lessons from political economy and process philosophy. *Research in Ethical Issues in Organizations, 8*, 63–83.

Pearce, C. L., & Conger, J. A. (Eds.). (2002). *Shared leadership: Reframing the hows and whys of leadership*. Thousand Oaks, CA: SAGE.

Pettigrew, A. M. (1997). What is processual analysis? *Scandinavian Journal of Management, 13*, 337–348.

Phipps, R. (2009). The philosophy of an open, infinite and integrated universe. In M. Dibben & R. Newton (Eds.), *Applied process thought II* (pp. 149–203). Frankfurt, Germany: Ontos-Verlag.

Prigogine, I. (1980). *From being to becoming: Time and complexity in the physical sciences*. San Francisco, CA: W.H. Freeman.

Qin, X., Ren, R., Zhang, Z., & Johnson, R. E. (2015). Fairness heuristics and substitutability effects: Inferring the fairness of outcomes, procedures, and interpersonal treatment when employees lack clear information. *Journal of Applied Psychology, 100*, 235–250.

Riggio, R. E., Zhu, W., Reina, C., & Maroosis, J. (2010). Virtue-based measurement of ethical leadership: The Leadership Virtues Questionnaire. *Consulting Psychology Journal, 62(4)*, 235–250.

Scandura, T. A., & Graen, G. B. (1984). Moderating effects of initial leader-member exchange status on the effects of a leadership intervention. *Journal of Applied Psychology, 69,* 428–436.

Seigworth, G. J., & Gregg, M. (2010). An inventory of shimmers. In M. Gregg & G. Seigworth (Eds.), *The affect theory reader* (pp. 1–25). Durham, NC: Duke University Press.

Sherburne, D. W. (1966). *A key to Whitehead's process and reality.* Chicago, IL: University of Chicago Press.

Shotter, J. (2005). Inside the moment of managing: Wittgenstein and the everyday dynamics of our expressive-responsive activities. *Organization Studies, 26,* 113–135.

Shotter, J., & Cunliffe, A. L. (2003). Managers as practical authors: Everyday conversations for action. In D. Holman & R. Thorpe (Eds.), *Management and language: The manager as practical author* (pp. 15–37). London, England: SAGE.

Smircich, L., & Morgan, G. (1982). Leadership: The management of meaning. *Journal of Applied Behavioral Science, 18,* 257–273.

Sparrowe, R. T., & Liden, R. C. (1997). Process and structure in leader-member exchange. *Academy of Management Review, 22,* 522–552.

Thompson, D., & Riggio, R. E. (2010). Introduction to special issue on defining and measuring character in leadership. *Consulting Psychology Journal, 62,* 211–215.

Tourish, D. (2014). Leadership, more or less? A processual, communication perspective on the role of agency in leadership theory. *Leadership, 10,* 79–98.

Tsoukas, H., & Chia, R. (2002). On organizational becoming: Rethinking organizational change. *Organization Science, 13,* 567–582.

Uhl-Bien, M. (2006). Relational leadership theory: Exploring the social processes of leadership and organizing. *The Leadership Quarterly, 17,* 654–676.

Uhl-Bien, M., & Marion, R. (2009). Complexity leadership in bureaucratic forms of organizing: A meso model. *The Leadership Quarterly, 20,* 631–650.

Uhl-Bien, M., & Ospina, S. (2012). Mapping the terrain: Convergence and divergence around relational leadership. In M. Uhl-Bien & S. Ospina (Eds.), *Advancing relational leadership: A dialogue among perspectives* (pp. xix–xivii). Charlotte, NC: Information Age.

Weik, E. (2004). From time to action: The contribution of Whitehead's philosophy to a theory of action. *Time and Society, 13,* 301–319.

Whitehead, A. N. (1927). *Symbolism: Its meaning and effect.* New York, NY: Fordham University Press.

Whitehead, A. N. (1929/1978). *Process and reality* [Corrected Edition]. New York, NY: Free Press.

Whitehead, A. N. (1956). *Modes of thought.* New York, NY: Columbia University Press.

Whitehead, A. N. (1967a). *Adventures of ideas.* New York, NY: Free Press.

Whitehead, A. N. (1967b). *Science and the modern world.* New York, NY: Free Press.

Williams, J. (2003). Gilles Deleuze's difference and repetition: A critical introduction and guide. Edinburgh, Scotland: Edinburgh University Press.

Wood, M. (2005). The fallacy of misplaced leadership. *Journal of Management Studies, 42,* 1101–1121.

Wood, M., & Dibben, M. (2015). Leadership as relational process. *Process Studies, 44,* 24–47.

Wood, M., & Ladkin, D. (2008). The event's the thing: Brief encounters with the leaderful moment. In K.T. James & J. Collins (Eds.), *Leadership perspectives: Knowledge into action* (pp. 15–28). New York, NY: Palgrave Macmillan.

CHAPTER 10

ETHICS AND ACCOUNTABILITY IN THE AGE OF PREDATORY GLOBALIZATION

An Impossibility Theorem?

Ali Farazmand
Florida Atlantic University

ABSTRACT

The challenges of ethics and accountability have always been a central concern in public governance and administration throughout history, yet the apparently ugly side of various forms of corruption, both concepts are in practice more complex and subtle than expected. This essay offers a general discussion of public service ethics and accountability in the age of corporate and predatory globalization, with an intention to offer a primer for practicing public administrators. Particular attention is paid to key theories of ethics and accountability, globalization with emphasis on "predatory globalization," marketization and sweeping privatization, the new public management (NPM), with implications for public service ethics and administration. The concept of "agencification" is introduced to show the transformed role of the state and public administration under "corpocracy" with declining spirit of ethics

Radical Thoughts on Ethical Leadership, pages 199–220
Copyright © 2017 by Information Age Publishing

and integrity, as well as the growing challenge of "impossibility theorem" in public service and administration. "Virtue ethics," "professionalism," ethics education, and character development are suggested as key theoretical and practical groundings to enhance ethical and accountability capacity in modern governance and public administration.

The issues of ethics and accountability, as related to leadership, have always been a major concern in governance. Since the ancient time, philosophers, thinkers, revolutionaries, and conscientious administrators have raised the concerns and often advised kings, princes, ministers, and other political rulers/officials on how to conduct the functions of governments and administration, and on how to treat citizens or subject peoples. Philosophers extensively wrote on this issue; indeed, a major pillar of all philosophical thinking and writing was, and still is, the subject of "ethics." In the East and West (China, Egypt, Persia, and Ottoman, and Rome) philosophers often wrote books of advice to kings and rulers about ethical values, virtues, and the good, the bad, and the ugly. They served officials and rulers with ethical advice.

Accountability didn't have as early origin as ethics did, except for the obligation to be accountable to rulers, kings, ministers, and other high authorities by subordinators. Yet accountability has had a high value as well throughout later times, despite pretentions of those in authorities to not feeling obligated to respond to anyone but themselves. Much of these concerns for leaders' ethics and accountability have also appeared or reflected directly or indirectly in novels, diaries, and historical bureaucratic records (Eisenstadt, 1963; Farazmand, 2009). However, systematic studies and writings on public administrative ethics and accountability are more recent undertakings. It is only the last half century that have the issues of ethics and accountability been so seriously paid attention to in public administration and policy. This has been for good reasons, a movement that still has a long way to go but is making significant progress with considerable impacts. Yet, many challenges make the goals of public service ethics and accountability difficult if not impossible to achieve. Of these, predatory corporate globalization is the most forbidding one; predatory globalization is an antithesis of public service and administration (Farazmand, 2012).

First we visit here the empire of the subject matter, followed by a brief sketch of some of the main theories of ethics, as well as the concepts and mechanisms of leader accountability. Then predatory globalization is briefly presented to explain why the challenge of achieving the goals of public service ethics and accountability in modern governance and administration is difficult if not impossible to overcome. Finally, an argument is made to performance with professional competence for results balanced by the imperative of ethical and accountable standards in contemporary public governance and administration.

VISITING THE EMPIRE

Visiting the empire, to borrow Herbert Simons' idea of the 1970s, shows that there are many colonies, some more populated than others, and some more significant than others. In the case of ethics, the number of colonies may be many, and they include philosophy, sociology, psychology, management, political science, and public service and public administration. The concerns over ethics and accountability have been mostly noted with more scholarly and practical purposes. Philosophers address ethics as a core issue in their inquiry and in search of ultimate truth and an ideal society (e.g., Plato's [4th century BC] Republic; Farabi's [12th century AD] Virtuous City; Kant's (1956) "categorical imperative"; and Marx [1860s] Das Capital, Communist Manifesto). Political scientists and public administration scholars advocate a more ethically sound political order with practical applications in policy and administration, and with variations in contexts and approaches across the globe (e.g., Rohr, 1989, 1998; Waldo, 1980/1992), but they are even more concerned with accountability issues in modern public governance and administration (Waldo, 1989/1992; Behn, 2001; Frederickson, 2001; Romzek & Dubnick, 1987; Rosenbloom, 1995). Similarly, sociologists and social or organizational psychologists consider ethics as a core value in their theorizing and articulating pillars of good societies and communities (e.g., Parson, 1951; Veblen, 1898, 1911; Weber, 1947). Today, accountability is also a central issue of organization theory and behavior, while public ethics and integrity occupy a special place in contemporary public service and administration teaching and practice (Cooper, 2001; Fredrickson, 2001; Jurkiewicz, 2012, 2013). The challenge of achieving the goals of public ethics and accountability in governance and administration is a near impossible task due to the overwhelming forces of predatory globalization that pervade politics, administration, and economy across the world.

THEORIES OF ETHICS

Visiting the empire above leads to several theories of ethics and accountability. These are in three categories: philosophical, organizational/managerial, and professional.

Philosophical Based Theories of Ethics

Four theoretical perspectives comprise philosophical views on ethics with clear implications for leaders.

Categorical Imperative

Immanuel Kant's (1724–1804) "Categorical imperative" is a perspective that focuses on the "nature of human act'" regardless of the outcomes or consequences. An example is lying, which is by nature bad and unacceptable, and must be categorically rejected or punished. Another is killing, committing crimes, and the like. A key pillar of education for private and public life in ancient Persia was the "categorical rejection of lying as a punishable act" and "justice" (Farazmand, 2009; Frye, 1975; Olmstead, 1948). While lying was categorically rejected as a punishable crime, Persian justice system nevertheless always considered human acts and behaviors in balance. For example, if a person committing lies, and in doing so had served a family, a community, or a system from destruction, it would be considered in rendering verdicts (Herodotus, 1954, 1984). Lying and borrowing money were considered correlated closely, as people in debt were often considered resorting to excuses, including lies, to justify/rationalize their failure to pay back their debt in time; both debt and lying were discouraged, but lying was a punishable act throughout the entire world-state Persian Empire, which ruled virtually the entire known world for over 230 years beginning with 559 BC, when Cyrus the Great founded the Empire (Herodotus, 1954, 1984). However, even more importantly, "lying" was viewed as a "vice" by Persians and was taught as destructive and corruptive to public and private life, because it worked against the three cardinal "virtues" or principles of "Good Thought, Good Deed, and Good Talk," as preached by Persian Prophet Zoroaster, which along with justice and competency served as the key pillars of the educational foundation throughout the Empire. Zoroastrianism was the first monotheistic religion in the world, espousing the one single God Ahura Mazda (Great God/Lord) and good versus evil, light versus darkness, and virtues versus vices. It was the pioneer of other Godly religions, such as Judaism, Christianity, and Islam (Frye, 1975; Olmstead, 1948; Cook, 1983; Farazmand, 2009). In philosophical terms, *deontological* perspective offers single-rule and multiple-rule *principles* that determine the ethical situations and imperatives—of these two, the single-rule rule view is consistent with the Kantian categorical imperatives—like the principle of "lying is bad" and unethical (see Chandler, 2001, pp. 181–182).

Consequentialism

The second philosophical perspective on ethics is the theory of "consequentialism," which judges human act in terms of its consequences; good consequences justify actions, while bad consequences should deter actions. There is a causal relationship between consequences and human action. This raises two questions: Should ends justify means? Any means? If actions producing bad consequences, whose acts and for who or whom should the consequences be judged? People differ in ideological, moral, cultural, and personal values and preferences. During the crusader wars, both Christians and Muslims justified their killing the others as "good" and viewed such actions ethically and morally justifiable according to their own beliefs. Today, capitalists and promoters of market ideology in the West (and East) propagate against socialism and view their own actions—including killing socialists in wars and otherwise—justifiable. This is justified in rationalization of their own actions. Another example: ISIS's mass murdering of other religious people—Shi'as, Sunnis, Izadis, Christians, etc.—may be justified according to its own belief, but can it be accepted by the world of people outside them? Does the result of the atomic bombs dropped on Hiroshima and Nakazaki in Japan justify the action of the United States? In philosophical terms, this is also called *teleological* perspective, referring to "results" and "consequences" (Chandler, 2001, 179–180).

Utilitarianism

The third philosophical perspective is the "theory of utilitarianism," which holds that actions producing "good results" for a larger majority would be justified—the utility of an action as long it serves a large group or groups of people would be instrumentally good. Utilitarianism, according to Jeremy Bentham (1748–1832) and John Stuart Mill (1806–1873), is instrumental and instrumental rationality serves ethical conducts deemed acceptable. Questions arise with utilitarianism when the rights of minorities, excluded people, and marginalized people are at stake. The majority of German people supported the Third Reich and Hitler—he was elected too—but was the Nazi actions acceptable to socialists, communists, non-Nazis in Germany? How about the rest of the world population Hitler invaded and subjugated? In philosophical terms, the *deontological principles* of *utilitarianism* of either Bentham (1834) or Mill (1965) offer solutions to some problems (Bentham, 1834; Mill, 1965), but give rise to other problems, a paradoxical view philosophers of the same thinking have not been able to answer yet.

Virtuous Ethics

The fourth philosophical perspective is the theory of virtuous ethics, which holds both actions and consequences together; virtues by intent, action, and consequences or ending results. Living a private and public life by virtues in thought, action, and results of action is considered ethical and acceptable. Piety is an example of living virtuous. Public administrators acting virtuously are considered ethically sound, and they serve the broad based public interests, public goods, and are accountable. In the ancient world, education of virtues, justice, and "good deeds, good thoughts, and good talks" were considered ethically sound and parts of educational development in the Persian Empire (Farazmand, 2009; Frye, 1975; Olmstead, 1948), and by some teaching in China via Confucian doctrines.

Organizational and Institutional-Based Theories of Ethics

Organizational based theories of ethics may also refer to bureaucratic, managerial, and administrative ethics. The fundamental *principle* guiding ethical conduct covers mainly the actual behavior displaced through performance in organizational contexts. Performance based on principles of merit and standards favor universalism in administrative treatment of employees, but they may at the same time disfavor or discriminate against those not meeting such standards or meritorious criteria (e.g., minorities, people of other race, color, religion, or political and ideological orientations). Organizational values promoting ethical values rest on *the principles* of inclusivity, anti-favoritism and nepotism, representativeness, responsiveness, and universalism; they categorically reject such destructive anomalies of favoritism, corruption, conflicts of interests, bribery, and lying. They offer institutional mechanisms such as the constitution as a basis of ethics (Rohr, 1978/1989), and both formal and informal institutional norms and values for ethical behaviors (Cooper, 1998).

Religion, culture, and laws also provide institutional foundations for ethical teaching and practice. In philosophical terms, the ontological and deontological values of organizational, bureaucratic, managerial, and administrative ethics are manifest *behaviors* (Skinner, 1971/2002), *while desiring intent, attitudinal, or inner motives in either formative or process stages leading to behaviors* (Farazmand, forthcoming a & b). Institutionally, this theoretical perspective is found in expressions through such terms as constitutionally based *bureaucratic ethics* (Rohr, 1978/1989); organizational *values* (Hart, 2001); and *administrative ethics* (Cooper, 1998, 2001).

The above theories of ethics have practical applications. The categorical imperative dictates, for example, favoritism and embezzlement as unethical and destructive in public service and administration, while making explanation of "situations" demanding flexibility difficult if not impossible. Both utilitarianism and deontological perspectives guide public servants to deal with the consequences or ends as goals—achieving goals and producing results (services by any means) no matter how, and achieving efficiency even at the expense of ethical misconduct or violation of individual rights. Virtue ethics has more profound implications in real life of public as well as private life, and the best approach to using virtue ethics is to make it part of the educational culture from a very early age.

Public service is best served by these virtuous principles (honesty, integrity, respect of others, hard work, equality, fairness, etc.), principles that not only guide public service delivery with virtues and ethical behavior, but also offer profound guidance to the life of people as persons, hence producing ethical people with high character and integrity. Finally, the practical values of organizational ethics are self-explanatory; they are more operational and pragmatic and have standard yardsticks to operate with (e.g., code of ethics, laws, regulations, guidelines, processes and procedures, etc).

Professional-Based Theories of Ethics

Professional based perspectives on ethics are explained by three theoretical grounds: One relies on the Weberian (1947) word of "expertise" and the role of professional experts played in policy process and administration. They offer objective expert information useful and necessary to policy process and public administration. This notion makes ethical grounding on the basis of disciplinary professional expertise and knowledge, hence ethically sound—a chemist, a biologist, and a lawyer seeing things through their "narrow" lenses and generalize them to the universe. The second perspective views "professionalism" as a noble source of ethical foundation in public service and administration, because professionalism is grounded on the principles of accountability, rationality, objectivity, fairness, social equity, and sound ethical characters as well as commitment to competency and performance—this notion also conveys a moral tone to administrative ethics—trust professionalism because it resists/rejects corruption and promotes virtuous and righteous effects (Farazmand, 1997b, 2002a).

The third professional grounding of ethics is based on a new and beyond Weberian notion of professional knowledge as a holistic, multi-dimensionally grounded in not only narrow based expertise and technical information, but also one that is broadly molded by values of integrity, honesty, public spiritedness, and commitment to public service and public values—it conveys the rigor of hard technical expertise and knowledge on the one hand, and the normative values of life and organizations in the universe. This perspective combines the first two views into one and creates a synthesis of professionalism armed by virtues, characters, as well as commitment to technical expertise. Professionals of this category are experts, virtuous actors in policy and administrative processes, ethicists with high-road (to borrow John Rohr's, 1978/1989 dichotomous High Road and Low Road) grains, and ability as well as courage to change lives and make history. They resist unethical temptations, exercise ethical principles with accountability, and resist what they may see against broad-based public interests and public values, while at the same time create new norms of practice in public service and administration (Farazmand, 2002, 2009). They are exemplar professionals.

COMPETING VALUES IN PUBLIC SERVICE AND ADMINISTRATION

Public service and administration carry values, and they are not always consistent; indeed, they contradict in action. The cardinal purposes of public service and administration is to serve society at large, the public interests, provide public goods in efficient manner, serve fairness and justice, and manage the economy and political as well as military affairs. In doing so, some values tend to compete against others in the operational processes. Societies are composed of people of various socio-economic and cultural, and ethnic, classes and mixes. The poor and the working class always strive to improve their lots and expect/demand opportunities for upward mobility with a fair distribution of national wealth that can help them lift up their status. The rich and well to do, on the other hand, tend to want more of what they have, strive to use wealth as a source of power to influence for what they aspire, and hence get on the driving seats. In the middle, the middle class people—people who work hard, make reasonably well, and strive to move upward to the status of the rich and affluent.

Each of these three groups or classes of people in societies have legitimate claim on governments and their administrative systems. Yet for the governments and administrations to perform in delivering services with values attached, there may be different approaches to choose from, and this is where the role of the state and public administration becomes an issue, a controversially contentious issue (Farazmand, 2005). The options are: (a) a strong role of the government along with private, (b) a weak role of the state with a powerful private sector, and (c) a mixed; all three depicting an economic role that favor some groups or classes while disfavoring others. Public administration and political science scholars have also debated extensively on the role of the state and public administration, a debate that has continued to occupy a major space in social sciences (Mosher, 1968; Waldo, 1980/1992). To maintain a balance is a difficult decision to make, decisions that are a function of many factors that include economic, political, ideological, and cultural in nature. Obviously, the rich is better organized, has more resources to devote toward what it wants, and has the ability and power to influence the policy decisions and their outcomes.

Thus the role of government is often moved back and forth and from left to right, depending on what interest group(s) or class(es) of power has more power to influence the decision choices and their outcomes. The poor and working class calls for more equity, fairness, and equal treatment, and allocation of national resources in a manner that would help them; the rich and affluent prefers and pushes for more distributional policy that favors business enterprises with discretionary choices; they want efficiency, results-oriented behaviors, little or no regulations, no government interference in their functions, and expediency in actions. But the middle class is often divided between the two—those committed to fairness and equal opportunity favor policy choices that tend to benefit the poor and underclass, and those who aspire to join the rank of the rich—or work as their agents (leaders, supervisors, professionals working in such enterprises)—favor policy choices that benefit the rich.

The clash of interests is also reflected in the clash of values. Two sets of values characterize administrative—and managerial and organizational—decisions and actions; they also characterize leader behavior in public service. On the one hand, all administrators are required to run public service organizations—ranging from the core government agencies to semi-core and semi-public agencies like government corporations—with efficiency, effectiveness, and economy. These three Es are the cardinal administrative values shared by both public and private organizations universally speaking; they are expected of all sound administrators, leaders, and officials running any organization. On the other hand, unlike private sector organizations, government agencies are also tasked and expected to uphold and promote the constitutional and political values of liberty, equality, equity, law and order, fairness, representation, responsiveness, and accountability in their functions of both making and delivering public services (Rohr, 1978/1989; Rosenbloom, 1995).

The two sets of values are often in conflict. Pursuing organizational or administrative values of economy, efficiency, and effectiveness may produce high performance and productivity, but it can potentially result in violation of political values of representation, fairness, inclusivity, responsiveness, equal treatment, conflict of interests, and favoritism. Leaders are often tempted to take shortcuts, hire and promote competent individuals as they wish, but by doing so they may violate laws and regulations promoting equal employment opportunity rights, or constitutional rights of public employees, or exclude a wide range of "other" competent employees from minorities and those unaware of such opportunities. Conflicts of interests, favoritism, nepotism, corruption, bribery, embezzlement, workplace sexual harassment, and a host of related conducts or tolerance of such misconducts are *unethical acts with detrimental consequences* and can have legal and judicial ramifications to the organization, management, and employee-management relations. Once an unethical conduct, say favoritism and nepotism, infects an organization, it penetrates the system throughout and corrupts it culturally, a disease that would become deadly and almost impossible to eradicate.

The clash of values can happen under any of the three major roles of government. Public sector bureaucracy is often strong and expansive under dictatorships, while it can be either small or large under democracy and representative governments. Strong bureaucracy is also an instrument of power functional to system maintenance and enhancement (Weber, 1984). Examples include the Chilean public bureaucracy under the dictator Pinochet after the military coup of September 11, 1973 for the next 20 years, with another example being the Iranian bureaucracy under the dictatorship of the Shah after the military coup of August 1953 for the next twenty five years (Farazmand, 1989a). On the other hand, the United States federal/state/local bureaucracies were very large and expansive for a long time of fifty years until 1980, when Ronald Reagan took over the presidency and reversed the trend by downsizing, outsourcing, and contracting and privatizing the federal bureaucracy, a trend that followed by the state and local governments to date. In either case, the constitutionally representative system of government has also had its large and small public sector roles in economy and society. Neither the Chilean nor the Iranian large public sector systems with large bureaucracies performed ethically or with accountability, nor the representative government of the United States has proven or guaranteed ethical and accountable administrative systems. Flaws are found in both systems, while expectations are more positive about the American system.

The reforms since the 1980s—sweeping privatization, commercialization, and corporatization, as well as the NPM with a managerial ideology of business market supremacy model—have led to a much smaller and reduced public sector organizational capacity—both institutionally and human as well as financial capital. There have been serious consequences for ethics and accountability in public service and administration. This trend has also been exported globally and most governments worldwide have gone through this administrative and political transformation. There has been a paradigmatic shift, since the fall of the Soviet Union, from the strong public sector administrative state to a hollowed, smaller, privatized, and outsourced government characterized by strong military-security bureaucracy, business ideology, and corpocracy (Farazmand, 1997a, 2002b, 2012; Parenti, 2010) with the corporate elite in the driving seats of governments. Starting with Ronald Reagan and Margaret Thatcher who claimed "government as the problem not the solution," the entire world of America and the United Kingdom as well as their global sphere of hegemony came under this new slogan armed with commercialization and privatization pushing politicians and public administrators to adopt the business model of management to public sector organizations.

The pressures on public administrators to do more with less and produce results at the expense of accountability and ethical behavior has led to an intensified clash of administrative and political/democratic values to an alarming epidemic level (Fredrickson, 1993, 2001; Farazmand, 2002a, 2002b, 2012). The central problems emerging from this global push have been increased corruption, conflicts of interests, and loss of accountability in public service delivery systems through privatization, outsourcing, and contracting out. Predatory corporate globalization of the world has also aggravated this problem worldwide.

GLOBALIZATION, PRIVATIZATION, AND NPM

Elsewhere (Farazmand, 1999, 2002b, 2012), I have discussed in detail the issues of globalization, privatization, the NPM, and predatory globalization. A bird's eye view account is given here to relate to the purpose of this article. Globalization is a term almost everyone has heard about and has developed opinions on. Long before the buzz word became known worldwide, I wrote and argued that globalization is nothing new; it has been around for the thousands of years. The first globalizer was Cyrus the Great, founder of the first World State Persian Empire (559–337 BC), when he conquered virtually the entire known world and established a democratic, tolerance-based governance system with a vision of uniting the world's numerous peoples by "synthesizing the world's civilizations" under the Persian rule (Frye, 1975; Olmstead, 1948). Later, others like Romans, Arabs, Persians, Ottomans, British, French, Spaniards, and Portuguese tried it, but the Soviet-American global rivalry was the most intense quest for such a global world order. With the fall of the Soviet Union in 1991, Americans have tried rigorously to force a new global world order on the nations, staged wars of different forms, and have had some success, but their global quest has been met with strong resistance from both strong and weaker global players—examples being a reasserting Russia, China, Iran, Brazil, Venezuela, and a number of other nations forming the so called BRICS. The globalization has also been met by global movements of anti-globalization and counter-globalization

Perspectives on globalization abound, but generally three views form the core of our points here: one for, one against, and one in the middle. Those arguing for globalization, which by the way by 1990s has become the subject of thousands of publications, assert that with the fall of the Soviet Union, the triumph of market and corporate capitalism has made the existence of governments and states irrelevant because corporations can do everything they do, that market is more efficient than government administration, that the age of poverty, war, and conflicts is over, and that peace and prosperity will prevail worldwide (see, for example, Fukuyama, 1992; Ohmae,

1990; and others). Opponents of globalization have rejected the proponents' view calling it naïve at best and corporate apologetic at worst, and argued vividly and forcefully that the world will be a much worse place to live, the environments will be destroyed by corporate globalization, poverty and wars would increase not decrease, and corporate capitalism's consumer culture is destroying cultural identities and values of various peoples worldwide. They reject globalization altogether, calling it "global pillage" with a "race to the bottom" for billions of people worldwide (see e.g., Brecher & Costello, 1994; Korten, 1995, 2001; Mele, 1996, and call for "localization" and return back to local economies and cultures.

In between the two perspectives rises the third perspective dubbed the "realists" with divergent views, theorists who argue for inevitability of corporate globalization as the last organizational form of capitalism, something that must pass its stage in the 21st century, but they offer practical solutions to solving the problems of globalization (Farazmand, 1999; Scholte, 1995/2005). They argue that total resistance is self-defeating, but select policy choices are available to national sovereignties—reject what is considered bad and destructive, accept what is good and useful, and adapt to changing conditions with independent authority (see e.g., Farazmand, 1999; Korten, 2001). This author falls in this category and argues that globalization is a "process through which worldwide transformation is taking place" (Farazmand, 1999, p. 509) with profound consequences for governments, public administration, economics, cultures, and societies, but the state is here to stay, however with a changed character and behavior (see Farazmand, 1999; 2002b; 2009; 2012). The state and public administration has changed in character in that it has become an "agent of the corporate globalization," and its behaviors have been characterized by promoting, enforcing, and enhancing the rules and values of the corporate globalizers in a new market-dominated global order with business model values.

Sweeping privatization, outsourcing, contracting out, and the so-called "NPM" modeled after the private sector business management ideology and formula have achieved the objectives of corporate globalization of the world (see Farazmand, 1999, 2002b, and 2009). Further, the nature of corporate globalization has also changed from a traditional market capitalism to one that is predatory operating with absolute rates of surplus accumulation or profit, hence the age of "predatory capitalism and predatory globalization" (Falk, 1999; Farazmand, 2012; Galbraith, 2006). Predatory capitalism and predatory globalization are the "antithesis of public administration" and broad based public interests, because they stand against anything that public administration with truly broad based public interests, public integrity, and public goods stand for. Public administration has been transformed from "administration of public affairs" to "administration of the public," acting as an agent of the predatory corporate globalization to provide security and social control for capital accumulation, hence the theory of "agencification," a term I have coined to describe the new role of the state and public administration in the twenty first century (see Farazmand, 2002a, b, 2012).

The NPM and sweeping privatization have been used by both corporations and government organizations to achieve and promote the strategic goals of corporate globalization and agencification has played a key role in achieving this mission. Sweeping privatization has transferred "public assets and public functions" from the public sector to the private business sector run by large corporations for profit and market expansion. At the same time, NPM has relentlessly propagated and promoted the ideology of business "managerialism" with normative and formative values of market-based business models in pubic management. The former has changed the structural configurations of the public-private sector relations, while the latter has changed the culture of public service and administration—from a self-conscious enterprise with confidence in public interests and public service to being forced to accept the managerial ideology that public administration is bad and business model of management is good—a new orthodoxy, which has left no room for any alternative; "either our way or highway." Several fundamental problems have emerged as a result of this transformation the last three decades: growing corruption, accentuation of further ethical and legal problems (Farazmand, 2002a, b, 2012; Jurkiewicz, 2013), and increasing accountability challenges.

Accountability problems have emerged more alarmingly since NPM was adopted as the new orthodoxy with results-oriented ideology, which created an impetus for bypassing rules and processes to achieve results at almost any cost, but by lowering and reducing the "transaction costs," a practice used in private business organizations. Rules, regulations, and procedures developed to safeguard against abuse, conflict of interests, violation of individual rights, and unfair and inequity practices were thrown out of windows in a rush to deregulation, privatization, outsourcing, commercialization, and corporatization since the 1980s. This has caused severe accountability problems, as it is not clear who is accountable to whom any more, as contractors and privatized "agents" subcontract out and are not accountable to the public citizens anymore. However, the end of the day, government is and must be accountable for its actions and inactions to the public.

Corruption has followed as a result of massive abuses of public funds, embezzlement, growing conflicts of interest in public procurements, and nepotism as well as favoritism in both military and civilian organizations. In capitalism and market-dominated environments, business-type practices of favors, business gifts, calculated business expenses to acquire more business contracts is normal, but in the public sector the laws govern operations of public management. Violation of laws, rules, and procedures is considered illegal and lead to corruption. As a result, unethical conducts have increased throughout public sector organizations, and ethical problems have become epidemic worldwide (Jurkiewicz, 2012). Money corrupts, and cash money corrupts even more, and money is the core of capitalist system. It is the engine of capitalism. The number of books and articles published on ethics and accountability concerns in public administration and policy the last three decades has been staggering. Until two decades ago, most public administration programs did not have any courses in ethics and accountability in their curricula; today most such programs and schools have separate courses as a core of their curriculums.

As an accrediting agency, the National Association of Schools of Public Affairs and Administration (NASPAA) has required inclusion in the Master of Public Administration (MPA) programs of training and education for public service courses and materials in ethics and accountability to promote anti-corruption and increase ethical and accountability mechanisms in public administration. Elaborate "codes" of ethics, training and education of ethics and accountability, and organizational policies and mechanisms in combating corruption and unethical behaviors of various kinds are now parts of most public organizational systems. Scholars are engaging in ethical discourse with deeper and more sophisticated analytical conceptualization (Dubnick, 2011), an intellectual endeavor that contributes further to a broader knowledge of ethics and integrity in public service and administration While the utilitarian, consequential, and categorical imperative theories of ethics may be used together to form a "unified theory of ethics" (Garofalo & Geuras, 1999), it is the virtuous ethics that might be a better or best approach to promote public ethics and integrity. That requires extensive embodiment of ethics education in our schools systems all the way from the elementary to the graduate levels. We need more solid character development while teaching our students with necessary "competencies" to produce results.

Professionalism armed with ethical and accountability mechanisms, led by a cardinal principle of sound character, can and must be promoted to guard against perpetrators of corruption, unfair practices, and unethical conducts. The push for high performance results must be balanced by preservation of public integrity, ethical values, and accountability standards (Farazmand, 2002b), and predatory capitalism must be resisted by all means. Public administrators have moral and professional responsibilities to resist any practices that feed into predatory capitalism and globalization, because it destroys public trust, integrity, and public interest—something public administration stands for. There is a long journey, but we must take it to restore public trust and save public service and integrity.

ACHIEVING ACCOUNTABILITY:
AN IMPOSSIBILITY THEOREM?

The above discussions on public service ethics and accountability begs a new question? What to do with the accountability problem in public service and administration, and how to achieve accountability and democratic administration in the age of predatory globalization.

Perspectives on democratic accountability abound with little agreements among them (Behn 2001). Just as perspectives on globalization vary, concepts and theories of accountability vary representing different ideological as well as political narratives. Classical and neoclassical economic theorists favoring corporate globalization often complain about the lack of accountability of bureaucracy and unelected professional bureaucrats or administrators who by virtue of their expertise and legal appointment are involved in the public policy process of formulation, development, and implementation (Downs, 1967; Niskanen, 1971; Ostrom, 1974). To them, only elected officials are accountable to citizens in a democratic polity. To these scholars, the problem of accountability is solved by sweeping privatization, marketization, and commercialization public services, government agencies, and their functions.

However, aside from ideological orientations, the problem of accountability is much wider and more comprehensive, and encompasses a spectrum of public life well beyond elected or unelected officials. It is not uncommon to hear or read about corruptions and accountability breaches in among elected or appointed officials on all partisan lines. Here, scholars share one point in common: on corruption and accountability lapses in public service and administration, and on how to achieve accountability to citizens.

Generally, three perspectives address the accountability problem with solutions. One is the broad "ruling class" perspective represented by Marxian and neo-Marxian theory. According to this perspective, a small group of ruling class in capitalism lives, prospers, and rules on the principles of money and profits, exploitation of the majority working class, and dispensation of money as a lubricant of the system perpetuation. It uses a functionary body of middle class "agents" in charge of administration, management, supervision, and those involved in politics, whether partisan, programmatic, bureaucratic, or policy in nature. To this perspective, capitalism corrupts and corruption is functional to system maintenance and enhancement, citizens are powerless and irrelevant as power elites decide and rule through its public as well as private corporate institutions and organizations, and accountability is more a flawed concept than a serious concern (see, for example, Mills, 1956; Parenti, 2010). Corporate globalization of the world and the surge of predatory globalization tend to have reinforced this critical perspective citing consequential examples: causing accentuated problems of corruption, loss of accountability through mergers and mega mergers as well as sweeping privatization and outsourcing of public institutions and funds, the widening have-and have-not gaps forcing millions of working class people in a race to the bottom, and lack of accountability among corporations and top political, administrative/bureaucratic, and military elites to anyone (see e.g., Brecher & Costello, 1994; Korten, 2001; Parenti, 2010).

The second perspective is offered by scholars less concerned with partisan or social class lines; they are concerned with the problems of accountability in all respects. To them, all officials in public life are and should be subject to public scrutiny and their actions or inactions must be subject to accountability. Any breach of accountability must be punished by constitutional, legal, and financial sanctions, regardless of the level or position of officials in the system. Most public administration scholars, philosophers, social scientists, and processionals committed to the noble profession of public service may fall in this category (see e.g., Jurkiewikz, 2012; Thayer 1997; Behn, 2001; Waldo, 1992). To these scholars, theories of virtue ethics and categorical imperatives noted earlier in this article, and "principled professionalism" (Farazmand, 2002a, forthcoming a, b) complement and reinforce this perspective. While approaches vary among these scholars, there are those who specifically argue for constitutionally empowered, neutrally competent, and independent professional "civil servants" who should be given authority to act as "guardians" of public trust and broad public interests (Rohr, 1978/1989; Rosen, 1998; Thayer, 1997; Waldo, 1980/1992).

The third perspective is that of the public choice theory noted earlier in this essay. To this perspective and its extended ideology of NPM the solution is privatization, marketization, and outsourcing (Behn, 2001; Osborne & Gaebler, 1992; Savas, 1987).

The problem of accountability is many dimensional, bit it is addressed at both micro and macro levels. At the micro level, the individual incidents of corruption, conflict of interests, wrongdoing, and unethical conducts explain cases of the problem are addressed, which demand measures of safeguard and protection. At the macro level, the broader issues of citizen trust in government and democracy and democratic administration are at stake. The solutions to the macro and micro accountability problems are also offered by three perspectives: one from public choice theory discussed above, which argues for a democratic administration through overlapping jurisdictions, organizational overlaps, taking work and politics as well as services to the local levels, where people/citizens can and should directly engage local politicians and public leaders and hold them accountable (Niskanen, 1971; Ostrom, 1974). Another one is the Marxian and neo-Marxian class view (Marx, 1967; Parenti, 2010; Schumepeter,

1942) that offers social revolutions replacing capitalism with socialism as a way out of class exploitation, corruption, and systemic changes—working class taking over and controlling and managing public resources through democratic centralism and other means of collective decision-making and administration that would serve the democratic rights of the vast majority of working class people (see, e.g., Lenin, 1917/1992). The third theoretical view offering solutions to accountability problems is the theory of representative bureaucracy and democratic democracy through bureaucratic accountability. This perspective argues that democracy is served by bureaucratic representation as an institutional mechanism (see Krislove & Rosenbloom, 1981; Rosenbloom, 1995).

The bureaucratic democracy model argues for: (a) a representative bureaucracy, an institutional system that provides social and policy representations of citizens in the bureaucracy and administration, one that is both responsive and accountable to broad-based and special citizenries. While social representation affords reflection of social groups—racial, gender, and ethnic based—who by performing tasks in the bureaucracy serve democracy and democratic interests of citizens. The second way the bureaucracy serves democracy and democratic accountability is through democratic administration hierarchically organized: Public organizations are organized hierarchically, at the top of which the directors and chiefs are appointed by elected officials or politically appointed bosses and their political appointees or political executives (an example is the Secretary of the State appointing his/her political executives, who would then appoint strategic officials who then appoint key administrators, and so on all the way down to the lowest level of the system). Career officials appointed to positions by the virtue of their specialized knowledge, expertise, experience, and skills perform tasks and report upward to the bosses, who provide accountability to political officials—both appointed and elected—who are to be held accountable to citizens; hence achieving bureaucratic accountability. According to this perspective, bureaucratic democracy assures accountability through organizational structures and processes that keep authority and accountability in balance.

The above theories and perspectives on accountability and democratic administration offer positive features, but they also carry serious problems of their own. For example, the public choice theory and NPM solutions to accountability problem through privatization and outsourcing may actually cause more accountability problems than it claims to solve, as outsourced contractors and subcontractors may be responsible to contract bosses but they may not be accountable to citizens, and privatized public functions are accountable to private stakeholders not public citizens. The traditional administrative models may have accountability mechanisms in place, but the slow process of bureaucratic system may undermine such accountability measures in action as well. Moreover, bureaucratic/administrative elites often engage in intimate relationships with political and partisan elites acting as key actors in the policy and administrative systems; they may hinder rather than enhance public accountability in administration. Similarly, the theory of representative bureaucracy may offer a degree of democratic administration and democratic accountability, but there is no guarantee that those ethnic, racial, or gender based employees in bureaucratic positions would necessarily represent and promote the interests of the groups or classes with whom they are associated with. Many people once positioned in key spots may forget where they came from and may not represent or promote the interests of the poor and working people in practice they are supposed to represent.

Finally, a fourth perspective on the accountability problem has recently emerged with the rise and spread of the "predatory globalization" with many implications worldwide. This perspective has raised the possibility of what I have called an "impossibility theorem" of accountability and in the age of predatory globalization (Farazmand, 2005).

The logic applied is quite simple: Predatory globalization is based on predatory corporate capitalism (but not all capitalist enterprises are predatory), which aims primarily at maximizing surplus values/profits at virtually any cost to others, and with no limit—it seeks absolute profit. When applied globally, globalization becomes predatory through its relentless push and pursuit for such absolute rates of profits and uses every possible means—peaceful as well as violent—to achieve its strategic goals. In its pursuit of such goals, it seeks monopolistic and oligopolistic strategies and alliances to succeed, and if faced local challenges or obstacles, it seeks the backing and intervention—military, as well as political and economic pressures and even violence of wars—from its state of origin. Examples of such predatory global corporations and predatory globalization are: (a) the September 11, 1973 Chilean military coup staged by the U.S. Central Intelligence Agency (CIA) and General Electric (GE), International Telephone and Telegraph (ITT), and other corporations, and carried out by the local agent General Pinochet who after killing the democratically elected president Salvatore Allende denationalized and reprivatized the Chilean Copper industry; (b) the August military coup d'etat of 1953 led by U.S. CIA, which toppled the democratically elected Prime Minister Mosaddegh and reinstalled the dictator Shah in power (Farazmand, 1989a; Korten, 2001; Morgan, 2006). Predatory capitalism and globalization has also been active at home in the United States, with a clear example of predatory lending on the housing situation prior to the bubble burst of 2008.

Under predatory capitalism and predatory globalization, achieving public accountability is an almost impossible task. Maximizing profits and production is tantamount to complying with government regulations—even if applied—on quality, standards, and control of public funds—or "accountability" requirements. The more of the latter means the less of the former, and this is not acceptable to giant corporate power structures (Korten, 1995, 2001). The financial and political abilities of giant corporate elites to lobby and influence politicians and change or control national legislation to their benefit is an assurance mechanism that turns the power of the state to their benefit and undermine almost any major accountability measure in public service and administration to work (for more on this, see Falk, 1999; Farazmand, 2012; Galbraith, 2006). This simple logic makes it almost impossible to achieve public accountability at the mass scale; hence an "impossibility theorem" (Farazmand, 2005), calling for stronger role of government in economy, politics, and administration.

At the micro-organizational level, scholars (e.g., Rosenbloom, 1995) note how difficult it is for the citizens to hold public administrators accountable. This is due to several facts: (a) administrators have specialized knowledge and expertise in various areas of public policy and management that general citizens don't have and cannot understand; (b) the language of bureaucracy is complicated with details of procedures, terms, and jargons; and (c) there are many legal avenues and reasons, including for example national security and fear of lawsuits, that is why it is difficult for public citizens to obtain information from administrative agencies. To counter these obstacles, scholars suggest citizens becoming "bureaucrats themselves" (Rosenbloom, 1980). This is another area of accountability subject that is understudied and in need of further inquiries.

REFERENCES

Behn, R. (2001). *Rethinking democratic accountability*. Washington, DC: The Brookings Institution.

Bentham, J. (1834). *Deontology*. Edinburgh, Scotland: William Tart.

Brecher, J., & Costello, T. (1994). *Global village or global pillage*. Boston, MA: South End Press.

Chandler, R. (2001). "The deontological dimensions of administrative ethics revisited." In T. Cooper (Ed.), *Handbook of administrative ethics* (2nd ed., pp. 179–194). New York, NY: Marcel Dekker.

Cook, J. M. (1983). *The Persian empire*. New York, NY: Schoken Books.

Cooper, T. (1998). *Responsible administrator* (4th ed.). New York, NY: Jossey-Bass, John Wiley.

Cooper, T. (2001). "The emergence of administrative ethics as a field of study." In T. Cooper (Ed.), *Handbook of administrative ethics*, (pp. 3–30) New York, NY: Marcel Dekker.

Downs, A. (1967). *Inside bureaucracy*. Boston, MA: Little Brown.

Dubnick, M. (2011). Accountability and ethics: Reconsidering the relationships, encyclopedia of public administration and public policy (2nd ed.). Taylor & Frances.

Eisenstadt, E. S. (1963). *The political systems of empires: A study of historical bureaucratic societies.* Glencoe, Scotland: Free Press.

Falk, R. (1999). *Predatory globalization: A critique.* Oxford, England: Blackwell.

Farazmand, A. (1989a). *The state, bureaucracy, and revolution.* New York, NY: Praeger.

Farazmand, A. (1989b).Crisis in the U.S. administrative state. *Administration and Society, 21*(2), 173–199.

Farazmand, A. (1997a).Bureaucracy, professionalism, and modern governance: a Comparative analysis. In Ali Farazmand (Ed.), *Modern systems of government: Exploring the role of bureaucrats and politicians* (pp. 48–73). Thousand Oaks, CA: SAGE.

Farazmand, A. (1997b). Ethics, professionalism, and the image of the public service. Paper presented at the 13th UN Conference of the group of experts on the United Nations Program on Public Administration and Finance, 27 May–4 June, UN publications ST/SG/AC.6/1997/1 . . . 3,6 May.

Farazmand, A. (1999). Globalization and public administration. *Public Administration Review, 59*(6), 509–522.

Farazmand, A. (2002a). Administrative ethics and professional competence: Accountability and performance under globalization. *International Review of Administrative Sciences, 68*(2), 127–143.

Farazmand, A. (2002b). "Globalization, privatization, and the future of modern governance: A critical assessment." *Public Money and Finance, 2*(1), 125–153.

Farazmand, A. (2005). Role of government in an era of total quality management (TQM) and globalization: Challenges and opportunities." *Public Organization Review: A Global Journal, 5,* 201–217.

Farazmand, A. (2009). Building administrative capacity for the age of rapid globalization: A modest prescription for survival in the twenty-first century. *Public Administration Review, 69*(6), 1007–1020.

Farazmand, A. (2012). "The future of public administration: Challenges and opportunities." *Administration & Society, 44*(4), 487–517.

Frederickson, G. (1993). *Ethics and public administration.* New York, NY: M. E. Sharpe.

Frederickson, G. (2001). "Research and knowledge in administrative ethics." In T. Cooper (Ed.), *Handbook of administrative ethics* (pp. 31–46). New York, NY: Marcel Dekker.

Frye, R. (1975). *The golden age of Persia.* New York, NY: The World.

Fukuyama, F. (1992). *The end of history and of the last man.* New York, NY: Avon.

Galbraith, J. K. (2006, May 4). Taming Predatory Capitalism. *The Nation.* Retrieved from http://www/thenation.com/20060417/forum/4

Garofalo, C., & Geuras, D. (1999). *Ethics in the public services: The moral mind at work.* Washington, DC: Georgetown University Press.

Hart, D. (2001). "Administration and the ethics of virtue: In all things, choose first for good character and then for technical expertise." In T. Cooper (Ed.), *Handbook of administrative ethics* (pp. 131–150). New York, NY: Marcel Dekker.

Heredotus. (1954/1984). *The Histories* (Aubrey de Selincourt, Trans.; A.R. Burn, Introduction). New York, NY: Penguin Books.

Jurkiewicz, C. (2012). Advancing ethical competency through pedagogy. In T. L. Cooper, & D. C. Menzel (Ed.), *Achieving ethical competence for public service leadership* (pp. 131–154). Armonk, NY: M. E. Sharpe.

Jurkiewicz, C. (2013). Advancing ethical competency through pedagogy. In T. L. Cooper & D. C. Menzel, D. C. (Ed.), *Achieving ethical competence for public service leadership* (pp. 131–154. Armonk, NY: M. E. Sharpe.

Kant, I. (1956). *Critique of practical reason*, translated by Lewis White Beck. Indianapolis, OH: Bobbs-Merrill.

Korten, D. (1995). *When corporations rule the world.* West Hartford, CT: Kumarian Press.

Korten, D. (2001). *When corporations rule the world* (2nd ed.). San Francisco, CA: Kohler.

Krislove, S., & Rosenbloom, D. (1981). *Representative bureaucracy and the American political system.* New York, NY: Oxford University Press.

Lenin, V. I. (1917/1992). *The state and revolution.* New York, NY: Penguin Books.

Marx, K. (1967). *The writings of the younger Marx on Philosophy and society* (L. D. Easton & K. H. Guddat, Ed. & Trans.). Garden City, NJ: Doubleday.

Marx, K. (1976). *Das Kapital.* Harmonstsworth, England: Penguin.

Mele, C. (1996). "Globalization, culture, and the neighborhood change: Reinventing the lower east side of New York." *Urban Affairs Review*, 32(1), 3–32.

Mill, J. S. (1965). *Utilitarianism* (J. B. Schneewind, Ed.). New York, NY: Collier.

Mills, C. W. (1956). *The power elite.* New York, NY: Oxford University Press.

Morgan, G. (2006). *Images of organization.* Thousand Oaks, CA: SAGE.

Mosher, F. (1968). *Democracy and the public service* (2nd ed). New York, NY: Oxford University Press.

Niskanen, W. (1971). *Bureaucracy and representative government.* Chicago, IL: Aldine Atherton.

Ohmae, K.(1990). *The borderless world: The rise of regional economies.* London, England: Harper-Collins

Olmstead, A. T. (1948). *History of the Persian empire: The Achaemenid period.* Chicago. IL: The University of Chicago Press.

Osborne, D., & Gaebler, T. (1992). *Reinventing government.* Reading, MA: Addison-Wesley.

Ostrom, V. (1974). *The intellectual crisis in American public administration.* University, AL: University of Alabama Press.

Parenti, M. (2010). *Democracy for the few.* New York, NY: St. Martin's Press.

Parson, T. (1951). *The social systems.* New York, NY: Free Press.

Rohr, J. (1978/1989). *Ethics for bureaucrats* (1st and 2nd ed). New York, NY: Marcel Dekker.

Romzek, B. S., Dubnick, M. J. (1987). M. J. Accountability in the public sector: Lessons from the challenger tragedy. *Public Administration Review, 47*(3), 227–239.

Rosen, B. (1998). *Holding government bureaucracies accountable.* Westport, CN: Praeger.

Rosenbloom, D. (1980). *Bureaucratic government: USA.* New York, NY: St. Martin's Press.

Rosenbloom, D. (1995). *Public administration and the public sector: Understanding management, politics, and law* (4th ed). New York, NY: McGraw-Hill.

Savas, E. S. (1987). *Privatization: The key to better government.* Chatham, NJ: Chatham House.

Scholte, J. A. (1995/2005). *Globalization: An introduction* (2nd ed.). New York, NY: Palgrave Macmillan.

Schumpeter, J. (1942). *Capitalism, socialism, and democracy.* New York, NY: Harper Brothers.

Skinner, B. F. (1971/2002). *Beyond freedom and dignity.* Indianapolis, OH: Hackett.

Thayer, F. (1997). "The U.S. Civil service: 1883–1993 (R.I.P)." In A. Farazmand (Ed.), *Modern systems of government: Exploring the role of bureaucrats and politicians* (pp. 95–124). Thousand Oaks, CA: SAGE.

Veblen, T. (1898)."Why economics is not an evolutionary science." *Quarterly Journal of Economics, 12,* 373–397.

Veblen, T. (1911). *The place of science in modern civilization and other essays.* New York, NY: Huebsch.

Waldo, D. (1980/1992). *The enterprise of public administration.* Novato, CA: Chandler & Sharp.

Weber, M. (1984). "Bureaucracy." In F. Fischer & C. Sirriani (Eds), *Critical studies in organization and bureaucracy* (pp. 24–39). Philadelphia, PA: Temple University Press.

Weber, M. (1947). *The theory of social and economic organizations* (A. M. Henderson & T. Parsons, Trans.). Oxford, England: Oxford University Press.

ABOUT THE EDITORS

Carole L. Jurkiewicz, PhD, is the Sherry H. Penney Endowed Professor of Leadership at the University of Massachusetts Boston. Her work focuses upon individual and organizational performance as a function of leader ethicality, and cross-sector applied organizational ethics. She has edited/authored over thirty books and published over 120 articles in the areas of organizational and individual performance, ethics, power, and leadership, bringing to her academic career many years' experience as an executive in private and nonprofit organizations. She is the editor-in-chief of *Public Integrity*, serves on the board of a number of scholarly journals and professional associations, and has consulted with a wide range of organizations including Sloan Kettering, AT&T, IBM, USPS, National Public Radio, Spinal Cord Injury Network, Habitat for Humanity, and the American Marketing Association, as well as numerous other governmental agencies and departments at the federal, state, and local levels.

Robert A. Giacalone, PhD, is currently The Raymond and Eleanor Smiley Chair in Business Ethics at the Boler School of Business, John Carroll University. In his current position, he also serves as the Director of The Ginn Institute for Corporate Social Responsibility. In addition to serving on several journal editorial boards, Dr. Giacalone has edited/authored 10 books and over 160 articles on ethics and values, impression management, and

Radical Thoughts on Ethical Leadership, page 221
Copyright © 2017 by Information Age Publishing
All rights of reproduction in any form reserved.

exit interviewing. His articles have appeared in journals such as the *Academy of Management Learning and Education, Journal of Applied Psychology, Human Relations, Business and Society Review, Journal of Business Ethics, Journal of Organizational Behavior,* and *Journal of Social Psychology.*

ABOUT THE CONTRIBUTORS

Scott Allison has authored numerous books, including *Heroes* and *Heroic Leadership*. He is Professor of Psychology at the University of Richmond. His other books include *Heroic Humility, Conceptions of Leadership, Frontiers in Spiritual Leadership,* and the *Handbook of Heroism and Heroic Leadership*. His work has appeared in *USA Today,* National Public Radio, the *New York Times,* the *Los Angeles Times, Slate Magazine,* MSNBC, CBS, *Psychology Today,* and the *Christian Science Monitor.*

Geoffrey G. Bell, PhD is an associate professor of strategic management at the Labovitz School of Business and Economics at the University of Minnesota Duluth. He graduated with a PhD in Strategic Management from the Carlson School of Management. His research interests include the influence of geography and networks on firm performance and the development of Radical management theory based upon virtue ethics. He is also active in pedagogical research.

Mark Dibben, PhD is an associate professor of management at the University of Tasmania and visiting professor of applied process thought at the Center for Process Studies in the Claremont School of Theology, California. His research interests are in what he terms applied process thought, the thoroughgoing serious-minded application of process philosophy to topics in the sciences and social sciences; he has published a book and two edited books founded in this topic and is academic director of the International Process Network, the overarching co-ordinating body of thirty-plus process

Radical Thoughts on Ethical Leadership, pages 223–228
Copyright © 2017 by Information Age Publishing
All rights of reproduction in any form reserved.

philosophy research centers around the globe. Other recent work includes sport-as-business and management history, as well as "ecological management" having process philosophy as its premise. In this respect, Dr. Dibben is Honorary Research Fellow in the Centre for Agroecology, Water, and Resilience at Coventry University and Distinguished Fellow of the Schumacher Institute, both in the United Kingdom.

J. Patrick Dobel is the John and Marguerite Corbally Chair in Public Service (emeritus) at the University of Washington. He teaches strategy, leadership, and public ethics at the Evans School of Public Policy and Governance. Professor Dobel has consulted with many public and nonprofit organizations and chaired numerous ethics commissions.

Bruno Dyck, an organizational theorist at the University of Manitoba, earned his PhD in Business at the University of Alberta. His research examines the role of values in management theory and practice, and he has published in leading journals on topics related to ethics, sustainability, religion, and organizational learning and change. He has also published two textbooks that contrast and compare conventional with sustainable approaches to management and OB.

Ali Farazmand is Professor of Public Administration at Florida Atlantic University, where he is also the MPA Program Coordinator. A PhD graduate of the Maxwell School of Syracuse University, he is the author of over 24 books and 150 journal articles and book chapters, including *Public Administration in a Globalized World* (Routledge), *Institutional Theory and Public Administration* (Springer), and *The Administrative State Revisited: Globalization and Transformation* (T&F). He is also editor in chief of *Public Organization Review* and *International Journal of Public Administration,* and *Global Encyclopedia of Public Administration and Public Policy.*

Robert A. Giacalone, PhD, is currently The Raymond and Eleanor Smiley Chair in Business Ethics at the Boler School of Business, John Carroll University. In his current position, he also serves as the Director of The Ginn Institute for Corporate Social Responsibility. In addition to serving on several journal editorial boards, Dr. Giacalone has edited/authored 10 books and over 160 articles on ethics and values, impression management, and exit interviewing. His articles have appeared in journals such as the *Academy of Management Learning and Education, Journal of Applied Psychology, Human Relations, Business and Society Review, Journal of Business Ethics, Journal of Organizational Behavior,* and *Journal of Social Psychology.*

Leonie Heres is assistant professor of Governance at the Utrecht University School of Governance, the Netherlands. Her research focuses on ethics and integrity, with a specific focus on the role of leadership and management in the moral behavior of and within organizations. Leonie is also an executive board member of the international academic research network on Public and Political Leadership (PUPOL). For more info and publications, see www.leonieheres.com

Leo (L.W.J.C.) Huberts is Professor of Public Administration at the Department of Political Science and Public Administration of the Vrije Universiteit Amsterdam in The Netherlands with special responsibility for the VU research group on Integrity and Quality of Governance and the global IIAS Study Group on Quality of Governance. He is author or editor of twenty books on influence on governmental policy, on public corruption and fraud, on the integrity and ethics of governance, including *Integrity of Governance: What It Is, What We Know, What Is Done, and Where to Go* (2014, Basingstoke: Palgrave Macmillan).

Carole L. Jurkiewicz, PhD, is the Sherry H. Penney Endowed Professor of Leadership at the University of Massachusetts Boston. Her work focuses upon individual and organizational performance as a function of leader ethicality, and cross-sector applied organizational ethics. She has edited/authored over thirty books and published over 120 articles in the areas of organizational and individual performance, ethics, power, and leadership, bringing to her academic career many years' experience as an executive in private and nonprofit organizations. She is the editor-in-chief of *Public Integrity*, serves on the board of a number of scholarly journals and professional associations, and has consulted with a wide range of organizations including Sloan Kettering, AT&T, IBM, USPS, National Public Radio, Spinal Cord Injury Network, Habitat for Humanity, and the American Marketing Association, as well as numerous other governmental agencies and departments at the federal, state, and local levels.

Karin Lasthuizen, PhD, is a professor and the inaugural Brian Picot Chair in Ethical Leadership at Victoria Business School, Victoria University of Wellington, New Zealand. Karin has over 60 publications on ethical leadership, ethics management, and (measurement of) corruption in national and international journals, books, magazines, and in the media. She co-authored the Routledge textbook *Ethics and Management in the Public Sector* (2013) with Alan Lawton and Julie Rayner. Karin is also co-founder of PUPOL—an international academic research network on public and political leadership.

Michael Macaulay is Associate Dean for Professional and Executive Education, at Victoria Business School, Victoria University of Wellington, New Zealand. He has published widely in the fields of integrity, ethics, and anti-corruption and is the co-chair of the European Group of Public Administration (EGPA) permanent study group on integrity and quality of governance. Michael has worked with numerous government agencies and NGOs in New Zealand and internationally, including the New Zealand Police, the United Nations Office on Drugs and Crime (UNODC) the Council of Europe and Transparency International. He has represented New Zealand at the many Open Government Partnership summits.

Rob Macklin, PhD, is a senior lecturer in management and business ethics at the Tasmanian School of Business & Economics of the University of Tasmania, Hobart. Dr Macklin's current research includes studies of mental illness at work from a labor process perspective, and investigations of management and leadership in residential aged care. He is also working on a philosophical/theological analyses of the role of agape in organizations informed by the work of Paul Tillich. In addition, he is working with colleagues on the development of a process philosophy approach to normative business ethics.

Mitchell J. Neubert is a professor of management and the Chavanne Chair of Christian Ethics in Business at Baylor University. Dr. Neubert's teaching and research focus on equipping leaders to lead individuals, teams, and organizations in a virtuous manner that results in positive change. He is a co-author of textbooks in organizational behavior and management. He also was a principle investigator on a National Science Foundation grant related to religion, work, and entrepreneurial behavior.

Ronald E. Riggio, PhD, is the Henry R. Kravis Professor of Leadership and Organizational Psychology and former director of the Kravis Leadership Institute at Claremont McKenna College. Dr. Riggio is a leadership scholar with more than a dozen authored or edited books and more than 150 articles/book chapters. His research interests are in leadership and organizational communication, particularly leader nonverbal communication and emotional competence. He is part of the Fullerton Longitudinal Study that is examining leadership development across the lifespan (beginning at 1 year of age and continuing through adulthood). Besides research on leadership development, he has been actively involved in training young (and not so young) leaders at the college level, and beyond.

Diane L. Swanson holds a PhD in Business Administration from the University of Pittsburgh. She is a professor of management and the Edgerley

Family Chair of Distinction at Kansas State University where she chairs the Business Ethics Education Initiative. She is also a Distinguished Visiting Scholar in the Center for Values-Driven Leadership at Benedictine University. Dr. Swanson, an award-winning author and educator, is recognized in several Who's Who bibliographical indices, has published widely on business ethics and corporate social responsibility, and has served on several editorial boards.

Allison Toner is a graduate of the University of Richmond with a major in Psychology and Political Science. She graduated cum laude after studying in the honors psychology program with Dr. Allison, with a focus on the key personality attributes of heroes and how these narratives play a part in American films. She is now working as a fashion merchandiser, using her psychology background to navigate the complex creative personalities that inhabit the retail industry.

Sandra Waddock is Galligan Chair of Strategy, Carroll School Scholar of Corporate Responsibility, and Professor of Management at Boston College's Carroll School of Management. She has published about 140 papers and thirteen books. Recipient of numerous awards, Waddock received the 2016 CSR Lifetime Achievement Award from Humboldt University in Berlin, the 2015 award for Leadership in Humanistic Management, and the 2014 Lifetime Achievement Award in Collaboration Research, among others. Current research interests are large systems change, the role of memes in change, developing a new narrative for business in society, stewardship of the future, corporate sustainability and responsibility, management education, and intellectual shamans. Her latest books are *Healing the World* (2017), *Intellectual Shamans* (Cambridge, 2015), *(Teaching) Managing Mindfully* (with Lawrence Lad and Judith Clair; 2017), and *Building the Responsible Enterprise* (with Andreas Rasche; 2012).

Dr. **Werner Webb** is chair of the department and associate professor at the Department of Public Administration and Management, University of South Africa. He has lectured Public Administration at various universities over the past more than 20 years and has presented academic papers at South African and international conferences. His research focus is public policy management, public service ethics, and corruption prevention. His current research project is funded by the National Research Foundation and is entitled *Managing Integrity: Causes, Consequences. and Remedies for Public Service Corruption.*

Martin Wood, PhD is a professor in the School of Management at RMIT, an Australian public research university located in Melbourne. He has previously held full-time academic appointments at the universities of York and Exeter and a research position at Warwick University in the U.K. His wide-ranging work cuts across established academic disciplines and applies themes from process philosophy to research in diverse fields of activity. Dr. Wood confronts the topic of leadership in a bold and unconventional way, articulating a relational model that focuses on leadership as a process without a fully determinate subject. In a recent project, he examines the experience of films, the ways they are made and the kinds of objects they are, and raises particular questions about whether a film can be a process for thinking inside the social sciences.